The New World Edition of the Works of Rudyard Kipling: Just So Stories for Little Children. Stalky & Co

Rudyard Kipling, Charles Wolcott Balestier

THE NEW WORLD EDITION
OF THE WORKS OF
RUDYARD KIPLING

JUST SO STORIES
FOR LITTLE CHILDREN

———

STALKY & CO.

BY

RUDYARD KIPLING

THIS AUTHORIZED EDITION IS
PUBLISHED EXCLUSIVELY
FOR
FUNK & WAGNALLS COMPANY

DOUBLEDAY, PAGE & COMPANY
GARDEN CITY, NEW YORK AND TORONTO

JUST SO STORIES

THE COUNTRY LIFE PRESS, GARDEN CITY, N. Y.

CONTENTS

HOW THE WHALE GOT HIS THROAT

(1897)

N the sea, once upon a time, O my Best Beloved, there was a Whale, and he ate fishes. He ate the starfish and the garfish, and the crab and the dab, and the plaice and the dace, and the skate and his mate, and the mackereel and the pickereel, and the really truly twirly-whirly eel. All the fishes he could find in all the sea he ate with his mouth—so! Till at last there was only one small fish left in all the sea, and he was a small 'Stute Fish, and he swam a little behind the Whale's right ear, so as to be out of harm's way. Then the Whale stood up on his tail and said, 'I'm hungry.' And the small 'Stute Fish said in a small 'stute voice, 'Noble and generous Cetacean, have you ever tasted Man?'

'No,' said the Whale. 'What is it like?'

'Nice,' said the small 'Stute Fish. 'Nice but nubbly.'

'Then fetch me some,' said the Whale, and he made the sea froth up with his tail.

'One at a time is enough,' said the 'Stute Fish. 'If you swim to latitude Fifty North, longitude Forty West (that is Magic), you will find, sitting on a raft, in the middle of the sea, with nothing on but a pair of blue

This is the picture of the Whale swallowing the Mariner with his infinite-resource-and-sagacity, and the raft and the jack-knife and his suspenders, which you must not forget. The buttony-things are the Mariner's suspenders, and you can see the knife close by them. He is sitting on the raft, but it has tilted up sideways, so you don't see much of it. The whity thing by the Mariner's left hand is a piece of wood that he was trying to row the raft with when the Whale came along. The piece of wood is called the jaws-of-a-gaff. The Mariner left it outside when he went in. The Whale's name was Smiler, and the Mariner was called Mr. Henry Albert Bivvens, A. B. The little 'Stute Fish is hiding under the Whale's tummy, or else I would have drawn him. The reason that the sea looks so ooshy-skooshy is because the Whale is sucking it all into his mouth so as to suck in Mr. Henry Albert Bivvens and the raft and the jack-knife and the suspenders. You must never forget the suspenders.

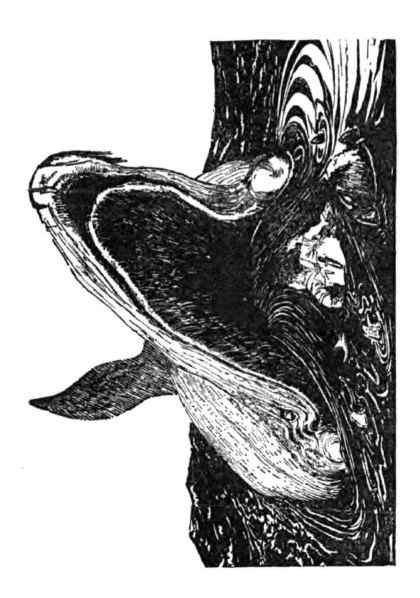

canvas breeches, a pair of suspenders (you must not forget the suspenders, Best Beloved), and a jack-knife, one shipwrecked Mariner, who, it is only fair to tell you, is a man of infinite-resource-and-sagacity.'

So the Whale swam and swam to latitude Fifty North, longitude Forty West, as fast as he could swim, and on a raft, in the middle of the sea, with nothing to wear except a pair of blue canvas breeches, a pair of suspenders (you must particularly remember the suspenders, Best Beloved), and a jack-knife, he found one single, solitary shipwrecked Mariner, trailing his toes in the water. (He had his Mummy's leave to paddle, or else he would never have done it, because he was a man of infinite-resource-and-sagacity.)

Then the Whale opened his mouth back and back and back till it nearly touched his tail, and he swallowed the shipwrecked Mariner, and the raft he was sitting on, and his blue canvas breeches, and the suspenders (which you must not forget), and the jack-knife. He swallowed them all down into his warm, dark, inside cupboards, and then he smacked his lips—so, and turned round three times on his tail.

But as soon as the Mariner, who was a man of infinite-resource-and-sagacity, found himself truly inside the Whale's warm, dark, inside cupboards, he stumped and he jumped and he thumped and he bumped, and he pranced and he danced, and he banged and he clanged, and he hit and he bit, and he leaped and he creeped, and he prowled and he howled, and he hopped and he dropped, and he cried and he sighed, and he crawled and he bawled, and he stepped and he lepped, and he danced hornpipes where he shouldn't, and the Whale felt most unhappy indeed. (Have you forgotten the suspenders?)

Here is the Whale looking for the little 'Stute Fish, who is hiding under the Door-sills of the Equator. The little 'Stute Fish's name was Pingle. He is hiding among the roots of the big seaweed that grows in front of the Doors of the Equator. I have drawn the Doors of the Equator. They are shut. They are always kept shut, because a door ought always to be kept shut. The ropy thing right across is the Equator itself; and the things that look like rocks are the two giants Moar and Koar, that keep the Equator in order. They drew the shadow-pictures on the Doors of the Equator, and they carved all those twisty fishes under the Doors. The beaky-fish are called beaked Dolphins, and the other fish with the queer heads are called Hammer-headed Sharks. The Whale never found the little 'Stute Fish till he got over his temper, and then they became good friends again.

HOW THE WHALE GOT HIS THROAT

So he said to the 'Stute Fish, 'This man is very nubbly, and besides he is making me hiccough. What shall I do?'

'Tell him to come out,' said the 'Stute Fish.

So the Whale called down his own throat to the ship-wrecked Mariner, 'Come out and behave yourself. I've got the hiccoughs.'

'Nay, nay!' said the Mariner. 'Not so, but far otherwise. Take me to my natal-shore and the white-cliffs-of-Albion, and I'll think about it.' And he began to dance more than ever.

'You had better take him home,' said the 'Stute Fish to the Whale. 'I ought to have warned you that he is a man of infinite-resource-and-sagacity.'

So the Whale swam and swam and swam, with both flippers and his tail, as hard as he could for the hic-coughs; and at last he saw the Mariner's natal-shore and the white-cliffs-of-Albion, and he rushed half-way up the beach, and opened his mouth wide and wide and wide, and said, 'Change here for Winchester, Ashuelot, Nashua, Keene, and stations on the Fitch-burg Road'; and just as he said 'Fitch' the Mariner walked out of his mouth. But while the Whale had been swimming, the Mariner, who was indeed a person of infinite-resource-and-sagacity, had taken his jack-knife and cut up the raft into a little square grating all running criss-cross, and he had tied it firm with his suspenders (Now you know why you were not to forget the suspenders!), and he dragged that grat-ing good and tight into the Whale's throat, and there it stuck! Then he recited the following Sloka, which, as you have not heard, I will now proceed to relate—

By means of a grating
I have stopped your ating.

11

For the Mariner he was also an Hi-ber-ni-an. And he stepped out on the shingle, and went home to his Mother, who had given him leave to trail his toes in the water; and he married and lived happily ever afterward. So did the Whale. But from that day on, the grating in his throat, which he could neither cough up nor swallow down, prevented him eating anything except very, very small fish; and that is the reason why whales nowadays never eat men or boys or little girls.

The small 'Stute Fish went and hid himself in the mud under the Door-sills of the Equator. He was afraid that the Whale might be angry with him.

The Sailor took the jack-knife home. He was wearing the blue canvas breeches when he walked out on the shingle. The suspenders were left behind, you see, to tie the grating with; and that is the end of that tale.

When the cabin port-holes are dark and green
    Because of the seas outside;
When the ship goes 'wop' (with a wiggle between)
And the steward falls into the soup-tureen,
    And the trunks begin to slide;
When Nursey lies on the floor in a heap,
And Mummy tells you to let her sleep,
And you aren't waked or washed or dressed,
Why, then you will know (if you haven't guessed)
You're 'Fifty North and Forty West!'

HOW THE CAMEL GOT HIS HUMP

(1897)

OW this is the next tale, and it tells how the Camel got his big hump.

In the beginning of years, when the world was so new-and-all, and the Animals were just beginning to work for Man, there was a Camel, and he lived in the middle of a Howling Desert because he did not want to work; and besides, he was a Howler himself. So he ate sticks and thorns and tamarisks and milkweed and prickles, most 'scruciating idle; and when anybody spoke to him he said 'Humph!' Just 'Humph!' and no more.

Presently the Horse came to him on Monday morning, with a saddle on his back and a bit in his mouth, and said, 'Camel, O Camel, come out and trot like the rest of us.'

'Humph!' said the Camel; and the Horse went away and told the Man.

Presently the Dog came to him, with a stick in his mouth, and said, 'Camel, O Camel, come and fetch and carry like the rest of us.'

15

This is the picture of the Djinn making the beginnings of the Magic that brought the Humph to the Camel. First he drew a line in the air with his finger, and it became solid; and then he made a cloud, and then he made an egg—you can see them at the bottom of the picture —and then there was a magic pumpkin that turned into a big white flame.   Then the Djinn took his magic fan and fanned that flame till the flame turned into a Magic by itself.   It was a good Magic and a very kind Magic really, though it had to give the Camel a Humph because the Camel was lazy.   The Djinn in charge of All Deserts was one of the nicest of the Djinns, so he would never do anything really unkind.

HOW THE CAMEL GOT HIS HUMP

'Humph!' said the Camel; and the Dog went away and told the Man.

Presently the Ox came to him, with the yoke on his neck, and said, 'Camel, O Camel, come and plough like the rest of us.'

'Humph!' said the Camel; and the Ox went away and told the Man.

At the end of the day the Man called the Horse and the Dog and the Ox together, and said, 'Three, O Three, I'm very sorry for you (with the world so new-and-all); but that Humph-thing in the Desert can't work, or he would have been here by now, so I am going to leave him alone, and you must work double-time to make up for it.'

That made the Three very angry (with the world so new-and-all), and they held a palaver, and an indaba, and a punchayet, and a pow-wow on the edge of the Desert; and the Camel came chewing milkweed most 'scruciating idle, and laughed at them. Then he said 'Humph!' and went away again.

Presently there came along the Djinn in charge of All Deserts, rolling in a cloud of dust (Djinns always travel that way because it is Magic), and he stopped to palaver and pow-wow with the Three.

'Djinn of All Deserts,' said the Horse, 'is it right for any one to be idle, with the world so new-and-all?'

'Certainly not,' said the Djinn.

'Well,' said the Horse, 'there's a thing in the middle of your Howling Desert (and he's a Howler himself) with a long neck and long legs, and he hasn't done a stroke of work since Monday morning. He won't trot.'

'Whew!' said the Djinn, whistling, 'that's my Camel, for all the gold in Arabia! What does he say about it?'

19

Here is the picture of the Djinn in charge of All Deserts guiding the Magic with his magic fan. The camel
is eating a twig of acacia, and he has just finished saying
'humph' once too often (the Djinn told him he would),
and so the Humph is coming. The long towelly thing
growing out of the thing like an onion is the Magic, and
you can see the Humph on its shoulder. The Humph
fits on the flat part of the Camel's back. The Camel is
too busy looking at his own beautiful self in the pool of
water to know what is going to happen to him.

Underneath the truly picture is a picture of the World-
so-new-and-all. There are two smoky volcanoes in it,
some other mountains and some stones and a lake and a
black island and a twisty river and a lot of other things,
as well as a Noah's Ark. I couldn't draw all the deserts
that the Djinn was in charge of, so I only drew one, but
it is a most deserty desert.

'He says "Humph!"' said the Dog; 'and he won't fetch and carry.'

'Does he say anything else?'

'Only "Humph!"; and he won't plough,' said the Ox.

'Very good,' said the Djinn. 'I'll humph him if you will kindly wait a minute.'

The Djinn rolled himself up in his dust-cloak, and took a bearing across the desert, and found the Camel most 'scruciatingly idle, looking at his own reflection in a pool of water.

'My long and bubbling friend,' said the Djinn, 'what's this I hear of your doing no work, with the world so new-and-all?'

'Humph!' said the Camel.

The Djinn sat down, with his chin in his hand, and began to think a Great Magic, while the Camel looked at his own reflection in the pool of water.

'You've given the Three extra work ever since Monday morning, all on account of your 'scruciating idleness,' said the Djinn; and he went on thinking Magics, with his chin in his hand.

'Humph!' said the Camel.

'I shouldn't say that again if I were you,' said the Djinn; 'you might say it once too often. Bubbles, I want you to work.'

And the Camel said 'Humph!' again; but no sooner had he said it than he saw his back, that he was so proud of, puffing up and puffing up into a great big lolloping humph.

'Do you see that?' said the Djinn. 'That's your very own humph that you've brought upon your very own self by not working. To-day is Thursday, and you've done no work since Monday, when the work began. Now you are going to work.'

'How can I,' said the Camel, 'with this humph on my back?'

'That's made a-purpose,' said the Djinn, 'all because you missed those three days. You will be able to work now for three days without eating, because you can live on your humph; and don't you ever say I never did anything for you. Come out of the Desert and go to the Three, and behave. Humph yourself!'

And the Camel humphed himself, humph and all, and went away to join the Three. And from that day to this the Camel always wears a humph (we call it 'hump' now, not to hurt his feelings); but he has never yet caught up with the three days that he missed at the beginning of the world, and he has never yet learned how to behave.

The Camel's hump is an ugly lump
   Which well you may see at the Zoo;
But uglier yet is the hump we get
   From having too little to do.

Kiddies and grown-ups too-oo-oo,
If we haven't enough to do-oo-oo,
     We get the hump—
     Cameelious hump—
The hump that is black and blue!

We climb out of bed with a frouzly head
   And a snarly-yarly voice.
We shiver and scowl and we grunt and we growl
   At our bath and our boots and our toys;

And there ought to be a corner for me
(And I know there is one for you)
     When we get the hump—
     Cameelious hump—
The hump that is black and blue!

The cure for this ill is not to sit still,
   Or frowst with a book by the fire;
But to take a large hoe and a shovel also,
   And dig till you gently perspire;

And then you will find that the sun and the wind,
And the Djinn of the Garden too,

JUST SO STORIES

Have lifted the hump—
The horrible hump—
The hump that is black and blue!

I get it as well as you-oo-oo—
If I haven't enough to do-oo-oo!
We all get hump—
Cameelious hump—
Kiddies and grown-ups too!

HOW THE RHINOCEROS GOT HIS SKIN

(1897)

NCE upon a time, on an uninhabited island on the shores of the Red Sea, there lived a Parsee from whose hat the rays of the sun were reflected in more-than-oriental splendour. And the Parsee lived by the Red Sea with nothing but his hat and his knife and a cooking-stove of the kind that you must particularly never touch. And one day he took flour and water and currants and plums and sugar and things, and made himself one cake which was two feet across and three feet thick. It was indeed a Superior Comestible (that's Magic), and he put it on the stove because he was allowed to cook on that stove, and he baked it and he baked it till it was all done brown and smelt most sentimental. But just as he was going to eat it there came down to the beach from the Altogether Uninhabited Interior one Rhinoceros with a horn on his nose, two piggy eyes, and few manners. In those days the Rhinoceros's skin fitted him quite tight. There were no wrinkles in it anywhere. He looked exactly like a Noah's Ark Rhinoceros, but of course much bigger.

27

This is the picture of the Parsee beginning to eat his cake on the Uninhabited Island in the Red Sea on a very hot day; and of the Rhinoceros coming down from the Altogether Uninhabited Interior, which, as you can truthfully see, is all rocky. The Rhinoceros's skin is quite smooth, and the three buttons that button it up are underneath, so you can't see them. The squiggly things on the Parsee's hat are the rays of the sun reflected in more-than-oriental splendour, because if I had drawn real rays they would have filled up all the picture. The cake has currants in it; and the wheel-thing lying on the sand in front belonged to one of Pharaoh's chariots when he tried to cross the Red Sea. The Parsee found it, and kept it to play with. The Parsee's name was Pestonjee Bomonjee, and the Rhinoceros was called Strorks, because he breathed through his mouth instead of his nose. I wouldn't ask anything about the cooking-stove if I were you.

HOW THE RHINOCEROS GOT HIS SKIN

All the same, he had no manners then, and he has no manners now, and he never will have any manners. He said, 'How!' and the Parsee left that cake and climbed to the top of a palm-tree with nothing on but his hat, from which the rays of the sun were always reflected in more-than-oriental splendour. And the Rhinoceros upset the oil-stove with his nose, and the cake rolled on the sand, and he spiked that cake on the horn of his nose, and he ate it, and he went away, waving his tail, to the desolate and Exclusively Uninhabited Interior which abuts on the islands of Mazanderan, Socotra, and the Promontories of the Larger Equinox. Then the Parsee came down from his palm-tree and put the stove on its legs and recited the following Sloka, which, as you have not heard, I will now proceed to relate:—

> Them that takes cakes
> Which the Parsee-man bakes
> Makes dreadful mistakes.

And there was a great deal more in that than you would think.

Because, five weeks later, there was a heat-wave in the Red Sea, and everybody took off all the clothes they had. The Parsee took off his hat; but the Rhinoceros took off his skin and carried it over his shoulder as he came down to the beach to bathe. In those days it buttoned underneath with three buttons and looked like a waterproof. He said nothing whatever about the Parsee's cake, because he had eaten it all; and he never had any manners, then, since, or henceforward. He waddled straight into the water and blew bubbles through his nose, leaving his skin on the beach.

Presently the Parsee came by and found the skin, and

31

This is the Parsee Pestonjee Bomonjee sitting in his palm-tree and watching the Rhinoceros Strorks bathing near the beach of the Altogether Uninhabited Island after Strorks had taken off his skin. The Parsee has rubbed the cake-crumbs into the skin, and he is smiling to think how they will tickle Strorks when Strorks puts it on again. The skin is just under the rocks below the palm-tree in a cool place; that is why you can't see it. The Parsee is wearing a new more-than-oriental-splendour hat of the sort that Parsees wear; and he has a knife in his hand to cut his name on palm-trees. The black things on the islands out at sea are bits of ships that got wrecked going down the Red Sea; but all the passengers were saved and went home.

The black thing in the water close to the shore is not a wreck at all. It is Strorks the Rhinoceros bathing without his skin. He was just as black underneath his skin as he was outside. I wouldn't ask anything about the cooking-stove if I were you.

he smiled one smile that ran all round his face two times. Then he danced three times round the skin and rubbed his hands. Then he went to his camp and filled his hat with cake-crumbs, for the Parsee never ate anything but cake, and never swept out his camp. He took that skin, and he shook that skin, and he scrubbed that skin, and he rubbed that skin just as full of old, dry, stale, tickly cake-crumbs and some burned currants as ever it could possibly hold. Then he climbed to the top of his palm-tree and waited for the Rhinoceros to come out of the water and put it on.

And the Rhinoceros did. He buttoned it up with the three buttons, and it tickled like cake-crumbs in bed. Then he wanted to scratch, but that made it worse; and then he lay down on the sands and rolled and rolled and rolled, and every time he rolled the cake-crumbs tickled him worse and worse and worse. Then he ran to the palm-tree and rubbed and rubbed and rubbed himself against it. He rubbed so much and so hard that he rubbed his skin into a great fold over his shoulders, and another fold underneath, where the buttons used to be (but he rubbed the buttons off), and he rubbed some more folds over his legs. And it spoiled his temper, but it didn't make the least difference to the cake-crumbs. They were inside his skin and they tickled. So he went home, very angry indeed and horribly scratchy; and from that day to this every rhinoceros has great folds in his skin and a very bad temper, all on account of the cake-crumbs inside.

But the Parsee came down from his palm-tree, wearing his hat, from which the rays of the sun were reflected in more-than-oriental splendour, packed up his cooking-stove, and went away in the direction of Orotavo, Amygdala, the Upland Meadows of Anantarivo, and the Marshes of Sonaput.

This Uninhabited Island
    Is off Cape Gardafui,
By the Beaches of Socotra
    And the Pink Arabian Sea:
But it's hot—too hot from Suez
    For the likes of you and me
        Ever to go
        In a P. and O.
    And call on the Cake-Parsee!

HOW THE LEOPARD GOT HIS SPOTS

(1901)

IN the days when everybody started fair, Best Beloved, the Leopard lived in a place called the High Veldt. 'Member it wasn't the Low Veldt, or the Bush Veldt, or the Sour Veldt, but the 'sclusively bare, hot, shiny High Veldt, where there was sand and sandy-coloured rock and 'sclusively tufts of sandy-yellowish grass. The Giraffe and the Zebra and the Eland and the Koodoo and the Harte-beest lived there; and they were 'sclusively sandy-yellow-brownish all over; but the Leopard, he was the 'sclusivest sandiest-yellowest-brownest of them all—a greyish-yellowish catty-shaped kind of beast, and he matched the 'sclusively yellowish-greyish-brownish colour of the High Veldt to one hair. This was very bad for the Giraffe and the Zebra and the rest of them; for he would lie down by a 'sclusively yellowish-greyish-brownish stone or clump of grass, and when the Giraffe or the Zebra or the Eland or the Koodoo or the Bush-Buck or the Bonte-Buck came by he would surprise them out of their jumpsome lives. He would indeed! And, also, there was an Ethiopian with bows and arrows (a 'sclusively greyish-brownish-yellowish man he was then),

39

who lived on the High Veldt with the Leopard; and the two used to hunt together—the Ethiopian with his bows and arrows, and the Leopard 'sclusively with his teeth and claws—till the Giraffe and the Eland and the Koodoo and the Quagga and all the rest of them didn't know which way to jump, Best Beloved. They didn't indeed!

After a long time—things lived for ever so long in those days—they learned to avoid anything that looked like a Leopard or an Ethiopian; and bit by bit—the Giraffe began it, because his legs were the longest—they went away from the High Veldt. They scuttled for days and days and days till they came to a great forest, 'sclusively full of trees and bushes and stripy, speckly, patchy-blatchy shadows, and there they hid: and after another long time, what with standing half in the shade and half out of it, and what with the slippery-slidy shadows of the trees falling on them, the Giraffe grew blotchy, and the Zebra grew stripy, and the Eland and the Koodoo grew darker, with little wavy grey lines on their backs like bark on a tree-trunk; and so, though you could hear them and smell them, you could very seldom see them, and then only when you knew precisely where to look. They had a beautiful time in the 'sclusively speckly-spickly shadows of the forest, while the Leopard and the Ethiopian ran about over the 'sclusively greyish-yellowish-reddish High Veldt outside, wondering where all their breakfasts and their dinners and their teas had gone. At last they were so hungry that they ate rats and beetles and rock-rabbits, the Leopard and the Ethiopian, and then they had the Big Tummy-ache, both together; and then they met Baviaan—the dog-headed, barking Baboon, who is Quite the Wisest Animal in All South Africa.

40

HOW THE LEOPARD GOT HIS SPOTS

Said Leopard to Baviaan (and it was a very hot day), 'Where has all the game gone?'

And Baviaan winked. He knew.

Said the Ethiopian to Baviaan, 'Can you tell me the present habitat of the aboriginal Fauna?' (That meant just the same thing, but the Ethiopian always used long words. He was a grown-up.)

And Baviaan winked. He knew.

Then said Baviaan, 'The game has gone into other spots; and my advice to you, Leopard, is to go into other spots as soon as you can.'

And the Ethiopian said, 'That is all very fine, but I wish to know whither the aboriginal Fauna has migrated.'

Then said Baviaan, 'The aboriginal Fauna has joined the aboriginal Flora because it was high time for a change; and my advice to you, Ethiopian, is to change as soon as you can.'

That puzzled the Leopard and the Ethiopian, but they set off to look for the aboriginal Flora, and presently, after ever so many days, they saw a great, high, tall forest full of tree trunks all 'sclusively speckled and sprottled and spottled, dotted and splashed and slashed and hatched and cross-hatched with shadows. (Say that quickly aloud, and you will see how very shadowy the forest must have been.)

'What is this,' said the Leopard, 'that is so 'sclusively dark, and yet so full of little pieces of light?'

'I don't know,' said the Ethiopian, 'but it ought to be the aboriginal Flora. I can smell Giraffe, and I can hear Giraffe, but I can't see Giraffe.'

'That's curious,' said the Leopard. 'I suppose it is because we have just come in out of the sunshine. I

41

This is Wise Baviaan, the dog-headed Baboon, who is Quite the Wisest Animal in All South Africa. I have drawn him from a statue that I made up out of my own head, and I have written his name on his belt and on his shoulder and on the thing he is sitting on. I have written it in what is not called Coptic and Hieroglyphic and Cuneiformic and Bengalic and Burmic and Hebric, all because he is so wise. He is not beautiful, but he is very wise; and I should like to paint him with paint-box colours, but I am not allowed. The umbrella-ish thing about his head is his Conventional Mane.

can smell Zebra, and I can hear Zebra, but I can't see Zebra.'

'Wait a bit,' said the Ethiopian. 'It's a long time since we've hunted 'em. Perhaps we've forgotten what they were like.'

'Fiddle!' said the Leopard. 'I remember them perfectly on the High Veldt, especially their marrow-bones. Giraffe is about seventeen feet high, of a 'sclusively fulvous golden-yellow from head to heel; and Zebra is about four and a half feet high, of a 'sclusively grey-fawn colour from head to heel.'

'Umm,' said the Ethiopian, looking into the speckly-spickly shadows of the aboriginal Flora-forest. 'Then they ought to show up in this dark place like ripe bananas in a smoke-house.'

But they didn't. The Leopard and the Ethiopian hunted all day; and though they could smell them and hear them, they never saw one of them.

'For goodness' sake,' said the Leopard at tea-time, 'let us wait till it gets dark. This daylight hunting is a perfect scandal.'

So they waited till dark, and then the Leopard heard something breathing sniffily in the starlight that fell all stripy through the branches, and he jumped at the noise, and it smelt like Zebra, and it felt like Zebra, and when he knocked it down it kicked like Zebra, but he couldn't see it. So he said, 'Be quiet, O you person without any form. I am going to sit on your head till morning, because there is something about you that I don't understand.'

Presently he heard a grunt and a crash and a scramble, and the Ethiopian called out, 'I've caught a thing that I can't see. It smells like Giraffe, and it kicks like Giraffe, but it hasn't any form.'

45

'Don't you trust it,' said the Leopard. 'Sit on its head till the morning—same as me. They haven't any form—any of 'em.'

So they sat down on them hard till bright morning-time, and then Leopard said, 'What have you at your end of the table, Brother?'

The Ethiopian scratched his head and said, 'It ought to be 'sclusively a rich fulvous orange-tawny from head to heel, and it ought to be Giraffe; but it is covered all over with chestnut blotches. What have you at your end of the table, Brother?'

And the Leopard scratched his head and said, 'It ought to be 'sclusively a delicate greyish-fawn, and it ought to be Zebra; but it is covered all over with black and purple stripes. What in the world have you been doing to yourself, Zebra? Don't you know that if you were on the High Veldt I could see you ten miles off? You haven't any form.'

'Yes,' said the Zebra, 'but this isn't the High Veldt. Can't you see?'

'I can now,' said the Leopard. 'But I couldn't all yesterday. How is it done?'

'Let us up,' said the Zebra, 'and we will show you.'

They let the Zebra and the Giraffe get up; and Zebra moved away to some little thorn-bushes where the sunlight fell all stripy, and Giraffe moved off to some tallish trees where the shadows fell all blotchy.

'Now watch,' said the Zebra and the Giraffe. 'This is the way it's done. One—two—three! And where's your breakfast?'

Leopard stared, and Ethiopian stared, but all they could see were stripy shadows and blotched shadows in the forest, but never a sign of Zebra and Giraffe. They had just walked off and hidden themselves in the shadowy forest.

'Hi! Hi!' said the Ethiopian. 'That's a trick worth learning. Take a lesson by it, Leopard. You show up in this dark place like a bar of soap in a coal-scuttle.'

'Ho! Ho!' said the Leopard. 'Would it surprise you very much to know that you show up in this dark place like a mustard-plaster on a sack of coals?'

'Well, calling names won't catch dinner,' said the Ethiopian. 'The long and the little of it is that we don't match our backgrounds. I'm going to take Baviaan's advice. He told me I ought to change; and as I've nothing to change except my skin I'm going to change that.'

'What to?' said the Leopard, tremendously excited.

'To a nice working blackish-brownish colour, with a little purple in it, and touches of slaty-blue. It will be the very thing for hiding in hollows and behind trees.'

So he changed his skin then and there, and the Leopard was more excited than ever; he had never seen a man change his skin before.

'But what about me?' he said, when the Ethiopian had worked his last little finger into his fine new black skin.

'You take Baviaan's advice too. He told you to go into spots.'

'So I did,' said the Leopard. 'I went into other spots as fast as I could. I went into this spot with you, and a lot of good it has done me.'

'Oh,' said the Ethiopian, 'Baviaan didn't mean spots in South Africa. He meant spots on your skin.'

'What's the use of that?' said the Leopard.

47

This is the picture of the Leopard and the Ethiopian after they had taken Wise Baviaan's advice and the Leopard had gone into other spots and the Ethiopian had changed his skin. The Ethiopian was really a negro, and so his name was Sambo. The Leopard was called Spots, and he has been called Spots ever since. They are out hunting in the spickly-speckly forest, and they are looking for Mr. One-Two-Three-Where's-your-Breakfast. If you look a little you will see Mr. One-Two-Three not far away. The Ethiopian has hidden behind a splotchy-blotchy tree because it matches his skin, and the Leopard is lying beside a spickly-speckly bank of stones because it matches his spots. Mr. One-Two-Three-Where's-your-Breakfast is standing up eating leaves from a tall tree. This is really a puzzle-picture like 'Find-the-Cat.'

'Think of Giraffe,' said the Ethiopian. 'Or if you prefer stripes, think of Zebra. They find their spots and stripes give them per-fect satisfaction.'

'Umm,' said the Leopard. 'I wouldn't look like Zebra—not for ever so.'

'Well, make up your mind,' said the Ethiopian, 'because I'd hate to go hunting without you, but I must if you insist on looking like a sunflower against a tarred fence.'

'I'll take spots, then,' said the Leopard; 'but don't make 'em too vulgar-big. I wouldn't look like Giraffe —not for ever so.'

'I'll make 'em with the tips of my fingers,' said the Ethiopian. 'There's plenty of black left on my skin still. Stand over!'

Then the Ethiopian put his five fingers close together (there was plenty of black left on his new skin still) and pressed them all over the Leopard, and wherever the five fingers touched they left five little black marks, all close together. You can see them on any Leopard's skin you like, Best Beloved. Sometimes the fingers slipped and the marks got a little blurred; but if you look closely at any Leopard now you will see that there are always five spots—off five fat black finger-tips.

'Now you are a beauty!' said the Ethiopian. 'You can lie out on the bare ground and look like a heap of pebbles. You can lie out on the naked rocks and look like a piece of pudding-stone. You can lie out on a leafy branch and look like sunshine sifting through the leaves; and you can lie right across the centre of a path and look like nothing in particular. Think of that and purr!'

'But if I'm all this,' said the Leopard, 'why didn't you go spotty too?'

'Oh, plain black's best for a nigger,' said the Ethiopian. 'Now come along and we'll see if we can't get even with Mr. One-Two-Three-Where's-your-Breakfast!'

So they went away and lived happily ever afterward, Best Beloved. That is all.

Oh, now and then you will hear grown-ups say, 'Can the Ethiopian change his skin or the Leopard his spots?' I don't think even grown-ups would keep on saying such a silly thing if the Leopard and the Ethiopian hadn't done it once—do you? But they will never do it again, Best Beloved. They are quite contented as they are.

I am the Most Wise Baviaan, saying in most wise tones,
'Let us melt into the landscape—just us two by our
   lones.'
People have come—in a carriage—calling. But Mummy
   is there.   .   .   .
Yes, I can go if you take me—Nurse says she don't care.
Let's go up to the pig-sties and sit on the farmyard rails!
Let's say things to the bunnies, and watch 'em skitter
   their tails!
Let's—oh, anything, daddy, so long as it's you and me,
And going truly exploring, and not being in till tea!
Here's your boots (I've brought 'em), and here's your
   cap and stick,
And here's your pipe and tobacco.   Oh, come along out
   of it—quick!

THE ELEPHANT'S CHILD

(1900)

N the High and Far-Off Times the Elephant, O Best Beloved, had no trunk. He had only a blackish, bulgy nose, as big as a boot, that he could wriggle about from side to side; but he couldn't pick up things with it. But there was one Elephant—a new Elephant—an Elephant's Child —who was full of 'satiable curtiosity, and that means he asked ever so many questions. And he lived in Africa, and he filled all Africa with his 'satiable curtiosities. He asked his tall aunt, the Ostrich, why her tail-feathers grew just so, and his tall aunt the Ostrich spanked him with her hard, hard claw. He asked his tall uncle, the Giraffe, what made his skin spotty, and his tall uncle, the Giraffe, spanked him with his hard, hard hoof. And still he was full of 'satiable curtiosity! He asked his broad aunt, the Hippopotamus, why her eyes were red, and his broad aunt, the Hippopotamus, spanked him with her broad, broad hoof; and he asked his hairy uncle, the Baboon, why melons tasted just so, and his hairy uncle, the Baboon, spanked him with his hairy, hairy paw. And still

he was full of 'satiable curtiosity! He asked questions about everything that he saw, or heard, or felt, or smelt, or touched, and all his uncles and his aunts spanked him. And still he was full of 'satiable curtiosity!

One fine morning in the middle of the Precession of the Equinoxes this 'satiable Elephant's Child asked a new fine question that he had never asked before. He asked, 'What does the Crocodile have for dinner?' Then everybody said, 'Hush!' in a loud and dretful tone, and they spanked him immediately and directly, without stopping, for a long time.

By and by, when that was finished, he came upon Kolokolo Bird sitting in the middle of a wait-a-bit thorn-bush, and he said, 'My father has spanked me, and my mother has spanked me; all my aunts and uncles have spanked me for my 'satiable curtiosity; and still I want to know what the Crocodile has for dinner!'

Then Kolokolo Bird said, with a mournful cry, 'Go to the banks of the great grey-green, greasy Limpopo River, all set about with fever-trees, and find out.'

That very next morning, when there was nothing left of the Equinoxes, because the Precession had preceded according to precedent, this 'satiable Elephant's Child took a hundred pounds of bananas (the little short red kind), and a hundred pounds of sugar-cane (the long purple kind), and seventeen melons (the greeny-crackly kind), and said to all his dear families, 'Good-bye. I am going to the great grey-green, greasy Limpopo River, all set about with fever-trees, to find out what the Crocodile has for dinner.' And they all spanked him once more for luck, though he asked them most politely to stop.

Then he went away, a little warm, but not at all

astonished, eating melons, and throwing the rind about, because he could not pick it up.

He went from Graham's Town to Kimberley, and from Kimberley to Khama's Country, and from Khama's Country he went east by north, eating melons all the time, till at last he came to the banks of the great grey-green, greasy Limpopo River, all set about with fever-trees, precisely as Kolokolo Bird had said.

Now you must know and understand, O Best Beloved, that till that very week, and day, and hour, and minute, this 'satiable Elephant's Child had never seen a Crocodile, and did not know what one was like. It was all his 'satiable curtiosity.

The first thing that he found was a Bi-Coloured-Python-Rock-Snake curled round a rock.

' 'Scuse me,' said the Elephant's Child most politely, 'but have you seen such a thing as a Crocodile in these promiscuous parts?'

'Have I seen a Crocodile?' said the Bi-Coloured-Python-Rock-Snake, in a voice of dretful scorn. 'What will you ask me next?'

' 'Scuse me,' said the Elephant's Child, 'but could you kindly tell me what he has for dinner?'

Then the Bi-Coloured-Python-Rock-Snake uncoiled himself very quickly from the rock, and spanked the Elephant's Child with his scalesome, flailsome tail.

'That is odd,' said the Elephant's Child, 'because my father and my mother, and my uncle and my aunt, not to mention my other aunt, the Hippopotamus, and my other uncle, the Baboon, have all spanked me for my 'satiable curtiosity—and I suppose this is the same thing.'

So he said good-bye very politely to the Bi-Coloured-

Python-Rock-Snake, and helped to coil him up on the rock again, and went on, a little warm, but not at all astonished, eating melons, and throwing the rind about, because he could not pick it up, till he trod on what he thought was a log of wood at the very edge of the great grey-green, greasy Limpopo River, all set about with fever-trees.

But it was really the Crocodile, O Best Beloved, and the Crocodile winked one eye—like this!

''Scuse me,' said the Elephant's Child most politely, 'but do you happen to have seen a Crocodile in these promiscuous parts?'

Then the Crocodile winked the other eye, and lifted half his tail out of the mud; and the Elephant's Child stepped back most politely, because he did not wish to be spanked again.

'Come hither, Little One,' said the Crocodile. 'Why do you ask such things?'

''Scuse me,' said the Elephant's Child most politely, 'but my father has spanked me, my mother has spanked me, not to mention my tall aunt, the Ostrich, and my tall uncle, the Giraffe, who can kick ever so hard, as well as my broad aunt, the Hippopotamus, and my hairy uncle, the Baboon, and including the Bi-Coloured-Python-Rock-Snake, with the scalesome, flailsome tail, just up the bank, who spanks harder than any of them; and so, if it's quite all the same to you, I don't want to be spanked any more.'

'Come hither, Little One,' said the Crocodile, 'for I am the Crocodile,' and he wept crocodile-tears to show it was quite true.

Then the Elephant's Child grew all breathless, and panted, and kneeled down on the bank and said, 'You

58

are the very person I have been looking for all these long days. Will you please tell me what you have for dinner?'

'Come hither, Little One,' said the Crocodile, 'and I'll whisper.'

Then the Elephant's Child put his head down close to the Crocodile's musky, tusky mouth, and the Crocodile caught him by his little nose, which up to that very week, day, hour, and minute, had been no bigger than a boot, though much more useful.

'I think,' said the Crocodile—and he said it between his teeth, like this—'I think to-day I will begin with Elephant's Child!'

At this, O Best Beloved, the Elephant's Child was much annoyed, and he said, speaking through his nose, like this, 'Led go! You are hurtig be!'

Then the Bi-Coloured-Python-Rock-Snake scuffled down from the bank and said, 'My young friend, if you do not now, immediately and instantly, pull as hard as ever you can, it is my opinion that your acquaintance in the large pattern leather ulster' (and by this he meant the Crocodile) 'will jerk you into yonder limpid stream before you can say Jack Robinson.'

This is the way Bi-Coloured-Python-Rock-Snakes always talk.

Then the Elephant's Child sat back on his little haunches, and pulled, and pulled, and pulled, and his nose began to stretch. And the Crocodile floundered into the water, making it all creamy with great sweeps of his tail, and he pulled, and pulled, and pulled.

And the Elephant's Child's nose kept on stretching; and the Elephant's Child spread all his little four legs and pulled, and pulled, and pulled, and his nose kept on

This is the Elephant's Child having his nose pulled by the Crocodile. He is much surprised and astonished and hurt, and he is talking through his nose and saying, 'Led go! You are hurtig be!' He is pulling very hard, and so is the Crocodile; but the Bi-Coloured-Python-Rock-Snake is hurrying through the water to help the Elephant's Child. All that black stuff is the banks of the great grey-green, greasy Limpopo River (but I am not allowed to paint these pictures), and the bottly-tree with the twisty roots and the eight leaves is one of the fever-trees that grow there.

Underneath the truly picture are shadows of African animals walking into an African ark. There are two lions, two ostriches, two oxen, two camels, two sheep, and two other things that look like rats, but I think they are rock-rabbits. They don't mean anything. I put them in because I thought they looked pretty. They would look very fine if I were allowed to paint them.

stretching; and the Crocodile threshed his tail like an oar, and he pulled, and pulled, and pulled, and at each pull the Elephant's Child's nose grew longer and longer —and it hurt him hijjus!

Then the Elephant's Child felt his legs slipping, and he said through his nose, which was now nearly five feet long, 'This is too butch for be!'

Then the Bi-Coloured-Python-Rock-Snake came down from the bank, and knotted himself in a double-clove-hitch round the Elephant's Child's hind-legs, and said, 'Rash and inexperienced traveller, we will now seriously devote ourselves to a little high tension, because if we do not, it is my impression that yonder self-propelling man-of-war with the armour-plated upper deck' (and by this, O Best Beloved, he meant the Crocodile) 'will permanently vitiate your future career.'

That is the way all Bi-Coloured-Python-Rock-Snakes always talk.

So he pulled, and the Elephant's Child pulled, and the Crocodile pulled; but the Elephant's Child and the Bi-Coloured-Python-Rock-Snake pulled hardest; and at last the Crocodile let go of the Elephant's Child's nose with a plop that you could hear all up and down the Limpopo.

Then the Elephant's Child sat down most hard and sudden; but first he was careful to say 'Thank you' to the Bi-Coloured-Python-Rock-Snake; and next he was kind to his poor pulled nose, and wrapped it all up in cool banana leaves, and hung it in the great grey-green, greasy Limpopo to cool.

'What are you doing that for?' said the Bi-Coloured-Python-Rock-Snake.

' 'Scuse me,' said the Elephant's Child, 'but my nose

This is just a picture of the Elephant's Child going to pull bananas off a banana-tree after he had got his fine new long trunk. I don't think it is a very nice picture; but I couldn't make it any better, because elephants and bananas are hard to draw. The streaky things behind the Elephant's Child mean squoggy marshy country somewhere in Africa. The Elephant's Child made most of his mud-cakes out of the mud that he found there. I think it would look better if you painted the banana-tree green and the Elephant's Child red.

is badly out of shape, and I am waiting for it to shrink.'

'Then you will have to wait a long time,' said the Bi-Coloured-Python-Rock-Snake. 'Some people do not know what is good for them.'

The Elephant's Child sat there for three days waiting for his nose to shrink. But it never grew any shorter, and, besides, it made him squint. For, O Best Beloved, you will see and understand that the Crocodile had pulled it out into a really truly trunk same as all Elephants have to-day.

At the end of the third day a fly came and stung him on the shoulder, and before he knew what he was doing he lifted up his trunk and hit that fly dead with the end of it.

' 'Vantage number one!' said the Bi-Coloured-Python-Rock-Snake. 'You couldn't have done that with a mere-smear nose. Try and eat a little now.'

Before he thought what he was doing the Elephant's Child put out his trunk and plucked a large bundle of grass, dusted it clean against his fore-legs, and stuffed it into his own mouth.

' 'Vantage number two!' said the Bi-Coloured-Python-Rock-Snake. 'You couldn't have done that with a mere-smear nose. Don't you think the sun is very hot here?'

'It is,' said the Elephant's Child, and before he thought what he was doing he schlooped up a schloop of mud from the banks of the great grey-green, greasy Limpopo, and slapped it on his head, where it made a cool schloopy-sloshy mud-cap all trickly behind his ears.

' 'Vantage number three!' said the Bi-Coloured-

67

Python-Rock-Snake. 'You couldn't have done that with a mere-smear nose. Now how do you feel about being spanked again?'

''Scuse me,' said the Elephant's Child, 'but I should not like it at all.'

'How would you like to spank somebody?' said the Bi-Coloured-Python-Rock-Snake.

'I should like it very much indeed,' said the Elephant's Child.

'Well,' said the Bi-Coloured-Python-Rock-Snake, 'you will find that new nose of yours very useful to spank people with.'

'Thank you,' said the Elephant's Child, 'I'll remember that; and now I think I'll go home to all my dear families and try.'

So the Elephant's Child went home across Africa frisking and whisking his trunk. When he wanted fruit to eat he pulled fruit down from a tree, instead of waiting for it to fall as he used to do. When he wanted grass he plucked grass up from the ground, instead of going on his knees as he used to do. When the flies bit him he broke off the branch of a tree and used it as a fly-whisk; and he made himself a new, cool, slushy-squshy mud-cap whenever the sun was hot. When he felt lonely walking through Africa he sang to himself down his trunk, and the noise was louder than several brass bands. He went especially out of his way to find a broad Hippopotamus (she was no relation of his), and he spanked her very hard, to make sure that the Bi-Coloured-Python-Rock-Snake had spoken the truth about his new trunk. The rest of the time he picked up the melon rinds that he had dropped on his way to the Limpopo—for he was a Tidy Pachyderm.

One dark evening he came back to all his dear families, and he coiled up his trunk and said, 'How do you do?' They were very glad to see him, and immediately said, 'Come here and be spanked for your 'satiable curtiosity.'

'Pooh,' said the Elephant's Child. 'I don't think you peoples know anything about spanking; but I do, and I'll show you.'

Then he uncurled his trunk and knocked two of his dear brothers head over heels.

'O Bananas!' said they, 'where did you learn that trick, and what have you done to your nose?'

'I got a new one from the Crocodile on the banks of the great grey-green, greasy Limpopo River,' said the Elephant's Child. 'I asked him what he had for dinner, and he gave me this to keep.'

'It looks very ugly,' said his hairy uncle, the Baboon.

'It does,' said the Elephant's Child. 'But it's very useful,' and he picked up his hairy uncle, the Baboon, by one hairy leg, and hove him into a hornet's nest.

Then that bad Elephant's Child spanked all his dear families for a long time, till they were very warm and greatly astonished. He pulled out his tall Ostrich aunt's tail-feathers; and he caught his tall uncle, the Giraffe, by the hind-leg, and dragged him through a thorn-bush; and he shouted at his broad aunt, the Hippopotamus, and blew bubbles into her ear when she was sleeping in the water after meals; but he never let any one touch Kolokolo Bird.

At last things grew so exciting that his dear families went off one by one in a hurry to the banks of the great grey-green, greasy Limpopo River, all set about with fever-trees, to borrow new noses from the Crocodile.

When they came back nobody spanked anybody any more; and ever since that day, O Best Beloved, all the Elephants you will ever see, besides all those that you won't, have trunks precisely like the trunk of the 'satiable Elephant's Child.

I keep six honest serving-men
   (They taught me all I knew);
Their names are What and Why and When
   And How and Where and Who.
I send them over land and sea,
   I send them east and west;
But after they have worked for me,
   I give them all a rest.

I let them rest from nine till five,
   For I am busy then,
As well as breakfast, lunch, and tea,
   For they are hungry men.
But different folk have different views;
   I know a person small—
She keeps ten million serving-men,
   Who get no rest at all!
She sends 'em abroad on her own affairs,
   From the second she opens her eyes—
One million Hows, two million Wheres,
   And seven million Whys!

THE SING-SONG OF OLD MAN KANGAROO

(1900)

OT always was the Kangaroo as now we do behold him, but a Different Animal with four short legs. He was grey and he was woolly, and his pride was inordinate: he danced on an outcrop in the middle of Australia, and he went to the Little God Nqa.

He went to Nqa at six before breakfast, saying, 'Make me different from all other animals by five this afternoon.'

Up jumped Nqa from his seat on the sand-flat and shouted, 'Go away!'

He was grey and he was woolly, and his pride was inordinate; he danced on a rock-ledge in the middle of Australia, and he went to the Middle God Nquing.

He went to Nquing at eight after breakfast, saying, 'Make me different from all other animals; make me, also, wonderfully popular by five this afternoon.'

Up jumped Nquing from his burrow in the spinifex and shouted, 'Go away!'

He was grey and he was woolly, and his pride was inordinate: he danced on a sandbank in the middle of Australia, and he went to the Big God Nqong.

73

This is a picture of Old Man Kangaroo when he was the Different Animal with four short legs. I have drawn him grey and woolly, and you can see that he is very proud because he has a wreath of flowers in his hair. He is dancing on an outcrop (that means a ledge of rock) in the middle of Australia at six o'clock before breakfast. You can see that it is six o'clock, because the sun is just getting up. The thing with the ears and the open mouth is Little God Nqa. Nqa is very much surprised, because he has never seen a Kangaroo dance like that before. Little God Nqa is just saying, 'Go away,' but the Kangaroo is so busy dancing that he has not heard him yet.

The Kangaroo hasn't any real name except Boomer. He lost it because he was so proud.

He went to Nqong at ten before dinner-time, saying, 'Make me different from all other animals; make me popular and wonderfully run after by five this afternoon.'

Up jumped Nqong from his bath in the salt-pan and shouted, 'Yes, I will!'

Nqong called Dingo—Yellow-Dog Dingo—always hungry, dusty in the sunshine, and showed him Kangaroo. Nqong said, 'Dingo! Wake up, Dingo! Do you see that gentleman dancing on an ashpit? He wants to be popular and very truly run after. Dingo, make him so!'

Up jumped Dingo—Yellow-Dog Dingo—and said, 'What, that cat-rabbit?'

Off ran Dingo—Yellow-Dog Dingo—always hungry, grinning like a coal-scuttle,—ran after Kangaroo.

Off went the proud Kangaroo on his four little legs like a bunny.

This, O Beloved of mine, ends the first part of the tale!

He ran through the desert; he ran through the mountains; he ran through the salt-pans; he ran through the reed-beds; he ran through the blue gums; he ran through the spinifex; he ran till his front legs ached.

He had to!

Still ran Dingo—Yellow-Dog Dingo—always hungry, grinning like a rat-trap, never getting nearer, never getting farther,—ran after Kangaroo.

He had to!

Still ran Kangaroo—Old Man Kangaroo. He ran through the ti-trees; he ran through the mulga; he ran through the long grass; he ran through the short grass; he ran through the Tropics of Capricorn and Cancer; he ran till his hind legs ached.

This is the picture of Old Man Kangaroo at five in the afternoon, when he had got his beautiful hind legs just as Big God Nqong had promised. You can see that it is five o'clock, because Big God Nqong's pet tame clock says so. That is Nqong, in his bath, sticking his feet out. Old Man Kangaroo is being rude to Yellow-Dog Dingo. Yellow-Dog Dingo has been trying to catch Kangaroo all across Australia. You can see the marks of Kangaroo's big new feet running ever so far back over the bare hills. Yellow-Dog Dingo is drawn black, because I am not allowed to paint these pictures with real colours out of the paint-box; and besides, Yellow-Dog Dingo got dreadfully black and dusty after running through the Flinders and the Cinders.

I don't know the names of the flowers growing round Nqong's bath. The two little squatty things out in the desert are the other two gods that Old Man Kangaroo spoke to early in the morning. That thing with the letters on it is Old Man Kangaroo's pouch. He had to have a pouch just as he had to have legs.

He had to!

Still ran Dingo—Yellow-Dog Dingo—hungrier and hungrier, grinning like a horse-collar, never getting nearer, never getting farther; and they came to the Wollgong River.

Now, there wasn't any bridge, and there wasn't any ferry-boat, and Kangaroo didn't know how to get over; so he stood on his legs and hopped.

He had to!

He hopped through the Flinders; he hopped through the Cinders; he hopped through the deserts in the middle of Australia. He hopped like a Kangaroo.

First he hopped one yard; then he hopped three yards; then he hopped five yards; his legs growing stronger; his legs growing longer. He hadn't any time for rest or refreshment, and he wanted them very much.

Still ran Dingo—Yellow-Dog Dingo—very much bewildered, very much hungry, and wondering what in the world or out of it made Old Man Kangaroo hop.

For he hopped like a cricket; like a pea in a saucepan; or a new rubber ball on a nursery floor.

He had to!

He tucked up his front legs; he hopped on his hind legs; he stuck out his tail for a balance-weight behind him; and he hopped through the Darling Downs.

He had to!

Still ran Dingo—Tired-Dog Dingo—hungrier and hungrier, very much bewildered, and wondering when in the world or out of it would Old Man Kangaroo stop.

Then came Nqong from his bath in the salt-pans, and said, 'It's five o'clock.'

Down sat Dingo—Poor-Dog Dingo—always hungry, dusty in the sunshine; hung out his tongue and howled.

Down sat Kangaroo—Old Man Kangaroo—stuck out his tail like a milking-stool behind him, and said, 'Thank goodness that's finished!'

Then said Nqong, who is always a gentleman, 'Why aren't you grateful to Yellow-Dog Dingo? Why don't you thank him for all he has done for you?'

Then said Kangaroo—Tired Old Kangaroo—'He's chased me out of the homes of my childhood; he's chased me out of my regular meal-times; he's altered my shape so I'll never get it back; and he's played Old Scratch with my legs.'

Then said Nqong, 'Perhaps I'm mistaken, but didn't you ask me to make you different from all other animals, as well as to make you very truly sought after? And now it is five o'clock.'

'Yes,' said Kangaroo. 'I wish that I hadn't. I thought you would do it by charms and incantations, but this is a practical joke.'

'Joke!' said Nqong, from his bath in the blue gums. 'Say that again and I'll whistle up Dingo and run your hind legs off.'

'No,' said the Kangaroo. 'I must apologise. Legs are legs, and you needn't alter 'em so far as I am concerned. I only meant to explain to Your Lordliness that I've had nothing to eat since morning, and I'm very empty indeed.'

'Yes,' said Dingo—Yellow-Dog Dingo,—'I am just in the same situation. I've made him different from all other animals; but what may I have for my tea?'

Then said Nqong from his bath in the salt-pan, 'Come and ask me about it to-morrow, because I'm going to wash.'

So they were left in the middle of Australia, Old Man Kangaroo and Yellow-Dog Dingo, and each said, 'That's your fault.'

This is the mouth-filling song
Of the race that was run by a Boomer,
Run in a single burst—only event of its kind—
Started by Big God Nqong from Warrigaborrigarooma,
Old Man Kangaroo first: Yellow-Dog Dingo behind.

Kangaroo bounded away,
His back-legs working like pistons—
Bounded from morning till dark,
Twenty-five feet to a bound.
Yellow-Dog Dingo lay
Like a yellow cloud in the distance—
Much too busy to bark.
My! but they covered the ground!

Nobody knows where they went,
Or followed the track that they flew in,
For that Continent
Hadn't been given a name.
They ran thirty degrees,
From Torres Straits to the Leeuwin
(Look at the Atlas, please),
And they ran back as they came.

S'posing you could trot
From Adelaide to the Pacific,
For an afternoon's run—
Half what these gentlemen did—
You would feel rather hot,
But your legs would develop terrific—
Yes, my importunate son,
You'd be a Marvellous Kid!

THE BEGINNING OF THE ARMADILLOES

(1900)

HIS, O Best Beloved, is another story of the High and Far-Off Times. In the very middle of those times was a Stickly-Prickly Hedgehog, and he lived on the banks of the turbid Amazon, eating shelly snails and things. And he had a friend, a Slow-Solid Tortoise, who lived on the banks of the turbid Amazon, eating green lettuces and things. And so that was all right, Best Beloved. Do you see?

But also, and at the same time, in those High and Far-Off Times, there was a Painted Jaguar, and he lived on the banks of the turbid Amazon too; and he ate everything that he could catch. When he could not catch deer or monkeys he would eat frogs and beetles; and when he could not catch frogs and beetles he went to his Mother Jaguar, and she told him how to eat hedgehogs and tortoises.

She said to him ever so many times, graciously waving her tail, 'My son, when you find a Hedgehog you must drop him into the water and then he will uncoil, and when you catch a Tortoise you must scoop him out

85

of his shell with your paw.' And so that was all right, Best Beloved.

One beautiful night on the banks of the turbid Amazon, Painted Jaguar found Stickly-Prickly Hedgehog and Slow-Solid Tortoise sitting under the trunk of a fallen tree. They could not run away, and so Stickly-Prickly curled himself up into a ball, because he was a Hedgehog, and Slow-Solid Tortoise drew in his head and feet into his shell as far as they would go, because he was a Tortoise; and so that was all right, Best Beloved. Do you see?

'Now attend to me,' said Painted Jaguar, 'because this is very important. My mother said that when I meet a Hedgehog I am to drop him into the water and then he will uncoil, and when I meet a Tortoise I am to scoop him out of his shell with my paw. Now which of you is Hedgehog and which is Tortoise? because, to save my spots, I can't tell.'

'Are you sure of what your Mummy told you?' said Stickly-Prickly Hedgehog. 'Are you quite sure? Perhaps she said that when you uncoil a Tortoise you must shell him out of the water with a scoop, and when you paw a Hedgehog you must drop him on the shell.'

'Are you sure of what your Mummy told you?' said Slow-and-Solid Tortoise. 'Are you quite sure? Perhaps she said that when you water a Hedgehog you must drop him into your paw, and when you meet a Tortoise you must shell him till he uncoils.'

'I don't think it was at all like that,' said Painted Jaguar, but he felt a little puzzled; 'but, please, say it again more distinctly.'

'When you scoop water with your paw you uncoil it with a Hedgehog,' said Stickly-Prickly. 'Remember that, because it's important.'

86

'But,' said the Tortoise, 'when you paw your meat you drop it into a Tortoise with a scoop. Why can't you understand?'

'You are making my spots ache,' said Painted Jaguar; 'and besides, I didn't want your advice at all. I only wanted to know which of you is Hedgehog and which is Tortoise.'

'I shan't tell you,' said Stickly-Prickly. 'But you can scoop me out of my shell if you like.'

'Aha!' said Painted Jaguar. 'Now I know you're Tortoise. You thought I wouldn't! Now I will.' Painted Jaguar darted out his paddy-paw just as Stickly-Prickly curled himself up, and of course Jaguar's paddy-paw was just filled with prickles. Worse than that, he knocked Stickly-Prickly away and away into the woods and the bushes, where it was too dark to find him. Then he put his paddy-paw into his mouth, and of course the prickles hurt worse than ever. As soon as he could speak he said, 'Now I know he isn't Tortoise at all. But'—and then he scratched his head with his un-prickly paw—'how do I know that this other is Tortoise?'

'But I am Tortoise,' said Slow-and-Solid. 'Your mother was quite right. She said that you were to scoop me out of my shell with your paw. Begin.'

'You didn't say she said that a minute ago,' said Painted Jaguar, sucking the prickles out of his paddy-paw. 'You said she said something quite different.'

'Well, suppose you say that I said that she said something quite different, I don't see that it makes any difference; because if she said what you said I said she said, it's just the same as if I said what she said she said. On the other hand, if you think she said that you were

87

This is an inciting map of the Turbid Amazon done in Red and Black. It hasn't anything to do with the story except that there are two Armadilloes in it—up by the top. The inciting part are the adventures that happened to the men who went along the road marked in red. I meant to draw Armadilloes when I began the map, and I meant to draw manatees and spider-tailed monkeys and big snakes and lots of Jaguars, but it was more inciting to do the map and the venturesome adventures in red. You begin at the bottom left-hand corner and follow the little arrows all about, and then you come quite round again to where the adventuresome people went home in a ship called the 'Royal Tiger.' This is a most adventuresome picture, and all the adventures are told about in writing, so you can be quite sure which is an adventure and which is a tree or a boat.

to uncoil me with a scoop, instead of pawing me into drops with a shell, I can't help that, can I?'

'But you said you wanted to be scooped out of your shell with my paw,' said Painted Jaguar.

'If you'll think again you'll find that I didn't say anything of the kind. I said that your mother said that you were to scoop me out of my shell,' said Slow-and-Solid.

'What will happen if I do?' said the Jaguar most sniffily and most cautious.

'I don't know, because I've never been scooped out of my shell before; but I tell you truly, if you want to see me swim away you've only got to drop me into the water.'

'I don't believe it,' said Painted Jaguar. 'You've mixed up all the things my mother told me to do with the things that you asked me whether I was sure that she didn't say, till I don't know whether I'm on my head or my painted tail; and now you come and tell me something I can understand, and it makes me more mixy than before. My mother told me that I was to drop one of you two into the water, and as you seem so anxious to be dropped I think you don't want to be dropped. So jump into the turbid Amazon and be quick about it.'

'I warn you that your Mummy won't be pleased. Don't tell her I didn't tell you,' said Slow-Solid.

'If you say another word about what my mother said—' the Jaguar answered, but he had not finished the sentence before Slow-and-Solid quietly dived into the turbid Amazon, swam under water for a long way, and came out on the bank where Stickly-Prickly was waiting for him.

'That was a very narrow escape,' said Stickly-Prickly.

91

'I don't like Painted Jaguar. What did you tell him that you were?'

'I told him truthfully that I was a truthful Tortoise, but he wouldn't believe it, and he made me jump into the river to see if I was, and I was, and he is surprised. Now he's gone to tell his Mummy. Listen to him!'

They could hear Painted Jaguar roaring up and down among the trees and the bushes by the side of the turbid Amazon, till his Mummy came.

'Son, son!' said his mother ever so many times, graciously waving her tail, 'what have you been doing that you shouldn't have done?'

'I tried to scoop something that said it wanted to be scooped out of its shell with my paw, and my paw is full of per-ickles,' said Painted Jaguar.

'Son, son!' said his mother ever so many times, graciously waving her tail, 'by the prickles in your paddy-paw I see that that must have been a Hedgehog. You should have dropped him into the water.'

'I did that to the other thing; and he said he was a Tortoise, and I didn't believe him, and it was quite true, and he has dived under the turbid Amazon, and he won't come up again, and I haven't anything at all to eat, and I think we had better find lodgings somewhere else. They are too clever on the turbid Amazon for poor me!'

'Son, son!' said his mother ever so many times, graciously waving her tail, 'now attend to me and remember what I say. A Hedgehog curls himself up into a ball and his prickles stick out every which way at once. By this you may know the Hedgehog.'

'I don't like this old lady one little bit,' said Stickly-Prickly, under the shadow of a large leaf. 'I wonder what else she knows?'

92

THE BEGINNING OF THE ARMADILLOES

'A Tortoise can't curl himself up,' Mother Jaguar went on, ever so many times, graciously waving her tail. 'He only draws his head and legs into his shell. By this you may know the Tortoise.'

'I don't like this old lady at all—at all,' said Slow-and-Solid Tortoise. 'Even Painted Jaguar can't forget those directions. It's a great pity that you can't swim, Stickly-Prickly.'

'Don't talk to me,' said Stickly-Prickly. 'Just think how much better it would be if you could curl up. This is a mess! Listen to Painted Jaguar.'

Painted Jaguar was sitting on the banks of the turbid Amazon sucking prickles out of his paw and saying to himself—

> 'Can't curl, but can swim—
> Slow-Solid, that's him!
> Curls up, but can't swim—
> Stickly-Prickly, that's him!'

'He'll never forget that this month of Sundays,' said Stickly-Prickly. 'Hold up my chin, Slow-and-Solid. I'm going to try to learn to swim. It may be useful.'

'Excellent!' said Slow-and-Solid; and he held up Stickly-Prickly's chin, while Stickly-Prickly kicked in the waters of the turbid Amazon.

'You'll make a fine swimmer yet,' said Slow-and-Solid. 'Now, if you can unlace my back-plates a little, I'll see what I can do towards curling up. It may be useful.'

Stickly-Prickly helped to unlace Tortoise's back-plates, so that by twisting and straining Slow-and-Solid actually managed to curl up a tiddy wee bit.

'Excellent!' said Stickly-Prickly; 'but I shouldn't do

93

This is a picture of the whole story of the Jaguar and the Hedgehog and the Tortoise and the Armadillo all in a heap. It looks rather the same any way you turn it. The Tortoise is in the middle, learning how to bend, and that is why the shelly plates on his back are so spread apart. He is standing on the Hedgehog, who is waiting to learn how to swim. The Hedgehog is a Japanesy Hedgehog, because I couldn't find our own Hedgehogs in the garden when I wanted to draw them. (It was daytime, and they had gone to bed under the dahlias.) Speckly Jaguar is looking over the edge, with his paddy-paw carefully tied up by his mother, because he pricked himself scooping the Hedgehog. He is much surprised to see what the Tortoise is doing, and his paw is hurting him. The snouty thing with the little eye that Speckly Jaguar is trying to climb over is the Armadillo that the Tortoise and the Hedgehog are going to turn into when they have finished bending and swimming. It is all a magic picture, and that is one of the reasons why I haven't drawn the Jaguar's whiskers. The other reason was that he was so young that his whiskers had not grown. The Jaguar's pet name with his Mummy was Doffles.

any more just now. It's making you black in the face. Kindly lead me into the water once again and I'll practise that side-stroke which you say is so easy.' And so Stickly-Prickly practised, and Slow-Solid swam alongside.

'Excellent!' said Slow-and-Solid. 'A little more practice will make you a regular whale. Now, if I may trouble you to unlace my back and front plates two holes more, I'll try that fascinating bend that you say is so easy. Won't Painted Jaguar be surprised!'

'Excellent!' said Stickly-Prickly, all wet from the turbid Amazon. 'I declare, I shouldn't know you from one of my own family. Two holes, I think, you said? A little more expression, please, and don't grunt quite so much, or Painted Jaguar may hear us. When you've finished, I want to try that long dive which you say is so easy. Won't Painted Jaguar be surprised!'

And so Stickly-Prickly dived, and Slow-and-Solid dived alongside.

'Excellent!' said Slow-and-Solid. 'A leetle more attention to holding your breath and you will be able to keep house at the bottom of the turbid Amazon. Now I'll try that exercise of wrapping my hind legs round my ears which you say is so peculiarly comfortable. Won't Painted Jaguar be surprised!'

'Excellent!' said Stickly-Prickly. 'But it's straining your back-plates a little. They are all overlapping now, instead of lying side by side.'

'Oh, that's the result of exercise,' said Slow-and-Solid. 'I've noticed that your prickles seem to be melting into one another, and that you're growing to look rather more like a pine-cone, and less like a chestnut-burr, than you used to.'

'Am I?' said Stickly-Prickly. 'That comes from my soaking in the water. Oh, won't Painted Jaguar be surprised!'

They went on with their exercises, each helping the other, till morning came; and when the sun was high they rested and dried themselves. Then they saw that they were both of them quite different from what they had been.

'Stickly-Prickly,' said Tortoise after breakfast, 'I am not what I was yesterday; but I think that I may yet amuse Painted Jaguar.'

'That was the very thing I was thinking just now,' said Stickly-Prickly. 'I think scales are a tremendous improvement on prickles—to say nothing of being able to swim. Oh, won't Painted Jaguar be surprised! Let's go and find him.'

By and by they found Painted Jaguar, still nursing his paddy-paw that had been hurt the night before. He was so astonished that he fell three times backward over his own painted tail without stopping.

'Good morning!' said Stickly-Prickly. 'And how is your dear gracious Mummy this morning?'

'She is quite well, thank you,' said Painted Jaguar; 'but you must forgive me if I do not at this precise moment recall your name.'

'That's unkind of you,' said Stickly-Prickly, 'seeing that this time yesterday you tried to scoop me out of my shell with your paw.'

'But you hadn't any shell. It was all prickles,' said Painted Jaguar. 'I know it was. Just look at my paw!'

'You told me to drop into the turbid Amazon and be drowned,' said Slow-Solid. 'Why are you so rude and forgetful to-day?'

THE BEGINNING OF THE ARMADILLOES

'Don't you remember what your mother told you?'
said Stickly-Prickly—

> 'Can't curl, but can swim—
> Stickly-Prickly, that's him!
> Curls up, but can't swim—
> Slow-Solid, that's him!'

Then they both curled themselves up and rolled
round and round Painted Jaguar till his eyes turned
truly cart-wheels in his head.

Then he went to fetch his mother.

'Mother,' he said, 'there are two new animals in the
woods to-day, and the one that you said couldn't swim,
swims, and the one that you said couldn't curl up, curls;
and they've gone shares in their prickles, I think, because both of them are scaly all over, instead of one
being smooth and the other very prickly; and, besides
that, they are rolling round and round in circles, and I
don't feel comfy.'

'Son, son!' said Mother Jaguar ever so many times,
graciously waving her tail, 'a Hedgehog is a Hedgehog,
and can't be anything but a Hedgehog; and a Tortoise
is a Tortoise, and can never be anything else.'

'But it isn't a Hedgehog, and it isn't a Tortoise. It's
a little bit of both, and I don't know its proper name.'

'Nonsense!' said Mother Jaguar. 'Everything has
its proper name. I should call it "Armadillo" till I
found out the real one. And I should leave it alone.'

So Painted Jaguar did as he was told, especially about
leaving them alone; but the curious thing is that from
that day to this, O Best Beloved, no one on the banks
of the turbid Amazon has ever called Stickly-Prickly
and Slow-Solid anything except Armadillo. There are

99

Hedgehogs and Tortoises in other places, of course (there are some in my garden); but the real old and clever kind, with their scales lying lippety-lappety one over the other, like pine-cone scales, that lived on the banks of the turbid Amazon in the High and Far-Off Days, are always called Armadilloes, because they were so clever.

So that's all right, Best Beloved. Do you see?

I've never sailed the Amazon,
  I've never reached Brazil;
But the 'Don' and 'Magdalena,'
  They can go there when they will!

        Yes, weekly from Southampton,
        Great steamers, white and gold,
        Go rolling down to Rio
        (Roll down—roll down to Rio!)
        And I'd like to roll to Rio
        Some day before I'm old!

I've never seen a Jaguar,
  Nor yet an Armadill—
O dilloing in his armour,
  And I s'pose I never will,

        Unless I go to Rio
        These wonders to behold—
        Roll down—roll down to Rio—
        Roll really down to Rio!
        Oh, I'd love to roll to Rio
        Some day before I'm old!

HOW THE FIRST LETTER WAS WRITTEN

(1901)

NCE upon a most early time was a Neolithic man. He was not a Jute or an Angle, or even a Dravidian, which he might well have been, Best Beloved, but never mind why. He was a Primitive, and he lived cavily in a Cave, and he wore very few clothes, and he couldn't read and he couldn't write and he didn't want to, and except when he was hungry he was quite happy. His name was Tegumai Bopsulai, and that means, 'Man-who-does-not-put-his-foot-forward-in-a-hurry'; but we, O Best Beloved, will call him Tegumai, for short. And his wife's name was Teshumai Tewindrow, and that means, 'Lady-who-asks-a-very-many-questions'; but we, O Best Beloved, will call her Teshumai, for short. And his little girl-daughter's name was Taffimai Metallumai, and that means, 'Small-person-without-any-manners-who-ought-to-be-spanked'; but I'm going to call her Taffy. And she was Tegumai Bopsulai's Best Beloved and her own Mummy's Best Beloved, and she was not spanked half as much as was good for her; and they were all three very happy. As soon as Taffy could run about she went everywhere

with her Daddy Tegumai, and sometimes they would
not come home to the Cave till they were hungry, and
then Teshumai Tewindrow would say, 'Where in the
world have you two been to, to get so shocking dirty?
Really, my Tegumai, you're no better than my Taffy.'

Now attend and listen!

One day Tegumai Bopsulai went down through the
beaver-swamp to the Wagai river to spear carp-fish for
dinner, and Taffy went too. Tegumai's spear was made
of wood with shark's teeth at the end, and before he had
caught any fish at all he accidentally broke it clean
across by jabbing it down too hard on the bottom of the
river. They were miles and miles from home (of course
they had their lunch with them in a little bag), and
Tegumai had forgotten to bring any extra spears.

'Here's a pretty kettle of fish!' said Tegumai. 'It
will take me half the day to mend this.'

'There's your big black spear at home,' said Taffy.
'Let me run back to the Cave and ask Mummy to give
it me.'

'It's too far for your little fat legs,' said Tegumai.
'Besides, you might fall into the beaver-swamp and be
drowned. We must make the best of a bad job.' He
sat down and took out a little leather mendy-bag, full
of reindeer-sinews and strips of leather, and lumps of
bees-wax and resin, and began to mend the spear.
Taffy sat down too, with her toes in the water and her
chin in her hand, and thought very hard. Then she
said—

'I say, Daddy, it's an awful nuisance that you and I
don't know how to write, isn't it? If we did we could
send a message for the new spear.'

'Taffy,' said Tegumai, 'how often have I told you not

104

to use slang? "Awful" isn't a pretty word,—but it would be a convenience, now you mention it, if we could write home.'

Just then a Stranger-man came along the river, but he belonged to a far tribe, the Tewaras, and he did not understand one word of Tegumai's language. He stood on the bank and smiled at Taffy, because he had a little girl-daughter of his own at home. Tegumai drew a hank of deer-sinews from his mendy-bag and began to mend his spear.

'Come here,' said Taffy. 'Do you know where my Mummy lives?' And the Stranger-man said 'Um!'— being, as you know, a Tewara.

'Silly!' said Taffy, and she stamped her foot, because she saw a shoal of very big carp going up the river just when her Daddy couldn't use his spear.

'Don't bother grown-ups,' said Tegumai, so busy with his spear-mending that he did not turn round.

'I aren't,' said Taffy. 'I only want him to do what I want him to do, and he won't understand.'

'Then don't bother me,' said Tegumai, and he went on pulling and straining at the deer-sinews with his mouth full of loose ends. The Stranger-man—a genuine Tewara he was—sat down on the grass, and Taffy showed him what her Daddy was doing. The Stranger-man thought, 'This is a very wonderful child. She stamps her foot at me and she makes faces. She must be the daughter of that noble Chief who is so great that he won't take any notice of me.' So he smiled more politely than ever.

'Now,' said Taffy, 'I want you to go to my Mummy, because your legs are longer than mine, and you won't fall into the beaver-swamp, and ask for Daddy's other spear—the one with the black handle that hangs over our fireplace.'

The Stranger-man (and he was a Tewara) thought, 'This is a very, very wonderful child. She waves her arms and she shouts at me, but I don't understand a word of what she says. But if I don't do what she wants, I greatly fear that that haughty Chief, Man-who-turns-his-back-on-callers, will be angry.' He got up and twisted a big flat piece of bark off a birch-tree and gave it to Taffy. He did this, Best Beloved, to show that his heart was as white as the birch-bark and that he meant no harm; but Taffy didn't quite understand.

'Oh!' said she. 'Now I see! You want my Mummy's living-address? Of course I can't write, but I can draw pictures if I've anything sharp to scratch with. Please lend me the shark's tooth off your necklace.'

The Stranger-man (and he was a Tewara) didn't say anything, so Taffy put up her little hand and pulled at the beautiful bead and seed and shark-tooth necklace round his neck.

The Stranger-man (and he was a Tewara) thought, 'This is a very, very wonderful child. The shark's tooth on my necklace is a magic shark's tooth, and I was always told that if anybody touched it without my leave they would immediately swell up or burst. But this child doesn't swell up or burst, and that important Chief, Man-who-attends-strictly-to-his-business, who has not yet taken any notice of me at all, doesn't seem to be afraid that she will swell up or burst. I had better be more polite.'

So he gave Taffy the shark's tooth, and she lay down flat on her tummy with her legs in the air, like some people on the drawing-room floor when they want to draw pictures, and she said, 'Now I'll draw you some beautiful pictures! You can look over my shoulder, but you mustn't joggle. First I'll draw Daddy fishing. It isn't very like him; but Mummy will know, because I've drawn his spear all broken. Well, now I'll draw the other spear that he wants, the black-handled spear. It looks as if it was sticking in Daddy's back, but that's because the shark's tooth slipped and this piece of bark isn't big enough. That's the spear I want you to fetch; so I'll draw a picture of me myself 'splaining to you. My hair doesn't stand up like I've drawn, but it's easier to draw that way. Now I'll draw you. I think you're very nice really, but I can't make you pretty in the picture, so you mustn't be 'fended. Are you 'fended?'

The Stranger-man (and he was a Tewara) smiled. He thought, 'There must be a big battle going to be fought somewhere, and this extraordinary child, who takes my magic shark's tooth but who does not swell up or burst, is telling me to call all the great Chief's tribe to help him. He is a great Chief, or he would have noticed me.'

'Look,' said Taffy, drawing very hard and rather scratchily, 'now I've drawn you, and I've put the spear that Daddy wants into your hand, just to remind you that you're to bring it. Now I'll show you how to find my Mummy's living-address. You go along till you come to two trees (those are trees), and then you go over a hill (that's a hill), and then you come into a beaver-swamp all full of beavers. I haven't put in all the beavers, because I can't draw beavers, but I've drawn their heads, and that's all you'll see of them when you cross the swamp. Mind you don't fall in!

Then our Cave is just beyond the beaver-swamp. It isn't as high as the hills really, but I can't draw things very small. That's my Mummy outside. She is beautiful. She is the most beautifullest Mummy there ever was, but she won't be 'fended when she sees I've drawn her so plain. She'll be pleased of me because I can draw. Now, in case you forget, I've drawn the spear that Daddy wants outside our Cave. It's inside really, but you show the picture to my Mummy and she'll give it you. I've made her holding up her hands, because I know she'll be so pleased to see you. Isn't it a beautiful picture? And do you quite understand, or shall I 'splain again?'

Now this is the picture that Taffy had drawn for him!

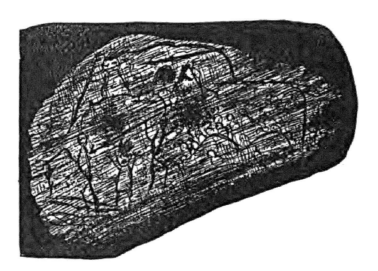

The Stranger-man (and he was a Tewara) looked at the picture and nodded very hard. He said to himself, 'If I do not fetch this great Chief's tribe to help him, he will be slain by his enemies who are coming up on all sides with spears. Now I see why the great Chief pretended not to notice me! He feared that his enemies were hiding in the bushes and would see him deliver a message to me. Therefore he turned his back, and let the wise and wonderful child draw the terrible picture showing me his difficulties. I will away and get help for him from his tribe.' He did not even ask Taffy the road, but raced off into the bushes like the wind, with the birch-bark in his hand, and Taffy sat down most pleased.

'What have you been doing, Taffy?' said Tegumai. He had mended his spear and was carefully waving it to and fro.

'It's a little berangement of my own, Daddy dear,' said Taffy. 'If you won't ask me questions, you'll know all about it in a little time, and you'll be surprised. You don't know how surprised you'll be, Daddy! Promise you'll be surprised.'

'Very well,' said Tegumai, and went on fishing.

The Stranger-man—did you know he was a Tewara? —hurried away with the picture and ran for some miles, till quite by accident he found Teshumai Tewindrow at the door of her Cave, talking to some other Neolithic ladies who had come in to a Primitive lunch. Taffy was very like Teshumai, specially about the upper part of the face and the eyes, so the Stranger-man—always a pure Tewara—smiled politely and handed Teshumai the birch-bark. He had run hard, so that he panted, and his legs were scratched with brambles, but he still tried to be polite.

As soon as Teshumai saw the picture she screamed like anything and flew at the Stranger-man. The other Neolithic ladies at once knocked him down and sat on him in a long line of six, while Teshumai pulled his hair.

'It's as plain as the nose on this Stranger-man's face,' she said. 'He has stuck my Tegumai all full of spears, and frightened poor Taffy so that her hair stands all on end; and not content with that, he brings me a horrid picture of how it was done. Look!' She showed the picture to all the Neolithic ladies sitting patiently on the Stranger-man. 'Here is my Tegumai with his arm broken; here is a spear sticking into his back; here is a man with a spear ready to throw; here is another man throwing a spear from a Cave, and here are a whole pack of people' (they were Taffy's beavers really, but they did look rather like people) 'coming up behind Tegumai. Isn't it shocking!'

'Most shocking!' said the Neolithic ladies, and they filled the Stranger-man's hair with mud (at which he was surprised), and they beat upon the Reverberating Tribal Drums, and called together all the chiefs of the Tribe of Tegumai, with their Hetmans and Dolmans, all Neguses, Woons, and Akhoonds of the organisation, in addition to the Warlocks, Angekoks, Juju-men, Bonzes, and the rest, who decided that before they chopped the Stranger-man's head off he should instantly lead them down to the river and show them where he had hidden poor Taffy.

By this time the Stranger-man (in spite of being a Tewara) was really annoyed. They had filled his hair quite solid with mud; they had rolled him up and down on knobby pebbles; they had sat upon him in a long line of six; they had thumped him and bumped him till he could hardly breathe; and though he did not understand their language, he was almost sure that the names the Neolithic ladies called him were not lady-like. However, he said nothing till all the Tribe of Tegumai

were assembled, and then he led them back to the bank
of the Wagai river, and there they found Taffy making
daisy-chains, and Tegumai carefully spearing small carp
with his mended spear.

'Well, you have been quick!' said Taffy. 'But why
did you bring so many people? Daddy dear, this is my
surprise. Are you surprised, Daddy?'

'Very,' said Tegumai; 'but it has ruined all my fishing
for the day. Why, the whole dear, kind, nice, clean,
quiet Tribe is here, Taffy.'

And so they were. First of all walked Teshumai
Tewindrow and the Neolithic ladies, tightly holding on
to the Stranger-man, whose hair was full of mud (al-
though he was a Tewara). Behind them came the
Head Chief, the Vice-Chief, the Deputy and Assistant
Chiefs (all armed to the upper teeth), the Hetmans and
Heads of Hundreds, Platoffs with their Platoons, and
Dolmans with their Detachments; Woons, Neguses,
and Akhoonds ranking in the rear (still armed to the
teeth). Behind them was the Tribe in hierarchical
order, from owners of four caves (one for each season), a
private reindeer-run, and two salmon-leaps, to feudal
and prognathous Villeins, semi-entitled to half a bear-
skin of winter nights, seven yards from the fire, and
adscript serfs, holding the reversion of a scraped marrow-
bone under heriot. (Aren't those beautiful words, Best
Beloved?) They were all there, prancing and shouting,
and they frightened every fish for twenty miles, and
Tegumai thanked them in a fluid Neolithic oration.

Then Teshumai Tewindrow ran down and kissed and
hugged Taffy very much indeed; but the Head Chief of
the Tribe of Tegumai took Tegumai by the top-knot
feathers and shook him severely.

111

This is the story of Taffimai Metallumai carved on an old tusk a very long time ago by the Ancient Peoples. If you read my story, or have it read to you, you can see how it is all told out on the tusk. The tusk was part of an old tribal trumpet that belonged to the Tribe of Tegumai. The pictures were scratched on it with a nail or something, and then the scratches were filled up with black wax, but all the dividing lines and the five little rounds at the bottom were filled with red wax. When it was new there was a sort of network of beads and shells and precious stones at one end of it; but now that has been broken and lost—all except the little bit that you see. The letters round the tusk are magic— Runic magic,—and if you can read them you will find out something rather new. The tusk is of ivory— very yellow and scratched. It is two feet long and two feet round, and weighs eleven pounds nine ounces.

113

'Explain! Explain! Explain!' cried all the Tribe of Tegumai.

'Goodness' sakes alive!' said Tegumai. 'Let go of my top-knot. Can't a man break his carp-spear without the whole countryside descending on him? You're a very interfering people.'

'I don't believe you've brought my Daddy's black-handled spear after all,' said Taffy. 'And what are you doing to my nice Stranger-man?'

They were thumping him by twos and threes and tens till his eyes turned round and round. He could only gasp and point at Taffy.

'Where are the bad people who speared you, my darling?' said Teshumai Tewindrow.

'There weren't any,' said Tegumai. 'My only visitor this morning was the poor fellow that you are trying to choke. Aren't you well, or are you ill, O Tribe of Tegumai?'

'He came with a horrible picture,' said the Head Chief,—'a picture that showed you were full of spears.'

'Er—um—P'raps I'd better 'splain that I gave him that picture,' said Taffy, but she did not feel quite comfy.

'You!' said the Tribe of Tegumai all together. 'Small-person - with - no - manners - who - ought - to - be - spanked! You?'

'Taffy dear, I'm afraid we're in for a little trouble,' said her Daddy, and put his arm round her, so she didn't care.

'Explain! Explain! Explain!' said the Head Chief of the Tribe of Tegumai, and he hopped on one foot.

'I wanted the Stranger-man to fetch Daddy's spear, so I drawded it,' said Taffy. 'There wasn't lots of

115

spears. There was only one spear. I drawded it three times to make sure. I couldn't help it looking as if it stuck into Daddy's head—there wasn't room on the birch-bark; and those things that Mummy called bad people are my beavers. I drawded them to show him the way through the swamp; and I drawded Mummy at the mouth of the Cave looking pleased because he is a nice Stranger-man, and I think you are just the stupidest people in the world,' said Taffy. 'He is a very nice man. Why have you filled his hair with mud? Wash him!'

Nobody said anything at all for a long time, till the Head Chief laughed; then the Stranger-man (who was at least a Tewara) laughed; then Tegumai laughed till he fell down flat on the bank; then all the Tribe laughed more and worse and louder. The only people who did not laugh were Teshumai Tewindrow and all the Neolithic ladies. They were very polite to all their husbands, and said 'Idiot!' ever so often.

Then the Head Chief of the Tribe of Tegumai cried and said and sang, 'O Small-person-without-any-manners-who-ought-to-be-spanked, you've hit upon a great invention!'

'I didn't intend to; I only wanted Daddy's black-handled spear,' said Taffy.

'Never mind. It is a great invention, and some day men will call it writing. At present it is only pictures, and, as we have seen to-day, pictures are not always properly understood. But a time will come, O Babe of Tegumai, when we shall make letters—all twenty-six of 'em,—and when we shall be able to read as well as to write, and then we shall always say exactly what we mean without any mistakes. Let the Neolithic ladies wash the mud out of the stranger's hair!'

'I shall be glad of that,' said Taffy, 'because, after all, though you've brought every single other spear in the Tribe of Tegumai, you've forgotten my Daddy's black-handled spear.'

Then the Head Chief cried and said and sang, 'Taffy dear, the next time you write a picture-letter, you'd better send a man who can talk our language with it, to explain what it means. I don't mind it myself, because I am a Head Chief, but it's very bad for the rest of the Tribe of Tegumai, and, as you can see, it surprises the stranger.'

Then they adopted the Stranger-man (a genuine Tewara of Tewar) into the Tribe of Tegumai, because he was a gentleman and did not make a fuss about the mud that the Neolithic ladies had put into his hair. But from that day to this (and I suppose it is all Taffy's fault), very few little girls have ever liked learning to read or write. Most of them prefer to draw pictures and play about with their Daddies—just like Taffy.

There runs a road by Merrow Down—
    A grassy track to-day it is—
An hour out of Guildford town,
    Above the river Wey it is.

Here, when they heard the horse-bells ring,
    The ancient Britons dressed and rode
To watch the dark Phœnicians bring
    Their goods along the Western Road.

Yes, here, or hereabouts, they met
    To hold their racial talks and such—
To barter beads for Whitby jet,
    And tin for gay shell torques and such.

But long and long before that time
    (When bison used to roam on it)
Did Taffy and her Daddy climb
    That down, and had their home on it.

Then beavers built in Broadstonebrook
    And made a swamp where Bramley stands;
And bears from Shere would come and look
    For Taffimai where Shamley stands.

The Wey, that Taffy called Wagai,
    Was more than six times bigger then;
And all the Tribe of Tegumai
    They cut a noble figure then!

HOW THE ALPHABET WAS MADE

(1901)

HE week after Taffimai Metal-lumai (we will still call her Taffy, Best Beloved) made that little mistake about her Daddy's spear and the Stranger-man and the picture-letter and all, she went carp-fishing again with her Daddy. Her Mummy wanted her to stay at home and help hang up hides to dry on the big drying-poles outside their Neolithic Cave, but Taffy slipped away down to her Daddy quite early, and they fished. Presently she began to giggle, and her Daddy said, 'Don't be silly, child.'

'But wasn't it inciting!' said Taffy. 'Don't you remember how the Head Chief puffed out his cheeks, and how funny the nice Stranger-man looked with the mud in his hair?'

'Well do I,' said Tegumai. 'I had to pay two deer-skins—soft ones with fringes—to the Stranger-man for the things we did to him.'

'We didn't do anything,' said Taffy. 'It was Mummy and the other Neolithic ladies—and the mud.'

121

'We won't talk about that,' said her Daddy. 'Let's have lunch.'

Taffy took a marrow-bone and sat mousy-quiet for ten whole minutes, while her Daddy scratched on pieces of birch-bark with a shark's tooth. Then she said, 'Daddy, I've thinked of a secret-surprise. You make a noise—any sort of noise.'

'Ah!' said Tegumai. 'Will that do to begin with?'

'Yes,' said Taffy. 'You look just like a carp-fish with its mouth open. Say it again, please.'

'Ah! ah! ah!' said her Daddy. 'Don't be rude, my daughter.'

'I'm not meaning rude, really and truly,' said Taffy. 'It's part of my secret-surprise-think. Do say "ah," Daddy, and keep your mouth open at the end, and lend me that tooth. I'm going to draw a carp-fish's mouth wide-open.'

'What for?' said her Daddy.

'Don't you see?' said Taffy, scratching away on the bark. 'That will be our little secret-s'prise. When I draw a carp-fish with his mouth open in the smoke at the back of our Cave—if Mummy doesn't mind—it will remind you of that ah-noise. Then we can play that it was me jumped out of the dark and s'prised you with that noise—same as I did in the beaver-swamp last winter.'

'Really?' said her Daddy, in the voice that grown-ups use when they are truly attending. 'Go on, Taffy.'

'Oh bother!' she said. 'I can't draw all of a carp-fish, but I can draw something that means a carp-fish's mouth. Don't you know how they stand on their heads rooting in the mud? Well, here's a pretence carp-fish (we can play that the rest of him is drawn). Here's just his mouth, and that means "ah."' And she drew this. (1.)

122

'That's not bad,' said Tegumai, and scratched on his own piece of bark for himself; 'but you've forgotten the feeler that hangs across his mouth.'

'But I can't draw, Daddy.'

'You needn't draw anything of him except just the opening of his mouth and the feeler across. Then we'll know he's a carp-fish, 'cause the perches and trouts haven't got feelers. Look here, Taffy.' And he drew this. (2.)

'Now I'll copy it,' said Taffy. 'Will you understand this when you see it?' And she drew this. (3.)

'Perfectly,' said her Daddy. 'And I'll be quite as s'prised when I see it anywhere, as if you had jumped out from behind a tree and said "Ah!"'

'Now, make another noise,' said Taffy, very proud.

'Yah!' said her Daddy, very loud.

'H'm,' said Taffy. 'That's a mixy noise. The end part is "ah"-carp-fish-mouth; but what can we do about the front part? "Yer-yer-yer" and "ah! Ya!"'

'It's very like the carp-fish-mouth noise. Let's draw another bit of the carp-fish and join 'em,' said her Daddy. He was quite incited too.

'No. If they're joined, I'll forget. Draw it separate. Draw his tail. If he's standing on his head the tail will come first. 'Sides, I think I can draw tails easiest,' said Taffy.

'A good notion,' said Tegumai. 'Here's a carp-fish tail for the "yer"-noise.' And he drew this. (4.)

'I'll try now,' said Taffy. ''Member I can't draw like you, Daddy. Will it do if I just draw the split part

123

of the tail, and a sticky-down line for where it joins?'
And she drew this. (5.)
Her Daddy nodded, and his eyes were
shiny bright with 'citement.
'That's beautiful,' she said. 'Now, make
another noise, Daddy.'
'Oh!' said her Daddy, very loud.
'That's quite easy,' said Taffy. 'You make your
mouth all round like an egg or a stone. So an egg or a
stone will do for that.'
'You can't always find eggs or stones. We'll have to
scratch a round something like one.' And he
drew this. (6.)
'My gracious!' said Taffy, 'what a lot of
noise-pictures we've made,—carp-mouth, carp-
tail, and egg! Now, make another noise,   6
Daddy.'
'Ssh!' said her Daddy, and frowned to himself, but
Taffy was too incited to notice.
'That's quite easy,' she said, scratching on the
bark.
'Eh, what?' said her Daddy. 'I meant I was thinking, and didn't want to be disturbed.'
'It's a noise, just the same. It's the noise a snake
makes, Daddy, when it is thinking and doesn't
want to be disturbed. Let's make the "ssh"-
noise a snake. Will this do?' And she drew
this. (7.)
7   'There,' she said. 'That's another s'prise-
secret. When you draw a hissy-snake by the door of
your little back-cave where you mend the spears, I'll
know you're thinking hard; and I'll come in most mousy-
quiet. And if you draw it on a tree by the river when

124

you're fishing, I'll know you want me to walk most most mousy-quiet, so as not to shake the banks.'

'Perfectly true,' said Tegumai. 'And there's more in this game than you think. Taffy, dear, I've a notion that your Daddy's daughter has hit upon the finest thing that there ever was since the Tribe of Tegumai took to using shark's teeth instead of flints for their spear-heads. I believe we've found out the big secret of the world.'

'Why?' said Taffy, and her eyes shone too with incitement.

'I'll show,' said her Daddy. 'What's water in the Tegumai language?'

'"Ya," of course, and it means river too—like Wagai-ya—the Wagai river.'

'What is bad water that gives you fever if you drink it—black water—swamp-water?'

'"Yo," of course.'

'Now look,' said her Daddy. 'S'pose you saw this scratched by the side of a pool in the beaver-swamp?' And he drew this. (8.)

'Carp-tail and round egg. Two noises mixed! "Yo," bad water,' said Taffy. ''Course I wouldn't drink that water because I'd know you said it was bad.'

'But I needn't be near the water at all. I might be miles away, hunting, and still—'

'And still it would be just the same as if you stood there and said, "G'way, Taffy, or you'll get fever." And that in a carp-fish-tail and a round egg! O Daddy, we must tell Mummy, quick!' and Taffy danced all round him.

'Not yet,' said Tegumai; 'not till we've gone a little

125

SO further. Let's see. "Yo" is bad water, but "so" is food cooked on the fire, isn't it?' And he drew this. (9.)

9

'Yes. Snake and egg,' said Taffy. 'So that means dinner's ready. If you saw that scratched on a tree you'd know it was time to come to the Cave. So'd I.'

'My Winkie!' said Tegumai. 'That's true too. But wait a minute. I see a difficulty. "So" means "come and have dinner," but "sho" means the drying-poles where we hang our hides.'

'Horrid old drying-poles!' said Taffy. 'I hate helping to hang heavy, hot, hairy hides on them. If you drew the snake and egg, and I thought it meant dinner, and I came in from the wood and found that it meant I was to help Mummy hang the hides on the drying-poles, what would I do?'

'You'd be cross. So'd Mummy. We must make a new picture for "sho." We must draw a spotty snake that hisses "sh-sh," and we'll play that the plain snake only hisses "ssss."'

'I couldn't be sure how to put in the spots,' said Taffy. 'And p'raps if you were in a hurry you might leave them out, and I'd think it was "so" when it was "sho," and then Mummy would catch me just the same. No! I think we'd better draw a picture of the horrid high drying-poles their very selves, and make quite sure. I'll put 'em in just after the hissy-snake. Look!' And she drew this. (10.)

SHO

10

'P'raps that's safest. It's very like our drying-poles, anyhow,' said her Daddy, laughing. 'Now I'll make a

126

new noise with a snake and drying-pole sound in it.
I'll say "shi." That's Tegumai for spear, Taffy.' And
he laughed.

'Don't make fun of me,' said Taffy, as she thought of
her picture-letter and the mud in the Stranger-man's
hair. 'You draw it, Daddy.'

'We won't have beavers or hills this time, eh?' said
her Daddy. 'I'll just draw a straight line
for my spear.' And he drew this. (11.)

'Even Mummy couldn't mistake that for
me being killed.'

'Please don't, Daddy. It makes me un-
comfy. Do some more noises. We're getting on beautifully.'

'Er-hm!' said Tegumai, looking up. 'We'll say "shu."
That means sky.'

Taffy drew the snake and the drying-pole. Then she
stopped. 'We must make a new picture for that end
sound, mustn't we?'

'"Shu-shu-u-u-u!"' said her Daddy. 'Why, it's
just like the round-egg-sound made thin.'

'Then s'pose we draw a thin round egg, and pretend
it's a frog that hasn't eaten anything for years.'

'N-no,' said her Daddy. 'If we drew that in a hurry
we might mistake it for the round egg itself. "Shu-shu-
shu!" I'll tell you what we'll do. We'll open a little
hole at the end of the round egg to show how the
O-noise runs out all thin, "ooo-oo-oo." Like
this.' And he drew this. (12.)

'Oh, that's lovely! Much better than a thin
frog. Go on,' said Taffy, using her shark's tooth.

Her Daddy went on drawing, and his hand shook with
incitement. He went on till he had drawn this. (13.)

SHU YA
13

'Don't look up, Taffy,' he said. 'Try if you can make out what that means in the Tegumai language. If you can, we've found the Secret.'

'Snake—pole—broken-egg—carp-tail and carp-mouth,' said Taffy. '"Shu-ya." Sky-water (rain).' Just then a drop fell on her hand, for the day had clouded over. 'Why, Daddy, it's raining. Was that what you meant to tell me?'

'Of course,' said her Daddy. 'And I told it you without saying a word, didn't I?'

'Well, I think I would have known it in a minute, but that raindrop made me quite sure. I'll always remember now. "Shu-ya" means rain, or "it is going to rain." Why, Daddy!' She got up and danced round him. 'S'pose you went out before I was awake, and drawed "shu-ya" in the smoke on the wall, I'd know it was going to rain and I'd take my beaver-skin hood. Wouldn't Mummy be surprised.'

Tegumai got up and danced. (Daddies didn't mind doing those things in those days.) 'More than that! More than that!' he said. 'S'pose I wanted to tell you it wasn't going to rain much and you must come down to the river, what would we draw? Say the words in Tegumai-talk first.'

'"Shu-ya-las, ya maru." (Sky-water ending. River come to.) What a lot of new sounds! I don't see how we can draw them.'

'But I do—but I do!' said Tegumai. 'Just attend a minute, Taffy, and we won't do any more to-day. We've got "shu-ya" all right, haven't we? but this "las" is a teaser. "La-la-la!"' and he waved his shark-tooth.

'There's the hissy-snake at the end and the carp-

128

mouth before the snake—"as-as-as." We only want "la-la,"' said Taffy.

'I know it, but we have to make "la-la." And we're the first people in all the world who've ever tried to do it, Taffimai!'

'Well,' said Taffy, yawning, for she was rather tired. '"Las" means breaking or finishing as well as ending, doesn't it?'

'So it does,' said Tegumai. '"Yo-las" means that there's no water in the tank for Mummy to cook with—just when I'm going hunting, too.'

'And "shi-las" means that your spear is broken. If I'd only thought of that instead of drawing silly beaver-pictures for the Stranger!'

'"La! La! La!"' said Tegumai, waving his stick and frowning. 'Oh bother!'

'I could have drawn "shi" quite easily,' Taffy went on. 'Then I'd have drawn your spear all broken —this way!' And she drew. (14.)

'The very thing,' said Tegumai. 'That's "la" all over. It isn't like any of the other marks, either.' And he drew this. (15.)

'Now for "ya." Oh, we've done that before. Now for "maru." "Mum-mum-mum." "Mum" shuts one's mouth up, doesn't it? We'll draw a shut mouth like this.' And he drew. (16.)

'Then the carp-mouth open. That makes "Ma-ma-ma!" But what about this "rrrrr"-thing, Taffy?'

'It sounds all rough and edgy, like your shark-tooth saw when you're cutting out a plank for the canoe,' said Taffy.

'You mean all sharp at the edges, like this?' said Tegumai. And he drew. (17.)

''Xactly,' said Taffy. 'But we don't want all those teeth: only put two.'

'I'll only put in one,' said Tegumai. 'If this game of ours is going to be what I think it will, the easier we make our sound-pictures the better for everybody.' And he drew. (18.)

'Now we've got it,' said Tegumai, standing on one leg. 'I'll draw 'em all in a string like fish.'

'Hadn't we better put a little bit of stick or something between each word, so's they won't rub up against each other and jostle, same as if they were carps?'

'Oh, I'll leave a space for that,' said her Daddy. And very incitedly he drew them all without stopping, on a big new bit of birch-bark. (19.)

¹⁹

'"Shu-ya-las ya-maru,"' said Taffy, reading it out sound by sound.

'That's enough for to-day,' said Tegumai. 'Besides, you're getting tired, Taffy. Never mind, dear. We'll finish it all to-morrow, and then we'll be remembered for years and years after the biggest trees you can see are all chopped up for firewood.'

So they went home, and all that evening Tegumai sat on one side of the fire and Taffy on the other, drawing 'ya's' and 'yo's' and 'shu's' and 'shi's' in the smoke on the wall and giggling together till her Mummy said. 'Really, Tegumai, you're worse than my Taffy.'

HOW THE ALPHABET WAS MADE

'Please don't mind,' said Taffy. 'It's only our secret-s'prise, Mummy dear, and we'll tell you all about it the very minute it's done; but please don't ask me what it is now, or else I'll have to tell.'

So her Mummy most carefully didn't; and bright and early next morning Tegumai went down to the river to think about new sound-pictures, and when Taffy got up she saw 'Ya-las' (water is ending or running out) chalked on the side of the big stone water-tank, outside the Cave.

'Um,' said Taffy. 'These picture-sounds are rather a bother! Daddy's just as good as come here himself and told me to get more water for Mummy to cook with.' She went to the spring at the back of the house and filled the tank from a bark bucket, and then she ran down to the river and pulled her Daddy's left ear—the one that belonged to her to pull when she was good.

'Now come 'along and we'll draw all the left-over sound-pictures,' said her Daddy, and they had a most inciting day of it, and a beautiful lunch in the middle, and two games of romps. When they came to T, Taffy said that as her name, and her Daddy's, and her Mummy's all began with that sound, they should draw a sort of family group of themselves holding hands. That was all very well to draw once or twice; but when it came to drawing it six or seven times, Taffy and Tegumai drew it

scratchier and scratchier, till at last the T-sound was only a thin long Tegumai with his arms out to hold Taffy and Teshumai. You can see from these three pictures partly how it happened. (20, 21, 22.)

Many of the other pictures were much too beautiful to begin with, especially before lunch; but as they were drawn over and over again on birch-bark, they became plainer and easier, till at last even Tegumai said he could find no fault with them. They turned the hissy-snake the other way round for the Z-sound, to show it was hissing backwards in a soft and gentle way (23); and they just made a twiddle for E, because it came into the pictures so often (24); and they drew pictures

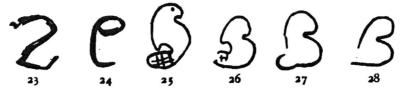

of the sacred Beaver of the Tegumais for the B-sound (25, 26, 27, 28); and because it was a nasty, nosy noise, they just drew noses for the N-sound, till they were tired (29); and they drew a picture of the big lake-pike's mouth for the greedy Ga-sound (30); and they drew the

pike's mouth again with a spear behind it for the scratchy, hurty Ka-sound (31); and they drew pictures

of a little bit of the winding Wagai river for the nice windy-windy Wa-sound (32, 33); and so on and so forth and so following till they had done and drawn all the sound-pictures that they wanted, and there was the Alphabet, all complete.

And after thousands and thousands and thousands of years, and after Hieroglyphics, and Demotics, and Nilotics, and Cryptics, and Cufics, and Runics, and Dorics, and Ionics, and all sorts of other ricks and tricks (because the Woons, and the Neguses, and the Akhoonds, and the Repositories of Tradition would never leave a good thing alone when they saw it), the fine old easy, understandable Alphabet—A, B, C, D, E, and the rest of 'em—got back into its proper shape again for all Best Beloveds to learn when they are old enough.

But I remember Tegumai Bopsulai, and Taffimai Metallumai and Teshumai Tewindrow, her dear Mummy, and all the days gone by. And it was so—just so—a long time ago—on the banks of the big Wagai!

One of the first things that Tegumai Bopsulai did after Taffy and he had made the Alphabet was to make a magic Alphabet-necklace of all the letters, so that it could be put in the Temple of Tegumai and kept for ever and ever. All the Tribe of Tegumai brought their most precious beads and beautiful things, and Taffy and Tegumai spent five whole years getting the necklace in order. This is a picture of the magic Alphabet-necklace. The string was made of the finest and strongest reindeer-sinew, bound round with thin copper wire.

Beginning at the top, the first bead is an old silver one that belonged to the Head Priest of the Tribe of Tegumai; then come three black mussel-pearls; next is a clay bead (blue and grey); next a nubbly gold bead sent as a present by a tribe who got it from Africa (but it must have been Indian really); the next is a long flat-sided glass bead from Africa (the Tribe of Tegumai took it in a fight); then come two clay beads (white and green), with dots on one, and dots and bands on the other; next are three rather chipped amber beads; then three clay beads (red and white), two with dots, and the big one in the middle with a toothed pattern. Then the letters begin, and between each letter is a little whitish clay bead with the letter repeated small. Here are the letters:—

A is scratched on a tooth—an elk-tush, I think.
B is the Sacred Beaver of Tegumai on a bit of old ivory.

135

C is a pearly oyster-shell—inside front.

D must be a sort of mussel-shell—outside front.

E is a twist of silver wire.

F is broken, but what remains of it is a bit of stag's horn.

G is painted black on a piece of wood. (The bead after G is a small shell, and not a clay bead. I don't know why they did that.)

H is a kind of big brown cowrie-shell.

I is the inside part of a long shell ground down by hand. (It took Tegumai three months to grind it down.)

J is a fish-hook in mother-of-pearl.

L is the broken spear in silver. (K ought to follow J, of course; but the necklace was broken once and they mended it wrong.)

K is a thin slice of bone scratched and rubbed in black.

M is on a pale grey shell.

N is a piece of what is called porphyry with a nose scratched on it. (Tegumai spent five months polishing this stone.)

O is a piece of oyster-shell with a hole in the middle.

P and Q are missing. They were lost, a long time ago, in a great war, and the tribe mended the necklace with the dried rattles of a rattlesnake, but no one ever found P and Q. That is how the saying began, 'You must mind your P's and Q's.'

R is, of course, just a shark's tooth.

S is a little silver snake.

T is the end of a small bone, polished brown and shiny.

136

U is another piece of oyster-shell.

W is a twisty piece of mother-of-pearl that they found inside a big mother-of-pearl shell, and sawed off with a wire dipped in sand and water. It took Taffy a month and a half to polish it and drill the holes.

X is silver wire joined in the middle with a raw garnet. (Taffy found the garnet.)

Y is the carp's tail in ivory.

Z is a bell-shaped piece of agate marked with Z-shaped stripes. They made the Z-snake out of one of the stripes by picking out the soft stone and rubbing in red sand and bees-wax. Just in the mouth of the bell you see the clay bead repeating the Z-letter.

These are all the letters.

The next bead is a small round greeny lump of copper ore; the next is a lump of rough turquoise; the next is a rough gold nugget (what they call water-gold); the next is a melon-shaped clay bead (white with green spots). Then come four flat ivory pieces, with dots on them rather like dominoes; then come three stone beads, very badly worn; then two soft iron beads with rust-holes at the edges (they must have been magic, because they look very common); and last is a very very old African bead, like glass—blue, red, white, black, and yellow. Then comes the loop to slip over the big silver button at the other end, and that is all.

I have copied the necklace very carefully. It weighs one pound seven and a half ounces. The black squiggle behind is only put in to make the beads and things look better.

Of all the Tribe of Tegumai
  Who cut that figure, none remain,—
On Merrow Down the cuckoos cry—
  The silence and the sun remain.

But as the faithful years return
  And hearts unwounded sing again,
Comes Taffy dancing through the fern
  To lead the Surrey spring again.

Her brows are bound with bracken-fronds,
  And golden elf-locks fly above;
Her eyes are bright as diamonds
  And bluer than the skies above.

In mocassins and deer-skin cloak,
  Unfearing, free and fair she flits,
And lights her little damp-wood smoke
  To show her Daddy where she flits.

For far—oh, very far behind,
  So far she cannot call to him,
Comes Tegumai alone to find
  The daughter that was all to him.

THE CRAB THAT PLAYED WITH THE SEA

(1902)

EFORE the High and Far-Off Times, O my Best Beloved, came the Time of the Very Beginnings; and that was in the days when the Eldest Magician was getting Things ready. First he got the Earth ready; then he got the Sea ready; and then he told all the Animals that they could come out and play. And the Animals said, 'O Eldest Magician, what shall we play at?' and he said, 'I will show you.' He took the Elephant—All-the-Elephant-there-was—and said, 'Play at being an Elephant,' and All-the-Elephant-there-was played. He took the Beaver—All-the-Beaver-there-was—and said, 'Play at being a Beaver,' and All-the-Beaver-there-was played. He took the Cow—All-the-Cow-there-was—and said, 'Play at being a Cow,' and All-the-Cow-there-was played. He took the Turtle—All-the-Turtle-there-was—and said, 'Play at being a Turtle,' and All-the-Turtle-there-was played. One by one he took all the beasts and birds and fishes and told them what to play at.

But towards evening, when people and things grow

143

restless and tired, there came up the Man (With his own little girl-daughter?)—Yes, with his own best-beloved little girl-daughter sitting upon his shoulder, and he said, 'What is this play, Eldest Magician?' And the Eldest Magician said, 'Ho, Son of Adam, this is the play of the Very Beginning; but you are too wise for this play.' And the Man saluted and said, 'Yes, I am too wise for this play; but see that you make all the Animals obedient to me.'

Now, while the two were talking together, Paü Amma the Crab, who was next in the game, scuttled off sideways and stepped into the sea, saying to himself, 'I will play my play alone in the deep waters, and I will never be obedient to this son of Adam.' Nobody saw him go away except the little girl-daughter where she leaned on the Man's shoulder. And the play went on till there were no more Animals left without orders; and the Eldest Magician wiped the fine dust off his hands and walked about the world to see how the Animals were playing.

He went North, Best Beloved, and he found All-the-Elephant-there-was digging with his tusks and stamping with his feet in the nice new clean earth that had been made ready for him.

'Kun?' said All-the-Elephant-there-was, meaning 'Is this right?'

'Payah kun,' said the Eldest Magician, meaning, 'That is quite right'; and he breathed upon the great rocks and lumps of earth that All-the-Elephant-there-was had thrown up, and they became the great Himalayan Mountains, and you can look them out on the map.

He went East, and he found All-the-Cow-there-was

144

feeding in the field that had been made ready for her, and she licked her tongue round a whole forest at a time, and swallowed it and sat down to chew her cud.

'Kun?' said All-the-Cow-there-was.

'Payah kun,' said the Eldest Magician; and he breathed upon the bare patch where she had eaten, and upon the place where she had sat down, and one became the great Indian Desert, and the other became the Desert of Sahara, and you can look them out on the map.

He went West, and he found All-the-Beaver-there-was making a beaver-dam across the mouths of broad rivers that had been got ready for him.

'Kun?' said All-the-Beaver-there-was.

'Payah kun,' said the Eldest Magician; and he breathed upon the fallen trees and the still water, and they became the Everglades in Florida, and you may look them out on the map.

Then he went South and found All-the-Turtle-there-was scratching with his flippers in the sand that had been got ready for him, and the sand and the rocks whirled through the air and fell far off into the sea.

'Kun?' said All-the-Turtle-there-was.

'Payah kun,' said the Eldest Magician; and he breathed upon the sand and the rocks, where they had fallen in the sea, and they became the most beautiful islands of Borneo, Celebes, Sumatra, Java, and the rest of the Malay Archipelago, and you can look them out on the map!

By and by the Eldest Magician met the Man on the banks of the Perak River, and said, 'Ho! Son of Adam, are all the Animals obedient to you?'

'Yes,' said the Man.

145

This is a picture of Pau Amma the Crab running away while the Eldest Magician was talking to the Man and his Little Girl Daughter. The Eldest Magician is sitting on his magic throne, wrapped up in his Magic Cloud. The three flowers in front of him are the three Magic Flowers. On the top of the hill you can see All-the-Elephant-there-was, and All-the-Cow-there-was, and All-the-Turtle-there-was going off to play as the Eldest Magician told them. The Cow has a hump, because she was All-the-Cow-there-was; so she had to have all there was for all the cows that were made afterwards. Under the hill there are Animals who have been taught the game they were to play. You can see All-the-Tiger-there-was smiling at All-the-Bones-there-were, and you can see All-the-Elk-there-was, and All-the-Parrot-there-was, and All-the-Bunnies-there-were on the hill. The other Animals are on the other side of the hill, so I haven't drawn them. The little house up the hill is All-the-House-there-was. The Eldest Magician made it to show the Man how to make houses when he wanted to. The Snake round that spiky hill is All-the-Snake-there-was, and he is talking to All-the-Monkey-there-was, and the Monkey is being rude to the Snake, and the Snake is being rude to the Monkey. The Man is very busy talking to the Eldest Magician. The Little Girl Daughter is looking at Pau Amma as he runs away. That humpy thing in the water in front is Pau Amma. He wasn't a common Crab in those days. He was a King Crab. That is why he looks different. The thing that looks like bricks that the Man is standing in, is the Big Miz-Maze. When the Man has done talking with the Eldest Magician he will walk in the

146

Big Miz-Maze, because he has to. The mark on the
stone under the Man's foot is a magic mark; and down

underneath I have drawn the three Magic Flowers all
mixed up with the Magic Cloud. All this picture is
Big Medicine and Strong Magic.

'Is all the Earth obedient to you?'

'Yes,' said the Man.

'Is all the Sea obedient to you?'

'No,' said the Man. 'Once a day and once a night the Sea runs up the Perak River and drives the sweet-water back into the forest, so that my house is made wet; once a day and once a night it runs down the river and draws all the water after it, so that there is nothing left but mud, and my canoe is upset. Is that the play you told it to play?'

'No,' said the Eldest Magician. 'That is a new and a bad play.'

'Look!' said the Man, and as he spoke the great Sea came up the mouth of the Perak River, driving the river backwards till it overflowed all the dark forests for miles, and miles, and flooded the Man's house.

'This is wrong. Launch your canoe and we will find out who is playing with the Sea,' said the Eldest Magician. They stepped into the canoe; the little girl-daughter came with them; and the man took his kris—a curving, wavy dagger with a blade like a flame,—and they pushed out on the Perak River. Then the Sea began to run back and back, and the canoe was sucked out of the mouth of the Perak River, past Selangor, past Malacca, past Singapore, out and out to the Island of Bintang, as though it had been pulled by a string.

Then the Eldest Magician stood up and shouted, 'Ho! beasts, birds, and fishes, that I took between my hands at the Very Beginning and taught the play that you should play, which one of you is playing with the Sea?'

Then all the beasts, birds, and fishes said together, 'Eldest Magician, we play the plays that you taught us

149

to play—we and our children's children. But not one of us plays with the Sea.'

Then the Moon rose big and full over the water, and the Eldest Magician said to the hunchbacked old man who sits in the Moon spinning a fishing-line with which he hopes one day to catch the world, 'Ho! Fisher of the Moon, are you playing with the Sea?'

'No,' said the Fisherman, 'I am spinning a line with which I shall some day catch the world; but I do not play with the Sea.' And he went on spinning his line.

Now there is also a Rat up in the Moon who always bites the old Fisherman's line as fast as it is made, and the Eldest Magician said to him, 'Ho! Rat of the Moon, are you playing with the Sea?'

And the Rat said, 'I am too busy biting through the line that this old Fisherman is spinning. I do not play with the Sea.' And he went on biting the line.

Then the little girl-daughter put up her little soft brown arms with the beautiful white shell bracelets and said, 'O Eldest Magician! when my father here talked to you at the Very Beginning, and I leaned upon his shoulder while the beasts were being taught their plays, one beast went away naughtily into the Sea before you had taught him his play.'

And the Eldest Magician said, 'How wise are little children who see and are silent! What was that beast like?'

And the little girl-daughter said, 'He was round and he was flat; and his eyes grew upon stalks; and he walked sideways like this; and he was covered with strong armour upon his back.'

And the Eldest Magician said, 'How wise are little

children who speak truth! Now I know where Pau Amma went. Give me the paddle!'

So he took the paddle; but there was no need to paddle, for the water flowed steadily past all the islands till they came to the place called Pusat Tasek—the Heart of the Sea—where the great hollow is that leads down to the heart of the world, and in that hollow grows the Wonderful Tree, Pauh Janggi, that bears the magic twin-nuts. Then the Eldest Magician slid his arm up to the shoulder through the deep warm water, and under the roots of the Wonderful Tree he touched the broad back of Pau Amma the Crab. And Pau Amma settled down at the touch, and all the Sea rose up as water rises in a basin when you put your hand into it.

'Ah!' said the Eldest Magician. 'Now I know who has been playing with the Sea'; and he called out, 'What are you doing, Pau Amma?'

And Pau Amma, deep down below, answered, 'Once a day and once a night I go out to look for my food. Once a day and once a night I return. Leave me alone.'

Then the Eldest Magician said, 'Listen, Pau Amma. When you go out from your cave the waters of the Sea pour down into Pusat Tasek, and all the beaches of all the islands are left bare, and the little fish die, and Raja Moyang Kaban, the King of the Elephants, his legs are made muddy. When you come back and sit in Pusat Tasek, the waters of the Sea rise, and half the little islands are drowned, and the Man's house is flooded, and Raja Abdullah, the King of the Crocodiles, his mouth is filled with the salt water.'

Then Pau Amma, deep down below, laughed and said, 'I did not know I was so important. Hencefor-

151

This is the picture of Pau Amma the Crab rising out of the sea as tall as the smoke of three volcanoes. I haven't drawn the three volcanoes, because Pau Amma was so big. Pau Amma is trying to make a Magic, but he is only a silly old King Crab, and so he can't do anything. You can see he is all legs and claws and empty hollow shell. The canoe is the canoe that the Man and the Girl Daughter and the Eldest Magician sailed from the Perak River in. The Sea is all black and bobbly, because Pau Amma has just risen up out of Pusat Tasek. Pusat Tasek is underneath, so I haven't drawn it. The Man is waving his curvy kris-knife at Pau Amma. The Little Girl Daughter is sitting quietly in the middle of the canoe. She knows she is quite safe with her Daddy. The Eldest Magician is standing up at the other end of the canoe beginning to make a Magic. He has left his magic throne on the beach, and he has taken off his clothes so as not to get wet, and he has left the Magic Cloud behind too, so as not to tip the boat over. The thing that looks like another little canoe outside the real canoe is called an outrigger. It is a piece of wood tied to sticks, and it prevents the canoe from being tipped over. The canoe is made out of one piece of wood, and there is a paddle at one end of it.

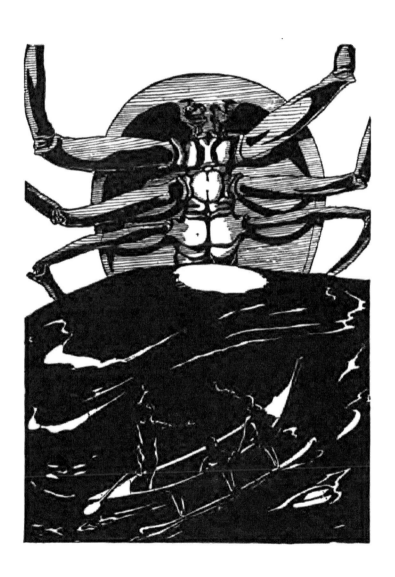

ward I will go out seven times a day, and the waters shall never be still.'

And the Eldest Magician said, 'I cannot make you play the play you were meant to play, Pau Amma, because you escaped me at the Very Beginning; but if you are not afraid, come up and we will talk about it.'

'I am not afraid,' said Pau Amma, and he rose to the top of the sea in the moonlight. There was nobody in the world so big as Pau Amma—for he was the King Crab of all Crabs. Not a common Crab, but a King Crab. One side of his great shell touched the beach at Sarawak; the other touched the beach at Pahang; and he was taller than the smoke of three volcanoes! As he rose up through the branches of the Wonderful Tree he tore off one of the great twin-fruits—the magic double-kernelled nuts that make people young,—and the little girl-daughter saw it bobbing alongside the canoe, and pulled it in and began to pick out the soft eyes of it with her little golden scissors.

'Now,' said the Magician, 'make a Magic, Pau Amma, to show that you are really important.'

Pau Amma rolled his eyes and waved his legs, but he could only stir up the Sea, because, though he was a King Crab, he was nothing more than a Crab, and the Eldest Magician laughed.

'You are not so important after all, Pau Amma,' he said. 'Now, let me try,' and he made a Magic with his left hand—with just the little finger of his left hand—and—lo and behold, Best Beloved, Pau Amma's hard, blue-green-black shell fell off him as a husk falls off a cocoa-nut, and Pau Amma was left all soft—soft as the little crabs that you sometimes find on the beach, Best Beloved.

'Indeed, you are very important,' said the Eldest Magician. 'Shall I ask the Man here to cut you with his kris? Shall I send for Raja Moyang Kaban, the King of the Elephants, to pierce you with his tusks? or shall I call Raja Abdullah, the King of the Crocodiles, to bite you?'

And Pau Amma said, 'I am ashamed! Give me back my hard shell and let me go back to Pusat Tasek, and I will only stir out once a day and once a night to get my food.'

And the Eldest Magician said, 'No, Pau Amma, I will not give you back your shell, for you will grow bigger and prouder and stronger, and perhaps you will forget your promise, and you will play with the Sea once more.'

Then Pau Amma said, 'What shall I do? I am so big that I can only hide in Pusat Tasek, and if I go anywhere else, all soft as I am now, the sharks and the dogfish will eat me. And if I go to Pusat Tasek, all soft as I am now, though I may be safe, I can never stir out to get my food, and so I shall die.' Then he waved his legs and lamented.

'Listen, Pau Amma,' said the Eldest Magician. 'I cannot make you play the play you were meant to play, because you escaped me at the Very Beginning; but if you choose, I can make every stone and every hole and every bunch of weed in all the seas a safe Pusat Tasek for you and your children for always.'

Then Pau Amma said, 'That is good, but I do not choose yet. Look! there is that Man who talked to you at the Very Beginning. If he had not taken up your attention I should not have grown tired of waiting and run away, and all this would never have happened. What will he do for me?'

THE CRAB THAT PLAYED WITH THE SEA

And the Man said, 'If you choose, I will make a Magic, so that both the deep water and the dry ground will be a home for you and your children—so that you shall be able to hide both on the land and in the sea.'

And Pau Amma said, 'I do not choose yet. Look! there is that girl who saw me running away at the Very Beginning. If she had spoken then, the Eldest Magician would have called me back, and all this would never have happened. What will she do for me?'

And the little girl-daughter said, 'This is a good nut that I am eating. If you choose, I will make a Magic and I will give you this pair of scissors, very sharp and strong, so that you and your children can eat cocoa-nuts like this all day long when you come up from the Sea to the land; or you can dig a Pusat Tasek for yourself with the scissors that belong to you when there is no stone or hole near by; and when the earth is too hard, by the help of these same scissors you can run up a tree.'

And Pau Amma said, 'I do not choose yet, for, all soft as I am, these gifts would not help me. Give me back my shell, O Eldest Magician, and then I will play your play.'

And the Eldest Magician said, 'I will give it back, Pau Amma, for eleven months of the year; but on the twelfth month of every year it shall grow soft again, to remind you and all your children that I can make magics, and to keep you humble, Pau Amma; for I see that if you can run both under the water and on land, you will grow too bold; and if you can climb trees and crack nuts and dig holes with your scissors, you will grow too greedy, Pau Amma.'

Then Pau Amma thought a little and said, 'I have made my choice. I will take all the gifts.'

157

Then the Eldest Magician made a Magic with the
right hand, with all five fingers of his right hand, and lo
and behold, Best Beloved, Pau Amma grew smaller and
smaller and smaller, till at last there was only a little
green crab swimming in the water alongside the canoe,
crying in a very small voice, 'Give me the scissors!'

And the girl-daughter picked him up on the palm of
her little brown hand, and sat him in the bottom of the
canoe and gave him her scissors, and he waved them in
his little arms, and opened them and shut them and
snapped them, and said 'I can eat nuts. I can crack
shells. I can dig holes. I can climb trees. I can
breathe in the dry air, and I can find a safe Pusat Tasek
under every stone.   I did not know I was so important.
Kun?'   (Is this right?)

'Payah kun,' said the Eldest Magician, and he
laughed and gave him his blessing; and little Pau Amma
scuttled over the side of the canoe into the water; and
he was so tiny that he could have hidden under the
shadow of a dry leaf on land or of a dead shell at the
bottom of the sea.

'Was that well done?' said the Eldest Magician.

'Yes,' said the Man.   'But now we must go back to
Perak, and that is a weary way to paddle.   If we had
waited till Pau Amma had gone out of Pusat Tasek and
come home, the water would have carried us there by
itself.'

'You are lazy,' said the Eldest Magician.   'So your
children shall be lazy.   They shall be the laziest people
in the world.   They shall be called the Malazy—the
lazy people'; and he held up his finger to the Moon and
said, 'O Fisherman, here is this Man too lazy to row
home.   Pull his canoe home with your line, Fisherman.'

'No,' said the Man. 'If I am to be lazy all my days, let the Sea work for me twice a day for ever. That will save paddling.'

And the Eldest Magician laughed and said, 'Payah kun' (That is right).

And the Rat of the Moon stopped biting the line; and the Fisherman let his line down till it touched the Sea, and he pulled the whole deep Sea along, past the Island of Bintang, past Singapore, past Malacca, past Selangor, till the canoe whirled into the mouth of the Perak River again.

'Kun?' said the Fisherman of the Moon.

'Payah kun,' said the Eldest Magician. 'See now that you pull the Sea twice a day and twice a night for ever, so that the Malazy fishermen may be saved paddling. But be careful not to do it too hard, or I shall make a Magic on you as I did to Pau Amma.'

Then they all went up the Perak River and went to bed, Best Beloved.

Now listen and attend!

From that day to this the Moon has always pulled the Sea up and down and made what we call the tides. Sometimes the Fisher of the Sea pulls a little too hard, and then we get spring-tides; and sometimes he pulls a little too softly, and then we get what are called neap-tides; but nearly always he is careful, because of the Eldest Magician.

And Pau Amma? You can see when you go to the beach, how all Pau Amma's babies make little Pusat Taseks for themselves under every stone and bunch of weed on the sands; you can see them waving their little scissors; and in some parts of the world they truly live on the dry land and run up the palm-trees and eat cocoa-

159

nuts, exactly as the girl-daughter promised. But once a year all Pau Ammas must shake off their hard armour and be soft—to remind them of what the Eldest Magician could do. And so it isn't fair to kill or hunt Pau Amma's babies just because old Pau Amma was stupidly rude a very long time ago.

Oh yes! And Pau Amma's babies hate being taken out of their little Pusat Taseks and brought home in pickle-bottles. That is why they nip you with their scissors, and it serves you right!

China-going P. and O.'s
Pass Pau Amma's playground close,
And his Pusat Tasek lies
Near the track of most B. I.'s
N. Y. K. and N. D. L.
Know Pau Amma's home as well
As the Fisher of the Sea knows
'Bens,' M. M.'s and Rubattinos.
But (and this is rather queer)
A. T. L.'s can not come here;
O. and O. and D. O. A.
Must go round another way.
Orient, Anchor, Bibby, Hall,
Never go that way at all.
U. C. S. would have a fit
If it found itself on it.
And if 'Beavers' took their cargoes
To Penang instead of Lagos,
Or a fat Shaw-Savill bore
Passengers to Singapore,
Or a White Star were to try a
Little trip to Sourabaya,
Or a B. S. A. went on
Past Natal to Cheribon,
Then great Mr. Lloyds would come
With a wire and drag them home!

You'll know what my riddle means
When you've eaten mangosteens.

Or if you can't wait till then, ask them to let you have the outside page of the 'Times'; turn over to page 2, where it is marked 'Shipping' on the top left hand; then take the Atlas (and that is the finest picture-book in the world) and see how the names of the places that the steamers go to fit into the names of the places on the map. Any steamer-child ought to be able to do that; but if you can't read, ask some one to show it you.

THE CAT THAT WALKED BY HIMSELF

(1902)

EAR and attend and listen; for this befell and behappened and became and was, O my Best Beloved, when the Tame animals were wild. The Dog was wild, and the Horse was wild, and the Cow was wild, and the Sheep was wild, and the Pig was wild—as wild as wild could be—and they walked in the Wet Wild Woods by their wild lones. But the wildest of all the wild animals was the Cat. He walked by himself, and all places were alike to him.

Of course the Man was wild too. He was dreadfully wild. He didn't even begin to be tame till he met the Woman, and she told him that she did not like living in his wild ways. She picked out a nice dry Cave, instead of a heap of wet leaves, to lie down in; and she strewed clean sand on the floor; and she lit a nice Fire of wood at the back of the Cave; and she hung a dried wild-horse skin, tail-down, across the opening of the Cave; and she said, 'Wipe your feet, dear, when you come in, and now we'll keep house.'

That night, Best Beloved, they ate wild sheep roasted on the hot stones, and flavoured with wild garlic and wild pepper; and wild duck stuffed with wild rice and wild fenugreek and wild coriander; and marrow-bones of wild oxen; and wild cherries, and wild grenadillas. Then the Man went to sleep in front of the fire ever so happy; but the Woman sat up, combing her hair. She took the bone of the shoulder of mutton—the big flat blade-bone—and she looked at the wonderful marks on it, and she threw more wood on the fire, and she made a Magic. She made the First Singing Magic in the world.

Out in the Wet Wild Woods all the wild animals gathered together where they could see the light of the fire a long way off, and they wondered what it meant.

Then Wild Horse stamped with his wild foot and said, 'O my Friends and O my Enemies, why have the Man and the Woman made that great light in that great Cave, and what harm will it do us?'

Wild Dog lifted up his wild nose and smelled the smell of the roast mutton, and said, 'I will go up and see and look, and say; for I think it is good. Cat, come with me.'

'Nenni!' said the Cat. 'I am the Cat who walks by himself, and all places are alike to me. I will not come.'

'Then we can never be friends again,' said Wild Dog, and he trotted off to the Cave. But when he had gone a little way the Cat said to himself, 'All places are alike to me. Why should I not go too and see and look and come away at my own liking?' So he slipped after Wild Dog softly, very softly, and hid himself where he could hear everything.

When Wild Dog reached the mouth of the Cave he lifted up the dried horse-skin with his nose and sniffed

164

the beautiful smell of the roast mutton, and the Woman, looking at the blade-bone, heard him, and laughed, and said, 'Here comes the first. Wild Thing out of the Wild Woods, what do you want?'

Wild Dog said, 'O my Enemy and Wife of my Enemy, what is this that smells so good in the Wild Woods?'

Then the Woman picked up a roasted mutton-bone and threw it to Wild Dog, and said, 'Wild Thing out of the Wild Woods, taste and try.' Wild Dog gnawed the bone, and it was more delicious than anything he had ever tasted, and he said, 'O my Enemy and Wife of my Enemy, give me another.'

The Woman said, 'Wild Thing out of the Wild Woods, help my Man to hunt through the day and guard this Cave at night, and I will give you as many roast bones as you need.'

'Ah!' said the Cat, listening. 'This is a very wise Woman, but she is not so wise as I am.'

Wild Dog crawled into the Cave and laid his head on the Woman's lap, and said, 'O my Friend and Wife of my Friend, I will help your Man to hunt through the day, and at night I will guard your Cave.'

'Ah!' said the Cat, listening. 'That is a very foolish Dog.' And he went back through the Wet Wild Woods waving his wild tail, and walking by his wild lone. But he never told anybody.

When the Man waked up he said, 'What is Wild Dog doing here?' And the Woman said, 'His name is not Wild Dog any more, but the First Friend, because he will be our friend for always and always and always. Take him with you when you go hunting.'

Next night the Woman cut great green armfuls of fresh grass from the water-meadows, and dried it before

This is the picture of the Cave where the Man and the Woman lived first of all. It was really a very nice Cave, and much warmer than it looks. The Man had a canoe. It is on the edge of the river, being soaked in water to make it swell up. The tattery-looking thing across the river is the Man's salmon-net to catch salmon with. There are nice clean stones leading up from the river to the mouth of the Cave, so that the Man and the Woman could go down for water without getting sand between their toes. The things like black-beetles far down the beach are really trunks of dead trees that floated down the river from the Wet Wild Woods on the other bank. The Man and the Woman used to drag them out and dry them and cut them up for firewood. I haven't drawn the horse-hide curtain at the mouth of the Cave, because the Woman has just taken it down to be cleaned. All those little smudges on the sand between the Cave and the river are the marks of the Woman's feet and the Man's feet.

The Man and the Woman are both inside the Cave eating their dinner. They went to another cosier Cave when the Baby came, because the Baby used to crawl down to the river and fall in, and the Dog had to pull him out.

the fire, so that it smelt like new-mown hay, and she sat at the mouth of the Cave and plaited a halter out of horse-hide, and she looked at the shoulder-of-mutton bone—at the big broad blade-bone—and she made a Magic. She made the Second Singing Magic in the world.

Out in the Wild Woods all the wild animals wondered what had happened to Wild Dog, and at last Wild Horse stamped with his foot and said, 'I will go and see and say why Wild Dog has not returned. Cat, come with me.'

'Nenni!' said the Cat. 'I am the Cat who walks by himself, and all places are alike to me. I will not come.' But all the same he followed Wild Horse softly, very softly, and hid himself where he could hear everything.

When the Woman heard Wild Horse tripping and stumbling on his long mane, she laughed and said, 'Here comes the second. Wild Thing out of the Wild Woods, what do you want?'

Wild Horse said, 'O my Enemy and Wife of my Enemy, where is Wild Dog?'

The Woman laughed, and picked up the blade-bone and looked at it, and said, 'Wild Thing out of the Wild Woods, you did not come here for Wild Dog, but for the sake of this good grass.'

And Wild Horse, tripping and stumbling on his long mane, said, 'That is true; give it me to eat.'

The Woman said, 'Wild Thing out of the Wild Woods, bend your wild head and wear what I give you, and you shall eat the wonderful grass three times a day.'

'Ah!' said the Cat, listening. 'This is a clever Woman, but she is not so clever as I am.'

Wild Horse bent his wild head, and the Woman

169

slipped the plaited-hide halter over it, and Wild Horse breathed on the Woman's feet and said, 'O my Mistress, and Wife of my Master, I will be your servant for the sake of the wonderful grass.'

'Ah!' said the Cat, listening. 'That is a very foolish Horse.' And he went back through the Wet Wild Woods, waving his wild tail and walking by his wild lone. But he never told anybody.

When the Man and the Dog came back from hunting, the Man said, 'What is Wild Horse doing here?' And the Woman said, 'His name is not Wild Horse any more, but the First Servant, because he will carry us from place to place for always and always and always. Ride on his back when you go hunting.'

Next day, holding her wild head high that her wild horns should not catch in the wild trees, Wild Cow came up to the Cave, and the Cat followed, and hid himself just the same as before; and everything happened just the same as before; and the Cat said the same things as before; and when Wild Cow had promised to give her milk to the Woman every day in exchange for the wonderful grass, the Cat went back through the Wet Wild Woods waving his wild tail and walking by his wild lone, just the same as before. But he never told anybody. And when the Man and the Horse and the Dog came home from hunting and asked the same questions same as before, the Woman said, 'Her name is not Wild Cow any more, but the Giver of Good Food. She will give us the warm white milk for always and always and always, and I will take care of her while you and the First Friend and the First Servant go hunting.'

Next day the Cat waited to see if any other Wild

170

THE CAT THAT WALKED BY HIMSELF

Thing would go up to the Cave, but no one moved in the Wet Wild Woods, so the Cat walked there by himself; and he saw the Woman milking the Cow, and he saw the light of the Fire in the Cave, and he smelt the smell of the warm white milk.

Cat said, 'O my Enemy and Wife of my Enemy, where did Wild Cow go?'

The Woman laughed and said, 'Wild Thing out of the Wild Woods, go back to the Woods again, for I have braided up my hair, and I have put away the magic blade-bone, and we have no more need of either friends or servants in our Cave.'

Cat said, 'I am not a friend, and I am not a servant. I am the Cat who walks by himself, and I wish to come into your Cave.'

Woman said, 'Then why did you not come with First Friend on the first night?'

Cat grew very angry and said, 'Has Wild Dog told tales of me?'

Then the Woman laughed and said, 'You are the Cat who walks by himself, and all places are alike to you. You are neither a friend nor a servant. You have said it yourself. Go away and walk by yourself in all places alike.'

Then Cat pretended to be sorry and said, 'Must I never come into the Cave? Must I never sit by the warm fire? Must I never drink the warm white milk? You are very wise and very beautiful. You should not be cruel even to a Cat.'

Woman said, 'I knew I was wise, but I did not know I was beautiful. So I will make a bargain with you. If ever I say one word in your praise, you may come into the Cave.'

This is the picture of the Cat that Walked by Him-self, walking by his wild lone through the Wet Wild Woods and waving his wild tail. There is nothing else in the picture except some toadstools. They had to grow there because the woods were so wet. The lumpy thing on the low branch isn't a bird. It is moss that grew there because the Wild Woods were so wet.

Underneath the truly picture is a picture of the cosy Cave that the Man and the Woman went to after the Baby came. It was their summer Cave, and they planted wheat in front of it. The man is riding on the Horse to find the Cow and bring her back to the Cave to be milked. He is holding up his hand to call the Dog, who has swum across to the other side of the river, look-ing for rabbits.

THE CAT THAT WALKED BY HIMSELF

'And if you say two words in my praise?' said the Cat.

'I never shall,' said the Woman, 'but if I say two words in your praise, you may sit by the Fire in the Cave.'

'And if you say three words?' said the Cat.

'I never shall,' said the Woman, 'but if I say three words in your praise, you may drink the warm white milk three times a day for always and always and always.'

Then the Cat arched his back and said, 'Now let the Curtain at the mouth of the Cave, and the Fire at the back of the Cave, and the Milk-pots that stand beside the Fire, remember what my Enemy and the Wife of my Enemy has said.'   And he went away through the Wet Wild Woods waving his wild tail and walking by his wild lone.

That night when the Man and the Horse and the Dog came home from hunting, the Woman did not tell them of the bargain that she had made with the Cat, because she was afraid that they might not like it.

Cat went far and far away and hid himself in the Wet Wild Woods by his wild lone for a long time till the Woman forgot all about him.   Only the Bat—the little upside-down Bat—that hung inside the Cave knew where Cat hid; and every evening Bat would fly to Cat with news of what was happening.

One evening Bat said, 'There is a Baby in the Cave. He is new and pink and fat and small, and the Woman is very fond of him.'

'Ah,' said the Cat, listening, 'but what is the Baby fond of?'

'He is fond of things that are soft and tickle,' said

175

the Bat. 'He is fond of warm things to hold in his arms when he goes to sleep. He is fond of being played with. He is fond of all those things.'

'Ah,' said the Cat, listening, 'then my time has come.'

Next night Cat walked through the Wet Wild Woods and hid very near the Cave till morning-time, and Man and Dog and Horse went hunting. The Woman was busy cooking that morning, and the Baby cried and interrupted. So she carried him outside the Cave and gave him a handful of pebbles to play with. But still the Baby cried.

Then the Cat put out his paddy-paw and patted the Baby on the cheek, and it cooed; and the Cat rubbed against its fat knees and tickled it under its fat chin with his tail. And the Baby laughed; and the Woman heard him and smiled.

Then the Bat—the little upside-down Bat—that hung in the mouth of the Cave said, 'O my Hostess and Wife of my Host and Mother of my Host's Son, a Wild Thing from the Wild Woods is most beautifully playing with your Baby.'

'A blessing on that Wild Thing whoever he may be,' said the Woman, straightening her back, 'for I was a busy woman this morning and he has done me a service.'

That very minute and second, Best Beloved, the dried horse-skin Curtain that was stretched tail-down at the mouth of the Cave fell down—'woosh!'—because it remembered the bargain she had made with the Cat; and when the Woman went to pick it up—lo and behold!—the Cat was sitting quite comfy inside the Cave.

'O my Enemy and Wife of my Enemy and Mother of my Enemy,' said the Cat, 'it is I: for you have spoken a word in my praise, and now I can sit within the Cave for always and always and always. But still I am the Cat who walks by himself, and all places are alike to me.'

The Woman was very angry, and shut her lips tight and took up her spinning-wheel and began to spin.

But the Baby cried because the Cat had gone away, and the Woman could not hush it, for it struggled and kicked and grew black in the face.

'O my Enemy and Wife of my Enemy and Mother of my Enemy,' said the Cat, 'take a strand of the thread that you are spinning and tie it to your spinning-whorl and drag it along the floor, and I will show you a Magic that shall make your Baby laugh as loudly as he is now crying.'

'I will do so,' said the Woman, 'because I am at my wits' end; but I will not thank you for it.'

She tied the thread to the little clay spindle-whorl and drew it across the floor, and the Cat ran after it and patted it with his paws and rolled head over heels, and tossed it backward over his shoulder and chased it between his hind-legs and pretended to lose it, and pounced down upon it again, till the Baby laughed as loudly as it had been crying, and scrambled after the Cat and frolicked all over the Cave till it grew tired and settled down to sleep with the Cat in its arms.

'Now,' said Cat, 'I will sing the Baby a song that shall keep him asleep for an hour.' And he began to purr, loud and low, low and loud, till the Baby fell fast asleep. The Woman smiled as she looked down upon the two of them, and said, 'That was wonderfully done. No question but you are very clever, O Cat.'

That very minute and second, Best Beloved, the smoke of the Fire at the back of the Cave came down in clouds from the roof—'puff!'—because it remembered the bargain she had made with the Cat; and when it had cleared away—lo and behold!—the Cat was sitting quite comfy close to the fire.

'O my Enemy and Wife of my Enemy and Mother of my Enemy,' said the Cat, 'it is I: for you have spoken a second word in my praise, and now I can sit by the warm Fire at the back of the Cave for always and always and always. But still I am the Cat who walks by himself, and all places are alike to me.'

Then the Woman was very very angry, and let down her hair and put more wood on the fire and brought out the broad blade-bone of the shoulder of mutton and began to make a Magic that should prevent her from saying a third word in praise of the Cat. It was not a Singing Magic, Best Beloved, it was a Still Magic; and by and by the Cave grew so still that a little wee-wee mouse crept out of a corner and ran across the floor.

'O my Enemy and Wife of my Enemy and Mother of my Enemy,' said the Cat, 'is that little mouse part of your Magic?'

'Ouh! Chee! No indeed!' said the Woman, and she dropped the blade-bone and jumped upon the foot-stool in front of the fire and braided up her hair very quick for fear that the mouse should run up it.

'Ah,' said the Cat, watching, 'then the mouse will do me no harm if I eat it?'

'No,' said the Woman, braiding up her hair, 'eat it quickly and I will ever be grateful to you.'

Cat made one jump and caught the little mouse, and the Woman said, 'A hundred thanks. Even the First Friend is not quick enough to catch little mice as you have done. You must be very wise.'

That very moment and second, O Best Beloved, the Milk-pot that stood by the fire cracked in two pieces—'ffft!'—because it remembered the bargain she had made with the Cat; and when the Woman jumped down from the footstool—lo and behold!—the Cat was lapping up the warm white milk that lay in one of the broken pieces.

'O my Enemy and Wife of my Enemy and Mother of my Enemy,' said the Cat, 'it is I: for you have spoken three words in my praise, and now I can drink the warm white milk three times a day for always and always and always. But still I am the Cat who walks by himself, and all places are alike to me.'

Then the Woman laughed and set the Cat a bowl of the warm white milk and said, 'O Cat, you are as clever as a man, but remember that your bargain was not made with the Man or the Dog, and I do not know what they will do when they come home.'

'What is that to me?' said the Cat. 'If I have my place in the Cave by the fire and my warm white milk three times a day I do not care what the Man or the Dog can do.'

That evening when the Man and the Dog came into the Cave, the Woman told them all the story of the bargain, while the Cat sat by the fire and smiled. Then the Man said, 'Yes, but he has not made a bargain with me or with all proper Men after me.' Then he took off his two leather boots and he took up his little stone axe (that makes three) and he fetched a piece of wood and a hatchet (that is five altogether), and he set them out in a row and he said, 'Now we will make our bargain. If you do not catch mice when you are in the Cave for always and always and always, I will throw these five things at you whenever I see you, and so shall all proper Men do after me.'

'Ah,' said the Woman, listening, 'this is a very clever Cat, but he is not so clever as my Man.'

The Cat counted the five things (and they looked very knobby) and he said, 'I will catch mice when I am in the Cave for always and always and always; but still I am the Cat who walks by himself, and all places are alike to me.'

'Not when I am near,' said the Man. 'If you had not said that last I would have put all these things away for always and always and always; but now I am going to throw my two boots and my little stone axe (that makes three) at you whenever I meet you. And so shall all proper Men do after me!'

Then the Dog said, 'Wait a minute. He has not made a bargain with me or with all proper Dogs after me.' And he showed his teeth and said, 'If you are not kind to the Baby while I am in the Cave for always and always and always, I will hunt you till I catch you, and when I catch you I will bite you. And so shall all proper Dogs do after me.'

'Ah,' said the Woman, listening, 'this is a very clever Cat, but he is not so clever as the Dog.'

Cat counted the Dog's teeth (and they looked very pointed) and he said, 'I will be kind to the Baby while I am in the Cave, as long as he does not pull my tail too hard, for always and always and always. But still I am the Cat that walks by himself, and all places are alike to me.'

'Not when I am near,' said the Dog. 'If you had not said that last I would have shut my mouth for always and always and always; but now I am going to hunt you up a tree whenever I meet you. And so shall all proper Dogs do after me.'

Then the Man threw his two boots and his little stone axe (that makes three) at the Cat, and the Cat ran out of the Cave and the Dog chased him up a tree; and from that day to this, Best Beloved, three proper Men out of five will always throw things at a Cat whenever they meet him, and all proper Dogs will chase him up a tree. But the Cat keeps his side of the bargain too. He will kill mice, and he will be kind to Babies when he is in the house, just as long as they do not pull his tail too hard. But when he has done that, and between times, and when the moon gets up and night comes, he is the Cat that walks by himself, and all places are alike to him. Then he goes out to the Wet Wild Woods or up the Wet Wild Trees or on the Wet Wild Roofs, waving his wild tail and walking by his wild lone.

Pussy can sit by the fire and sing,
    Pussy can climb a tree,
Or play with a silly old cork and string
    To 'muse herself, not me.
But I like Binkie my dog, because
    He knows how to behave;
So, Binkie's the same as the First Friend was,
    And I am the Man in the Cave!

Pussy will play man-Friday till
    It's time to wet her paw
And make her walk on the window-sill
    (For the footprint Crusoe saw);
Then she fluffles her tail and mews,
    And scratches and won't attend.
But Binkie will play whatever I choose,
    And he is my true First Friend!

Pussy will rub my knees with her head,
    Pretending she loves me hard;
But the very minute I go to my bed
    Pussy runs out in the yard,
And there she stays till the morning-light;
    So I know it is only pretend;
But Binkie, he snores at my feet all night,
    And he is my Firstest Friend!!

THE BUTTERFLY THAT STAMPED

(1902)

HIS, O my Best Beloved, is a story —a new and a wonderful story— a story quite different from the other stories—a story about The Most Wise Sovereign Suleiman-bin-Daoud—Solomon the Son of David.

There are three hundred and fifty-five stories about Suleiman-bin-Daoud; but this is not one of them. It is not the story of the Lapwing who found the Water; or the Hoopoe who shaded Suleiman-bin-Daoud from the heat. It is not the story of the Glass Pavement, or the Ruby with the Crooked Hole, or the Gold Bars of Balkis. It is the story of the Butterfly that Stamped.

Now attend all over again and listen!

Suleiman-bin-Daoud was wise. He understood what the beasts said, what the birds said, what the fishes said, and what the insects said. He understood what the rocks said deep under the earth when they bowed in towards each other and groaned; and he understood what the trees said when they rustled in the middle of the morning. He understood everything, from the

185

bishop on the bench to the hyssop on the wall; and Balkis, his Head Queen, the Most Beautiful Queen Balkis, was nearly as wise as he was.

Suleiman-bin-Daoud was strong. Upon the third finger of his right hand he wore a ring. When he turned it once, Afrits and Djinns came out of the earth to do whatever he told them. When he turned it twice, Fairies came down from the sky to do whatever he told them; and when he turned it three times, the very great angel Azrael of the Sword came dressed as a water-carrier, and told him the news of the three worlds,— Above—Below—and Here.

And yet Suleiman-bin-Daoud was not proud. He very seldom showed off, and when he did he was sorry for it. Once he tried to feed all the animals in all the world in one day, but when the food was ready, an Animal came out of the deep sea and ate it up in three mouthfuls. Suleiman-bin-Daoud was very surprised and said, 'O Animal, who are you?' And the Animal said, 'O King, live for ever! I am the smallest of thirty thousand brothers, and our home is at the bottom of the sea. We heard that you were going to feed all the animals in all the world, and my brothers sent me to ask when dinner would be ready.' Suleiman-bin-Daoud was more surprised than ever and said, 'O Animal, you have eaten all the dinner that I made ready for all the animals in the world.' And the Animal said, 'O King, live for ever, but do you really call that a dinner? Where I come from we each eat twice as much as that between meals.' Then Suleiman-bin-Daoud fell flat on his face and said, 'O Animal! I gave that dinner to show what a great and rich king I was, and not because I really wanted to be kind to the animals.

Now I am ashamed, and it serves me right.' Suleiman-bin-Daoud was a really truly wise man, Best Beloved. After that he never forgot that it was silly to show off; and now the real story part of my story begins.

He married ever so many wives. He married nine hundred and ninety-nine wives, besides the Most Beautiful Balkis; and they all lived in a great golden palace in the middle of a lovely garden with fountains. He didn't really want nine hundred and ninety-nine wives, but in those days everybody married ever so many wives, and of course the King had to marry ever so many more just to show that he was the King.

Some of the wives were nice, but some were simply horrid, and the horrid ones quarrelled with the nice ones and made them horrid too, and then they would all quarrel with Suleiman-bin-Daoud, and that was horrid for him. But Balkis the Most Beautiful never quarrelled with Suleiman-bin-Daoud. She loved him too much. She sat in her rooms in the Golden Palace, or walked in the Palace garden, and was truly sorry for him.

Of course if he had chosen to turn his ring on his finger and call up the Djinns and the Afrits they would have magicked all those nine hundred and ninety-nine quarrelsome wives into white mules of the desert or greyhounds or pomegranate seeds; but Suleiman-bin-Daoud thought that that would be showing off. So, when they quarrelled too much, he only walked by himself in one part of the beautiful Palace gardens and wished he had never been born.

One day, when they had quarrelled for three weeks —all nine hundred and ninety-nine wives together— Suleiman-bin-Daoud went out for peace and quiet as

This is the picture of the Animal that came out of the sea and ate up all the food that Suleiman-bin-Daoud had made ready for all the animals in all the world. He was really quite a nice Animal, and his Mummy was very fond of him and of his twenty-nine thousand nine hundred and ninety-nine other brothers that lived at the bottom of the sea. You know •that he was the smallest of them all, and so his name was Small Porgies. He ate up all those boxes and packets and bales and things that had been got ready for all the animals, without ever once taking off the lids or untying the strings, and it did not hurt him at all. The sticky-up masts behind the boxes of food belong to Suleiman-bin-Daoud's ships. They were busy bringing more food when Small Porgies came ashore. He did not eat the ships. They stopped unloading the foods and instantly sailed away to sea till Small Porgies had quite finished eating. You can see some of the ships beginning to sail away by Small Porgies' shoulder. I have not drawn Suleiman-bin-Daoud, but he is just outside the picture, very much astonished. The bundle hanging from the mast of the ship in the corner is really a package of wet dates for parrots to eat. I don't know the names of the ships. That is all there is in that picture.

usual; and among the orange-trees he met Balkis the
Most Beautiful, very sorrowful because Suleiman-bin-
Daoud was so worried. And she said to him, 'O my
Lord and Light of my Eyes, turn the ring upon your
finger and show these Queens of Egypt and Mesopotamia
and Persia and China that you are the great and terrible
King.' But Suleiman-bin-Daoud shook his head and
said, 'O my Lady and Delight of my Life, remember the
Animal that came out of the sea and made me ashamed
before all the animals in all the world because I showed
off. Now, if I showed off before these Queens of Persia
and Egypt and Abyssinia and China, merely because
they worry me, I might be made even more ashamed
than I have been.'

And Balkis the Most Beautiful said, 'O my Lord and
Treasure of my Soul, what will you do?'

And Suleiman-bin-Daoud said, 'O my Lady and
Content of my Heart, I shall continue to endure my
fate at the hands of these nine hundred and ninety-nine
Queens who vex me with their continual quarrelling.'

So he went on between the lilies and the loquats and
the roses and the cannas and the heavy-scented ginger-
plants that grew in the garden, till he came to the great
camphor-tree that was called the Camphor Tree of
Suleiman-bin-Daoud. But Balkis hid among the tall
irises and the spotted bamboos and the red lilies behind
the camphor-tree, so as to be near her own true love,
Suleiman-bin-Daoud.

Presently two Butterflies flew under the tree, quarrelling.

Suleiman-bin-Daoud heard one say to the other, 'I
wonder at your presumption in talking like this to me.
Don't you know that if I stamped with my foot all

Suleiman-bin-Daoud's Palace and this garden here would immediately vanish in a clap of thunder?'

Then Suleiman-bin-Daoud forgot his nine hundred and ninety-nine bothersome wives, and laughed, till the camphor-tree shook, at the Butterfly's boast. And he held out his finger and said, 'Little man, come here.'

The Butterfly was dreadfully frightened, but he managed to fly up to the hand of Suleiman-bin-Daoud, and clung there, fanning himself. Suleiman-bin-Daoud bent his head and whispered very softly, 'Little man, you know that all your stamping wouldn't bend one blade of grass. What made you tell that awful fib to your wife?—for doubtless she is your wife.'

The Butterfly looked at Suleiman-bin-Daoud and saw the most wise King's eyes twinkle like stars on a frosty night, and he picked up his courage with both wings, and he put his head on one side and said, 'O King, live for ever. She is my wife; and you know what wives are like.'

Suleiman-bin-Daoud smiled in his beard and said, 'Yes, I know, little brother.'

'One must keep them in order somehow,' said the Butterfly, 'and she has been quarrelling with me all the morning. I said that to quiet her.'

And Suleiman-bin-Daoud said, 'May it quiet her. Go back to your wife, little brother, and let me hear what you say.'

Back flew the Butterfly to his wife, who was all of a twitter behind a leaf, and she said, 'He heard you! Suleiman-bin-Daoud himself heard you!'

'Heard me!' said the Butterfly. 'Of course he did. I meant him to hear me.'

'And what did he say? Oh, what did he say?'

'Well,' said the Butterfly, fanning himself most importantly, 'between you and me, my dear—of course I don't blame him, because his Palace must have cost a great deal and the oranges are just ripening,—he asked me not to stamp, and I promised I wouldn't.'

'Gracious!' said his wife, and sat quite quiet; but Suleiman-bin-Daoud laughed till the tears ran down his face at the impudence of the bad little Butterfly.

Balkis the Most Beautiful stood up behind the tree among the red lilies and smiled to herself, for she had heard all this talk. She thought, 'If I am wise I can yet save my Lord from the persecutions of these quarrelsome Queens,' and she held out her finger and whispered softly to the Butterfly's Wife, 'Little woman, come here.'

Up flew the Butterfly's Wife, very frightened, and clung to Balkis's white hand.

Balkis bent her beautiful head down and whispered, 'Little woman, do you believe what your husband has just said?'

The Butterfly's Wife looked at Balkis, and saw the Most Beautiful Queen's eyes shining like deep pools with starlight on them, and she picked up her courage with both wings and said, 'O Queen, be lovely for ever. You know what men-folk are like.'

And the Queen Balkis, the Wise Balkis of Sheba, put her hand to her lips to hide a smile, and said, 'Little sister, I know.'

'They get angry,' said the Butterfly's Wife, fanning herself quickly, 'over nothing at all, but we must humour them, O Queen. They never mean half they say. If it pleases my husband to believe that I believe he can make Suleiman-bin-Daoud's Palace disappear by stamping his foot, I'm sure I don't care. He'll forget all about it to-morrow.'

'Little sister,' said Balkis, 'you are quite right; but next time he begins to boast, take him at his word. Ask him to stamp, and see what will happen. We know what men-folk are like, don't we? He'll be very much ashamed.'

Away flew the Butterfly's Wife to her husband, and in five minutes they were quarrelling worse than ever.

'Remember!' said the Butterfly. 'Remember what I can do if I stamp my foot.'

'I don't believe you one little bit,' said the Butterfly's Wife. 'I should very much like to see it done. Suppose you stamp now.'

'I promised Suleiman-bin-Daoud that I wouldn't,' said the Butterfly, 'and I don't want to break my promise.'

'It wouldn't matter if you did,' said his wife. 'You couldn't bend a blade of grass with your stamping. I dare you to do it,' she said. 'Stamp! Stamp! Stamp!'

Suleiman-bin-Daoud, sitting under the camphor-tree, heard every word of this, and he laughed as he had never laughed in his life before. He forgot all about his Queens; he forgot about the Animal that came out of the sea; he forgot about showing off. He just laughed with joy, and Balkis, on the other side of the tree, smiled because her own true love was so joyful.

Presently the Butterfly, very hot and puffy, came whirling back under the shadow of the camphor-tree and said to Suleiman, 'She wants me to stamp! She wants to see what will happen, O Suleiman-bin-Daoud! You know I can't do it, and now she'll never believe a word I say. She'll laugh at me to the end of my days!'

'No, little brother,' said Suleiman-bin-Daoud, 'she

194

will never laugh at you again,' and he turned the ring on his finger—just for the little Butterfly's sake, not for the sake of showing off,—and, lo and behold, four huge Djinns came out of the earth!

'Slaves,' said Suleiman-bin-Daoud, 'when this gentleman on my finger' (that was where the impudent Butterfly was sitting) 'stamps his left front forefoot you will make my Palace and these gardens disappear in a clap of thunder. When he stamps again you will bring them back carefully.'

'Now, little brother,' he said, 'go back to your wife and stamp all you've a mind to.'

Away flew the Butterfly to his wife, who was crying, 'I dare you to do it! I dare you to do it! Stamp! Stamp now! Stamp!' Balkis saw the four vast Djinns stoop down to the four corners of the gardens with the Palace in the middle, and she clapped her hands softly and said, 'At last Suleiman-bin-Daoud will do for the sake of a Butterfly what he ought to have done long ago for his own sake, and the quarrelsome Queens will be frightened!'

Then the Butterfly stamped. The Djinns jerked the Palace and the gardens a thousand miles into the air: there was a most awful thunder-clap, and everything grew inky black. The Butterfly's Wife fluttered about in the dark, crying, 'Oh, I'll be good! I'm so sorry I spoke! Only bring the gardens back, my dear darling husband, and I'll never contradict again.'

The Butterfly was nearly as frightened as his wife, and Suleiman-bin-Daoud laughed so much that it was several minutes before he found breath enough to whisper to the Butterfly, 'Stamp again, little brother. Give me back my Palace, most great magician.'

195

This is the picture of the four gull-winged Djinns lifting up Suleiman-bin-Daoud's Palace the very minute after the Butterfly had stamped. The Palace and the gardens and everything came up in one piece like a board, and they left a big hole in the ground all full of dust and smoke. If you look in the corner, close to the thing that looks like a lion, you will see Suleiman-bin-Daoud with his magic stick and the two Butterflies behind him. The thing that looks like a lion is really a lion carved in stone, and the thing that looks like a milk-can is really a piece of a temple or a house or something. Suleiman-bin-Daoud stood there so as to be out of the way of the dust and the smoke when the Djinns lifted up the Palace. I don't know the Djinns' names. They were servants of Suleiman-bin-Daoud's magic ring, and they changed about every day. They were just common gull-winged Djinns.

The thing at the bottom is a picture of a very friendly Djinn called Akraig. He used to feed the little fishes in the sea three times a day, and his wings were made of pure copper. I put him in to show you what a nice Djinn is like. He did not help to lift the Palace. He was busy feeding little fishes in the Arabian Sea when it happened.

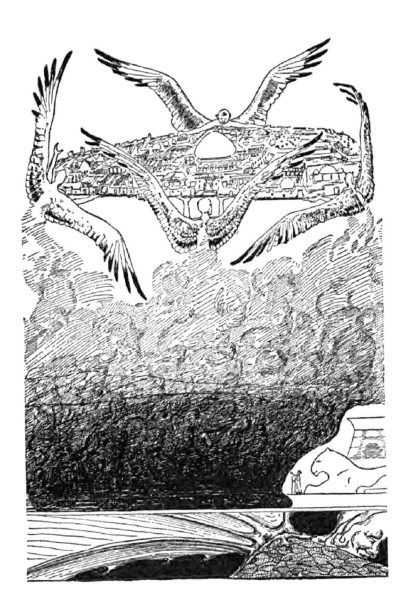

THE BUTTERFLY THAT STAMPED

'Yes, give him back his Palace,' said the Butterfly's Wife, still flying about in the dark like a moth. 'Give him back his Palace, and don't let's have any more horrid magic.'

'Well, my dear,' said the Butterfly as bravely as he could, 'you see what your nagging has led to. Of course it doesn't make any difference to me—I'm used to this kind of thing—but as a favour to you and to Suleiman-bin-Daoud I don't mind putting things right.'

So he stamped once more, and that instant the Djinns let down the Palace and the gardens, without even a bump. The sun shone on the dark-green orange-leaves; the fountains played among the pink Egyptian lilies; the birds went on singing; and the Butterfly's Wife lay on her side under the camphor-tree waggling her wings and panting, 'Oh, I'll be good! I'll be good!'

Suleiman-bin-Daoud could hardly speak for laughing. He leaned back all weak and hiccoughy, and shook his finger at the Butterfly and said, 'O great wizard, what is the sense of returning my Palace to me if at the same time you slay me with mirth!'

Then came a terrible noise, for all the nine hundred and ninety-nine Queens ran out of the Palace shrieking and shouting and calling for their babies. They hurried down the great marble steps below the fountain, one hundred abreast, and the Most Wise Balkis went statelily forward to meet them and said, 'What is your trouble, O Queens?'

They stood on the marble steps one hundred abreast and shouted, 'What is our trouble? We were living peacefully in our golden Palace, as is our custom, when upon a sudden the Palace disappeared, and we were left sitting in a thick and noisome darkness; and it

199

thundered, and Djinns and Afrits moved about in the darkness! That is our trouble, O Head Queen, and we are most extremely troubled on account of that trouble, for it was a troublesome trouble, unlike any trouble we have known.'

Then Balkis the Most Beautiful Queen—Suleiman-bin-Daoud's Very Best Beloved—Queen that was of Sheba and Sabie and the Rivers of the Gold of the South—from the Desert of Zinn to the Towers of Zimbabwe—Balkis, almost as wise as the Most Wise Suleiman-bin-Daoud himself, said, 'It is nothing, O Queens! A Butterfly has made complaint against his wife because she quarrelled with him, and it has pleased our Lord Suleiman-bin-Daoud to teach her a lesson in low-speaking and humbleness, for that is counted a virtue among the wives of the butterflies.'

Then up and spoke an Egyptian Queen—the daughter of a Pharaoh—and she said, 'Our Palace cannot be plucked up by the roots like a leek for the sake of a little insect. No! Suleiman-bin-Daoud must be dead, and what we heard and saw was the earth thundering and darkening at the news.'

Then Balkis beckoned that bold Queen without looking at her, and said to her and to the others, 'Come and see.'

They came down the marble steps, one hundred abreast, and beneath his camphor-tree, still weak with laughing, they saw the Most Wise King Suleiman-bin-Daoud rocking back and forth with a Butterfly on either hand, and they heard him say, 'O wife of my brother in the air, remember after this to please your husband in all things, lest he be provoked to stamp his foot yet again; for he has said that he is used to this

Magic, and he is most eminently a great magician—one who steals away the very Palace of Suleiman-bin-Daoud himself. Go in peace, little folk!' And he kissed them on the wings, and they flew away.

Then all the Queens except Balkis—the Most Beautiful and Splendid Balkis, who stood apart smiling—fell flat on their faces, for they said, 'If these things are done when a Butterfly is displeased with his wife, what shall be done to us who have vexed our King with our loud-speaking and open quarrelling through many days?'

Then they put their veils over their heads, and they put their hands over their mouths, and they tiptoed back to the Palace most mousy-quiet.

Then Balkis—the Most Beautiful and Excellent Balkis—went forward through the red lilies into the shade of the camphor-tree and laid her hand upon Suleiman-bin-Daoud's shoulder and said, 'O my Lord and Treasure of my Soul, rejoice, for we have taught the Queens of Egypt and Ethiopia and Abyssinia and Persia and India and China with a great and a memorable teaching.'

And Suleiman-bin-Daoud, still looking after the Butterflies where they played in the sunlight, said, 'O my Lady and Jewel of my Felicity, when did this happen? For I have been jesting with a Butterfly ever since I came into the garden.' And he told Balkis what he had done.

Balkis—the Tender and Most Lovely Balkis—said, 'O my Lord and Regent of my Existence, I hid behind the camphor-tree and saw it all. It was I who told the Butterfly's Wife to ask the Butterfly to stamp, because I hoped that for the sake of the jest my Lord would make some great Magic and that the Queens would see

201

it and be frightened.' And she told him what the Queens had said and seen and thought.

Then Suleiman-bin-Daoud rose up from his seat under the camphor-tree, and stretched his arms and rejoiced and said, 'O my Lady and Sweetener of my Days, know that if I had made a Magic against my Queens for the sake of pride or anger, as I made that feast for All the Animals, I should certainly have been put to shame. But by means of your wisdom I made the Magic for the sake of a jest and for the sake of a little Butterfly, and— behold—it has also delivered me from the vexations of my vexatious wives! Tell me, therefore, O my Lady and Heart of my Heart, how did you come to be so wise?'

And Balkis the Queen, beautiful and tall, looked up into Suleiman-bin-Daoud's eyes and put her head a little on one side, just like the Butterfly, and said, 'First, O my Lord, because I loved you; and secondly, O my Lord, because I know what women-folk are.'

Then they went up to the Palace and lived happily ever afterwards.

But wasn't it clever of Balkis?

There was never a Queen like Balkis,
    From here to the wide world's end;
But Balkis talked to a butterfly
    As you would talk to a friend.

There was never a King like Solomon,
    Not since the world began;
But Solomon talked to a butterfly
    As a man would talk to a man.

She was Queen of Sabæa—
    And he was Asia's Lord—
But they both of 'em talked to butterflies
    When they took their walks abroad!

                    THE   END

To
CORMELL PRICE
Headmaster, United Services College
Westward Ho! Bideford, North Devon
1874-1894

'LET us now praise famous men'—
      Men of little showing—
      For their work continueth,
And their work continueth,
Broad and deep continueth,
    Greater than their knowing!

Western wind and open surge
    Took us from our mothers;
Flung us on a naked shore
(Twelve bleak houses by the shore!
Seven summers by the shore!)
    'Mid two hundred brothers.

There we met with famous men
    Set in office o'er us;
And they beat on us with rods—
Faithfully with many rods—
Daily beat us on with rods,
    For the love they bore us.

Out of Egypt unto Troy—
    Over Himalaya—
Far and sure our bands have gone—
Hy-Brasil or Babylon,
Islands of the Southern Run,
    And Cities of Cathaia!

And we all praise famous men—
    Ancients of the College;
For they taught us common sense—
Tried to teach us common sense—
Truth and God's Own Common Sense,
    Which is more than knowledge!

Each degree of Latitude
    Strung about Creation
Seeth one (or more) of us
(Of one muster all of us),
Diligent in that he does,
    Keen in his vocation.

This we learned from famous men,
    Knowing not its uses,
When they showed, in daily work,
Man must finish off his work—
Right or wrong, his daily work—
    And without excuses.

Servants of the Staff and chain—
    Mine and fuse and grapnel—
Some before the face of Kings,
Stand before the face of Kings;
Bearing gifts to divers Kings—
    Gifts of case and shrapnel.

This we learned from famous men
    Teaching in our borders,
Who declared it was best,
Safest, easiest, and best—
Expeditious, wise, and best—
    To obey your orders.

Some beneath the further stars
　　Bear the greater burden:
Set to serve the lands they rule,
(Save he serve no man may rule),
Serve and love the lands they rule;
　　Seeking praise nor guerdon.

This we learned from famous men,
　　Knowing not we learned it.
Only, as the years went by—
Lonely, as the years went by—
Far from help as years went by,
　　Plainer we discerned it.

Wherefore praise we famous men
　　From whose bays we borrow—
They that put aside To-day—
All the joys of their To-day—
And with toil of their To-day
　　Bought for us To-morrow!

Bless and praise we famous men—
　　Men of little showing—
For their work continueth,
And their work continueth,
Broad and deep continueth,
　　Great beyond their knowing!

.

CONTENTS

'IN AMBUSH'

(1897)

IN summer all right-minded boys built huts in the furze-hill behind the College—little lairs whittled out of the heart of the prickly bushes, full of stumps, odd root-ends, and spikes, but, since they were strictly forbidden, palaces of delight. And for the fifth summer in succession, Stalky, M'Turk, and Beetle (this was before they reached the dignity of a study) had built, like beavers, a place of retreat and meditation, where they smoked.

Now there was nothing in their characters, as known to Mr. Prout, their house-master, at all commanding respect; nor did Foxy, the subtle red-haired school Sergeant, trust them. His business was to wear tennis-shoes, carry binoculars, and swoop hawk-like upon evil boys. Had he taken the field alone, that hut would have been raided, for Foxy knew the manners of his quarry; but Providence moved Mr. Prout, whose school-name, derived from the size of his feet, was Hoofer, to investigate on his own account; and it was the cautious Stalky who found the track of his pugs on the very floor of their lair one peaceful afternoon when Stalky would fain have forgotten Prout and his works in a volume of Surtees and a new briar-wood pipe. Crusoe, at sight of the foot-print, did not act more swiftly than Stalky.

3

He removed the pipes, swept up all loose match-ends, and departed to warn Beetle and M'Turk.

But it was characteristic of the boy that he did not approach his allies till he had met and conferred with little Hartopp, President of the Natural History Society, an institution which Stalky held in contempt. Hartopp was more than surprised when the boy meekly, as he knew how, begged to propose himself, Beetle, and M'Turk as candidates; confessed to a long-smothered interest in first-flowerings, early butterflies, and new arrivals, and volunteered, if Mr. Hartopp saw fit, to enter on the new life at once. Being a master, Hartopp was suspicious; but he was also an enthusiast, and his gentle little soul had been galled by chance-heard remarks from the three, and specially Beetle. So he was gracious to that repentant sinner, and entered the three names in his book.

Then, and not till then, did Stalky seek Beetle and M'Turk in their house form-room. They were stowing away books for a quiet afternoon in the furze, which they called the 'wuzzy.'

'All up!' said Stalky serenely. 'I spotted Heffy's fairy feet round our hut after dinner. 'Blessing they're so big.'

'Con-found! Did you hide our pipes!' said Beetle.

'Oh no. Left 'em in the middle of the hut, of course. What a blind ass you are, Beetle! D'you think nobody thinks but yourself? Well, we can't use the hut any more. Hoofer will be watchin' it.'

'"Bother! Likewise blow!"' said M'Turk thoughtfully, unpacking the volumes with which his chest was cased. The boys carried their libraries between their belt and their collar. 'Nice job! This means we're under suspicion for the rest of the term.'

'Why? All that Heffy has found is a hut. He and Foxy will watch it. It's nothing to do with us; only we mustn't be seen that way for a bit.'

'Yes, and where else are we to go?' said Beetle. 'You chose that place, too—an'—an' I wanted to read this afternoon.'

Stalky sat on a desk drumming his heels on the form.

'You're a despondin' brute, Beetle. Sometimes I think I shall have to drop you altogether. Did you ever know your Uncle Stalky forget you yet? "His rebus infectis"—after I'd seen Heffy's man-tracks marchin' round our hut, I found little Hartopp—"destricto ense"—wavin' a butterfly-net. I conciliated Hartopp. 'Told him that you'd read papers to the Bug-hunters if he'd let you join, Beetle. 'Told him you liked butterflies, Turkey. Anyhow, I soothed the Hartoffles, and we're Bug-hunters now.'

'What's the good of that?' said Beetle.

'Oh, Turkey, kick him!'

In the interests of science, bounds were largely relaxed for the members of the Natural History Society. They could wander, if they kept clear of all houses, practically where they chose; Mr. Hartopp holding himself responsible for their good conduct.

Beetle began to see this as M'Turk began the kicking.

'I'm an ass, Stalky!' he said, guarding the afflicted part. 'Pax, Turkey. I'm an ass.'

'Don't stop, Turkey. Isn't your Uncle Stalky a great man?'

'Great man,' said Beetle.

'All the same, bug-huntin's a filthy business,' said M'Turk. 'How the deuce does one begin?'

'This way,' said Stalky, turning to some fags' lockers

5

behind him. Fags are dabs at Natural History. 'Here's young Braybrooke's botany-case.' He flung out a tangle of decayed roots and adjusted the slide. ''Gives one no end of a professional air, I think. Here's Clay Minor's geological hammer. Beetle can carry that. Turkey, you'd better covet a butterfly-net from somewhere.'

'I'm blowed if I do,' said M'Turk simply, but with immense feeling. 'Beetle, give me the hammer.'

'All right. I'm not proud. Chuck us down that net on top of the lockers, Stalky.'

'That's all right. It's a collapsible jamboree, too. Beastly luxurious dogs these fags are. Built like a fishin'-rod. 'Pon my sainted Sam, but we look the complete Bug-hunters! Now, listen to your Uncle Stalky! We're goin' along the cliffs after butterflies. Very few chaps come there. We're goin' to leg it, too. You'd better leave your book behind.'

'Not much!' said Beetle firmly. 'I'm not goin' to be done out of my fun for a lot of filthy butterflies.'

'Then you'll sweat horrid. You'd better carry my Jorrocks. 'Twon't make you any hotter.'

They all sweated; for Stalky led them at a smart trot west away along the cliffs under the furze-hills, crossing combe after gorsy combe. They took no heed to flying rabbits or fluttering fritillaries, and all that Turkey said of geology was utterly unquotable.

'Are we going to Clovelly?' he puffed at last, and they flung themselves down on the short, springy turf between the drone of the sea below and the light summer wind among the inland trees. They were looking into a combe half full of old, high furze in gay bloom that ran up to a fringe of brambles and a dense wood of mixed

timber and hollies.   It was as though one-half the combe
were filled with golden fire to the cliff's edge.   The side
nearest to them was open grass, and fairly bristled with
notice-boards.

'Fee-rocious old cove, this,' said Stalky, reading the
nearest. ' "Prosecuted with the utmost rigour of the
law.   G. M. Dabney, Col., J. P.," an' all the rest of it.
'Don't seem to me that any chap in his senses would
trespass here, does it?'

'You've got to prove damage 'fore you can prosecute
for anything!   'Can't prosecute for trespass,' said M'-
Turk, whose father held many acres in Ireland. 'That's
all rot!'

' 'Glad of that, 'cause this looks like what we wanted.
Not straight across, Beetle, you blind lunatic!   Any
one could stop us half a mile off.   This way; and furl
up your beastly butterfly-net.'

Beetle disconnected the ring, thrust the net into a
pocket, shut up the handle to a two-foot stave, and slid
the cane-ring round his waist.   Stalky led inland to the
wood, which was, perhaps, a quarter of a mile from the
sea, and reached to the fringe of the brambles.

'Now we can get straight down through the furze to
the cliff, and never show up at all,' said the tactician.
'Beetle, go ahead and explore.   Snf!   Snf!   Beastly
stink of fox somewhere!'

On all fours, save when he clung to his spectacles,
Beetle wormed into the gorse, and presently announced
between grunts of pain that he had found a very fair fox-
track.   This was well for Beetle, since Stalky pinched
him 'a tergo.'   Down that tunnel they crawled.   It
was evidently a highway for the inhabitants of the
combe; and, to their inexpressible joy, ended, at the very

STALKY & CO.

edge of the cliff, in a few square feet of dry turf walled and roofed with impenetrable gorse.

'By gum! There isn't a single thing to do except lie down,' said Stalky, returning a knife to his pocket. 'Look here!'

He parted the tough stems before him, and it was as a window opened on a far view of Lundy, and the deep sea sluggishly nosing the pebbles a couple of hundred feet below. They could hear young jackdaws squawking on the ledges, the hiss and jabber of a nest of hawks somewhere out of sight; and, with great deliberation, Stalky spat on to the back of a young rabbit sunning himself far down where only a cliff-rabbit could have found foot-hold. Big gray and black gulls screamed against the jackdaws; the heavy-scented acres of bloom round them were alive with low-nesting birds, singing or silent as the shadow of the wheeling hawks passed and returned; and on the naked turf across the combe rabbits thumped and frolicked.

'Whew! What a place! Talk of natural history; this is it,' said Stalky, filling himself a pipe. 'Isn't it scrumptious? Good old sea!' He spat again approvingly, and was silent.

M'Turk and Beetle had taken out their books and were lying on their stomachs, chin in hand. The sea snored and gurgled; the birds, scattered for the moment by these new animals, returned to their businesses, and the boys read on in the rich, warm sleepy silence.

'Hullo, here's a keeper,' said Stalky, shutting 'Handley Cross' cautiously, and peering through the jungle. A man with a gun appeared on the sky-line to the east. 'Confound him, he's going to sit down!'

'He'd swear we were poachin' too,' said Beetle.

8

'What's the good of pheasants' eggs? They're always addled.'

''Might as well get up to the wood, I think,' said Stalky. 'We don't want G. M. Dabney, Col., J. P., to be bothered about us so soon. Up the wuzzy and keep quiet! He may have followed us, you know.'

Beetle was already far up the tunnel. They heard him gasp indescribably: there was the crash of a heavy body leaping through the furze.

'Aie! yeou little red rascal. I see yeou!' The keeper threw the gun to his shoulder, and fired both barrels in their direction. The pellets dusted the dry stems round them as a big fox plunged between Stalky's legs and ran over the cliff-edge.

They said nothing till they reached the wood, torn, dishevelled, hot, but unseen.

'Narrow squeak,' said Stalky. 'I'll swear some of the pellets went through my hair.'

'Did you see him?' said Beetle. 'I almost put my hand on him. Wasn't he a wopper! Didn't he stink! Hullo, Turkey, what's the matter? Are you hit?'

M'Turk's lean face had turned pearly white; his mouth, generally half open, was tight shut, and his eyes blazed. They had never seen him like this save once, in a sad time of civil war.

'Do you know that that was just as bad as murder?' he said, in a grating voice, as he brushed prickles from his head.

'Well, he didn't hit us,' said Stalky. 'I think it was rather a lark. Here, where are you going?'

'I'm going up to the house, if there is one,' said M'-Turk, pushing through the hollies. 'I am going to tell this Colonel Dabney.'

'Are you crazy? He'll swear it served us jolly well right. He'll report us. It'll be a public lickin'. Oh, Turkey, don't be an ass! Think of us!'

'You fool!' said M'Turk, turning savagely. 'D'you suppose I'm thinkin' of us? It's the keeper.'

'He's cracked,' said Beetle miserably, as they followed. Indeed, this was a new Turkey—a haughty, angular, nose-lifted Turkey—whom they accompanied through a shrubbery on to a lawn, where a white-whiskered old gentleman with a cleek was alternately putting and blaspheming vigorously.

'Are you Colonel Dabney?' M'Turk began in this new creaking voice of his.

'I—I am, and'—his eyes travelled up and down the boy—'who—what the devil d'you want? Ye've been disturbing my pheasants. Don't attempt to deny it. Ye needn't laugh at it. [M'Turk's not too lovely features had twisted themselves into a horrible sneer at the word 'pheasant.'] You've been bird's-nesting. You needn't hide your hat. I can see that you belong to the College. Don't attempt to deny it. Ye do! Your name and number at once, sir. Ye want to speak to me—Eh? You saw my notice-boards? 'Must have. Don't attempt to deny it. Ye did! Damnable! Oh, damnable!'

He choked with emotion. M'Turk's heel tapped the lawn and he stuttered a little—two sure signs that he was losing his temper. But why should he, the offender, be angry?

'Lo-look here, sir. Do—do you shoot foxes? Because, if you don't, your keeper does. We've seen him! I do-don't care what you call us—but it's an awful thing. It's the ruin of good feelin' among neighbours. A ma-man

10

ought to say once and for all how he stands about pre-
servin'. It's worse than murder, because there's no
legal remedy.' M'Turk was quoting confusedly from
his father, while the old gentleman made noises in his
throat.

'Do you know who I am?' he gurgled at last; Stalky
and Beetle quaking.

'No, sorr, nor do I care if ye belonged to the Castle
itself. Answer me now, as one gentleman to another.
Do ye shoot foxes or do ye not?'

And four years before Stalky and Beetle had carefully
kicked M'Turk out of his Irish dialect! Assuredly he
had gone mad or taken a sunstroke, and as assuredly he
would be slain—once by the old gentleman and once by
the Head. A public licking for the three was the least
they could expect. Yet—if their eyes and ears were to
be trusted—the old gentleman had collapsed. It might
be a lull before the storm, but—

'I do not.' He was still gurgling.

'Then you must sack your keeper. He's not fit to
live in the same county with a God-fearin' fox. An' a
vixen, too—at this time o' year!'

'Did ye come up on purpose to tell me this?'

'Of course I did, ye silly man,' with a stamp of the
foot. 'Would you not have done as much for me if
you'd seen that thing happen on my land, now?'

Forgotten—forgotten was the College and the decency due to elders! M'Turk was treading again the
barren purple mountains of the rainy West coast, where
in his holidays he was viceroy of four thousand naked
acres, only son of a three-hundred-year-old house, lord
of a crazy fishing-boat, and the idol of his father's shift-
less tenantry. It was the landed man speaking to his

11

equal—deep calling to deep—and the old gentleman acknowledged the cry.

'I apologise,' said he. 'I apologise unreservedly—to you, and to the Old Country. Now, will you be good enough to tell me your story?'

'We were in your combe,' M'Turk began, and he told his tale alternately as a schoolboy, and, when the iniquity of the thing overcame him, as an indignant squire; concluding: 'So you see he must be in the habit of it. I—we—one never wants to accuse a neighbour's man; but I took the liberty in this case—'

'I see. Quite so. For a reason ye had. Infamous—oh, infamous!' The two had fallen into step beside each other on the lawn, and Colonel Dabney was talking as one man to another. 'This comes of promoting a fisherman—a fisherman—from his lobster-pots. It's enough to ruin the reputation of an archangel. Don't attempt to deny it. It is! Your father has brought you up well. He has. I'd much like the pleasure of his acquaintance. Very much, indeed. And these young gentlemen? English they are. Don't attempt to deny it. They came up with you, too? Extraordinary! Extraordinary, now! In the present state of education I shouldn't have thought any three boys would be well enough grounded. . . . But out of the mouths of—No—no! Not that by any odds. Don't attempt to deny it. Ye're not! Sherry always catches me under the liver, but—beer, now? Eh? What d'you say to beer, and something to eat? It's long since I was a boy—abominable nuisances; but exceptions prove the rule. And a vixen, too!'

They were fed on the terrace by a gray-haired housekeeper. Stalky and Beetle merely ate, but M'Turk with bright eyes continued a free and lofty discourse; and ever the old gentleman treated him as a brother.

'My dear man, of course ye can come again. Did I not say exceptions prove the rule? The lower combe? Man, dear, anywhere ye please, so long as you do not disturb my pheasants. The two are not incompatible. Don't attempt to deny it. They're not! I'll never allow another gun, though. Come and go as ye please. I'll not see you, and ye needn't see me. Ye've been well brought up. Another glass of beer, now? I tell you a fisherman he was and a fisherman he shall be to-night again. He shall! 'Wish I could drown him. I'll convoy you to the Lodge. My people are not precisely—ah—broke to boy, but they'll know you again.'

He dismissed them with many compliments by the high Lodge-gate in the split-oak park palings and they stood still; even Stalky, who had played second, not to say a dumb, fiddle, regarding M'Turk as one from another world. The two glasses of strong home-brewed had brought a melancholy upon the boy, for, slowly strolling with his hands in his pockets, he crooned:—

'Oh, Paddy dear, and did ye hear the news that's goin' round?'

Under other circumstances Stalky and Beetle would have fallen upon him, for that song was barred utterly— anathema—the sin of witchcraft. But seeing what he had wrought, they danced round him in silence, waiting till it pleased him to touch earth.

The tea-bell rang when they were still half a mile from College. M'Turk shivered and came out of dreams.

The glory of his holiday estate had left him. He was a Colleger of the College, speaking English once more.

'Turkey, it was immense!' said Stalky generously. 'I didn't know you had it in you. You've got us a hut for the rest of the term, where we simply can't be collared. Fids! Fids! Oh, fids! I gloat! Hear me gloat!'

They spun wildly on their heels, jodelling after the accepted manner of a 'gloat,' which is not unremotely allied to Primitive Man's song of triumph, and dropped down the hill by the path from the gasometer just in time to meet their house-master, who had spent the afternoon watching their abandoned hut in the 'wuzzy.'

Unluckily, all Mr. Prout's imagination leaned to the darker side of life, and he looked on those young-eyed cherubims most sourly. Boys that he understood attended house-matches and could be accounted for at any moment. But he had heard M'Turk openly deride cricket—even house-matches; Beetle's views on the honour of the house he knew were incendiary; and he could never tell when the soft and smiling Stalky was laughing at him. Consequently—since human nature is what it is—those boys had been doing wrong somewhere. He hoped it was nothing very serious, but . . .

'Ti-ra-la-la-i-tu! I gloat! Hear me!' Stalky, still on his heels, whirled like a dancing dervish to the dining-hall.

'Ti-ra-la-la-i-tu! I gloat! Hear me!' Beetle spun behind him with outstretched arms.

'Ti-ra-la-la-i-tu! I gloat! Hear me!' M'Turk's voice cracked.

Now was there or was there not a distinct flavour of beer as they shot past Mr. Prout?

He was unlucky in that his conscience as a house-master impelled him to consult his associates. Had he taken his pipe and his troubles to little Hartopp's rooms he would, perhaps, have been saved confusion, for Hartopp believed in boys, and knew something about them. His fate led him to King, a fellow house-master, no friend of his, but a zealous hater of Stalky & Co.

'Ah-haa!' said King, rubbing his hands when the tale was told. 'Curious! Now my house never dream of doing these things.'

'But you see I've no proof, exactly.'

'Proof? With the egregious Beetle! As if one wanted it! I suppose it is not impossible for the Sergeant to supply it? Foxy is considered at least a match for any evasive boy in my house. Of course they were smoking and drinking somewhere. That type of boy always does. They think it manly.'

'But they've no following in the school, and they are distinctly—er—brutal to their juniors,' said Prout, who had from a distance seen Beetle return, with interest, his butterfly-net to a tearful fag.

'Ah! They consider themselves superior to ordinary delights. Self-sufficient little animals! There's something in M'Turk's Hibernian sneer that would make me a little annoyed. And they are so careful to avoid all overt acts, too. It's sheer calculated insolence. I am strongly opposed, as you know, to interfering with another man's house; but they need a lesson, Prout. They need a sharp lesson, if only to bring down their over-weening self-conceit. Were I you, I should devote myself for a week to their little performances. Boys of that order—I may flatter myself, but I think I know boys—don't join the Bug-hunters for love. Tell the

15

Sergeant to keep his eye open; and, of course, in my peregrinations I may casually keep mine open too.'

'Ti-ra-la-la-i-tu! I gloat! Hear me!' far down the corridor.

'Disgusting!' said King. 'Where do they pick up these obscene noises? One sharp lesson is what they want.'

The boys did not concern themselves with lessons for the next few days. They had all Colonel Dabney's estate to play with, and they explored it with the stealth of Red Indians and the accuracy of burglars. They could enter either by the Lodge-gates on the upper road —they were careful to ingratiate themselves with the Lodge-keeper and his wife—drop down into the combe, and return along the cliffs; or they could begin at the combe, and climb up into the road.

They were careful not to cross the Colonel's path—he had served his turn, and they would not out-wear their welcome—nor did they show up on the sky-line when they could move in cover. The shelter of the gorse by the cliff-edge was their chosen retreat. Beetle christened it the Pleasant Isle of Aves, for the peace and the shelter of it; and here, pipes and tobacco once cached in a convenient ledge an arm's length down the cliff, their position was legally unassailable.

For, observe, Colonel Dabney had not invited them to enter his house. Therefore, they did not need to ask specific leave to go visiting; and school rules were strict on that point. He had merely thrown open his grounds to them; and, since they were lawful Bug-hunters, their extended bounds ran up to his notice-boards in the combe and his Lodge-gates on the hill.

They were amazed at their own virtue.

'And even if it wasn't,' said Stalky, flat on his back, staring into the blue. 'Even suppose we were miles out of bounds, no one could get at us through this wuzzy, unless he knew the tunnel. Isn't this better than lyin' up just behind the Coll.—in a blue funk every time we had a smoke? Isn't your Uncle Stalky—?'

'No,' said Beetle—he was stretched at the edge of the cliff thoughtfully spitting. 'We've got to thank Turkey for this. Turkey is the Great Man. Turkey, dear, you're distressing Heffles.'

'Gloomy old ass!' said M'Turk, deep in a book.

'They've got us under suspicion,' said Stalky. 'Hoop-hats is so suspicious somehow; and Foxy always makes every stalk he does a sort of—sort of—'

'Scalp,' said Beetle. 'Foxy's a giddy Chingangook.'

'Poor Foxy!' said Stalky. 'He's goin' to catch us one of these days. 'Said to me in the Gym last night, "I've got my eye on you, Mister Corkran. I'm only warning you for your good." Then I said, "Well, you jolly well take it off again, or you'll get into trouble. I'm only warnin' you for your good." Foxy was wrath.'

'Yes, but it's only fair sport for Foxy,' said Beetle. 'It's Hefflelinga that has the evil mind. 'Shouldn't wonder if he thought we got tight.'

'I never got squiffy but once—that was in the holidays,' said Stalky reflectively; 'an' it made me horrid sick. 'Pon my sacred Sam, though, it's enough to drive a man to drink, havin' an animal like Hoof for house-master.'

'If we attended the matches an' yelled, "Well hit, sir," an' stood on one leg an' grinned every time Heffy said, "So ho, my sons. Is it thus?" an' said, "Yes, sir," an' "No, sir," an' "Oh, sir," an' "Please, sir," like a lot o' filthy fa-ags, Heffy 'ud think no end of us,' said M'Turk, with a sneer.

' 'Too late to begin that.'

'It's all right. The Hefflelinga means well. But he is an ass. And we show him that we think he's an ass. An' so Heffy don't love us. 'Told me last night after prayers that he was "in loco parentis,"' Beetle grunted.

'The deuce he did!' cried Stalky. 'That means he's maturin' something unusual dam' mean. 'Last time he told me that he gave me three hundred lines for dancin' the cachuca in Number Ten dormitory. "Loco parentis," by gum! But what's the odds, as long as you're 'appy? We're all right.'

They were, and their very rightness puzzled Prout, King, and the Sergeant. Boys with bad consciences show it. They slink out past the Fives Court in haste, and smile nervously when questioned. They return, disordered, in bare time to save a call-over. They nod and wink and giggle one to the other, scattering at the approach of a master. But Stalky and his allies had long outlived these manifestations of youth. They strolled forth unconcernedly, and returned, in excellent shape, after a light refreshment of strawberries and cream at the Lodge.

The Lodge-keeper had been promoted to keeper, vice the murderous fisherman, and his wife made much of the boys. The man, too, gave them a squirrel, which they presented to the Natural History Society; thereby checkmating little Hartopp, who wished to know what they were doing for Science. Foxy faithfully worked some deep Devon lanes behind a lonely cross-roads inn; and it was curious that Prout and King, members of Common-room seldom friendly, walked together in the same direction—that is to say, north-east. Now, the Pleasant Isle of Aves lay due south-west.

'They're deep—day-vilish deep,' said Stalky. 'Why are they drawin' those covers?'

'Me,' said Beetle sweetly. 'I asked Foxy if he had ever tasted the beer there. That was enough for Foxy, and it cheered him up a little. He and Heffy were sniffin' round our old hut so long I thought they'd like a change.'

'Well, it can't last for ever,' said Stalky. 'Heffy's bankin' up like a thunder-cloud, an' King goes rubbin' his beastly hands, an' grinnin' like a hyena. It's shockin' demoralisin' for King. He'll burst some day.'

That day came a little sooner than they expected—came when the Sergeant, whose duty it was to collect defaulters, did not attend an afternoon call-over.

'Tired of pubs, eh? He's gone up to the top of hill with his binoculars to spot us,' said Stalky. 'Wonder he didn't think of that before. Did you see old Heffy cock his eye at us when we answered our names? Heffy's in it, too. Ti-ra-la-la-i-tu! I gloat! Hear me! Come on!'

'Aves?' said Beetle.

'Of course, but I'm not smokin' aujourd'hui. Parceque je jolly well pense that we'll be suivi. We'll go along the cliffs, slow, an' give Foxy lots of time to parallel us up above.'

They strolled towards the swimming-baths, and presently overtook King.

'Oh, don't let me interrupt you,' he said. 'Engaged in scientific pursuits, of course? I trust you will enjoy yourselves, my young friends?'

19

STALKY & CO.

'You see!' said Stalky, when they were out of ear-shot. 'He can't keep a secret. He's followin' to cut off our line of retreat. He'll wait at the baths till Heffy comes along. They've tried every blessed place except along the cliffs, and now they think they've bottled us. No need to hurry.'

They walked leisurely over the combes till they reached the line of notice-boards.

'Listen a shake. Foxy's up wind comin' down hill like beans. When you hear him move in the bushes, go straight across to Aves. They want to catch us "fla-grante delicto."'

They dived into the gorse at right angles to the tunnel, openly crossing the grass, and lay still in Aves.

'What did I tell you?' Stalky carefully put away the pipes and tobacco. The Sergeant, out of breath, was leaning against the fence, raking the furze with his binoculars, but he might as well have tried to see through a sand-bag. Anon, Prout and King appeared behind him. They conferred.

'Aha! Foxy don't like the notice-boards, and he don't like the prickles either. Now we'll cut up the tunnel and go to the Lodge. Hullo! They've sent Foxy into cover.'

The Sergeant was waist-deep in crackling, swaying furze, his ears filled with the noise of his own progress. The boys reached the shelter of the wood and looked down through a belt of hollies.

'Hellish noise!' said Stalky critically. ''Don't think Colonel Dabney will like it. I move we go up to the Lodge and get something to eat. We might as well see the fun out.'

Suddenly the keeper passed them at a trot.

20

'Who'm they to combe-bottom for Lard's sake?
Master'll be crazy,' he said.

'Poachers simly,' Stalky replied in the broad Devon
that was the boy's 'langue de guerre.'

'I'll poach 'em to raights!' He dropped into the
funnel-like combe, which presently began to fill with
noises, notably King's voice crying, 'Go on, Sergeant!
Leave him alone, you, sir. He is executing my orders.'

'Who'm yeou to give arders here, gingy whiskers?
Yeou come up to the master. Come out o' that wuzzy!
[This is to the Sergeant.] Yiss, I reckon us knows the
boys yeou'm after. They've tu long ears an' vuzzy
bellies, an' you nippies they in yeour pockets when
they'm dead. Come on up to master! He'll boy yeou
all you'm a mind to. Yeou other folk bide your side
fence.'

'Explain to the proprietor. You can explain, Sergeant,' shouted King. Evidently the Sergeant had surrendered to the major force.

Beetle lay at full length on the turf behind the Lodge
literally biting the earth in spasms of joy.

Stalky kicked him upright. There was nothing of
levity about Stalky or M'Turk save a stray muscle
twitching on the cheek.

They tapped at the Lodge door, where they were
always welcome.

'Come yeou right in an' set down, my little dearrs,'
said the woman. 'They'll niver touch my man. He'll
poach 'em to rights. Iss fai! Fresh berries an' cream.
Us Dartymoor folk niver forgit their friends. But
them Bidevor poachers, they've no hem to their garments. Sugar? My man he've digged a badger for yeou,
my dearrs. 'Tis in the linhay in a box.'

21

'Us'll take un with us when we'm finished here. I reckon yeou'm busy. We'll bide here an'—'tis washin' day with yeou, simly,' said Stalky. 'We'm no company to make all vitty for. Niver yeou mind us. Yiss. There's plenty cream.'

The woman withdrew, wiping her pink hands on her apron, and left them in the parlour. There was a scuffle of feet on the gravel outside the heavily-leaded diamond panes, and then the voice of Colonel Dabney, something clearer than a bugle.

'Ye can read? You've eyes in your head? Don't attempt to deny it. Ye have!'

Beetle snatched a crochet-work antimacassar from the shiny horsehair sofa, stuffed it into his mouth, and rolled out of sight.

'You saw my notice-boards. Your duty? Curse your impudence, sir. Your duty was to keep off my grounds. Talk of duty to me! Why—why—why, ye misbegotten poacher, ye'll be teaching me my A B C next! Roarin' like a bull in the bushes down there! Boys? Boys? Boys? Keep your boys at home, then! I'm not responsible for your boys! But I don't believe it—I don't believe a word of it. Ye've a furtive look in your eye—a furtive, sneakin', poachin' look in your eye, that 'ud ruin the reputation of an archangel! Don't attempt to deny it! Ye have! A sergeant? More shame to you, then, an' the worst bargain Her Majesty ever made! A sergeant, to run about the country poachin' on your pension! Damnable! Oh, damnable! But I'll be considerate. I'll be merciful. By gad, I'll be the very essence o' humanity! Did ye, or did ye not, see my notice-boards? Don't attempt to deny it! Ye did. Silence, Sergeant!'

Twenty-one years in the army had left their mark on Foxy. He obeyed.

'Now. March!'

The high Lodge-gate shut with a clang. 'My duty! A sergeant to tell me my duty!' puffed Colonel Dabney. 'Good Lard! More sergeants!'

'It's King! It's King!' gulped Stalky, his head on the horsehair pillow. M'Turk was eating the rag-carpet before the speckless hearth, and the sofa heaved to the emotions of Beetle. Through the thick glass the figures without showed blue, distorted, and menacing.

'I—I protest against this outrage.' King had evidently been running up hill. 'The man was entirely within his duty. Let—let me give you my card.'

'He's in flannels!' Stalky buried his head again.

'Unfortunately—most unfortunately—I have not one with me, but my name is King, sir, a house-master of the College, and you will find me prepared—fully prepared—to answer for this man's action. We've seen three—'

'Did ye see my notice-boards?'

'I admit we did; but under the circumstances—'

'I stand "in loco parentis."' Prout's deep voice was added to the discussion. They could hear him pant.

'F'what?' Colonel Dabney was growing more and more Irish.

'I'm responsible for the boys under my charge.'

'Ye are, are ye? Then all I can say is that ye set them a very bad example—a dam' bad example, if I may say so. I do not own your boys. I've not seen your boys, an' I tell you that if there was a boy grinnin' in every bush on the place still ye've no shadow of a right here, comin' up from the combe that way, an' frightenin' everything in it. Don't attempt to deny it. Ye did. Ye should have come to the Lodge an' seen me like Christians, instead of chasin' your dam' boys through the length and breadth of my covers. "In loco parentis" ye are? Well, I've not forgotten my Latin either, an' I'll say to you: "Quis custodiet ipsos custodes?" If the masters trespass, how can we blame the boys?'

'But if I could speak to you privately,' said Prout.

'I'll have nothing private with you! Ye can be as private as ye please on the other side o' that gate, an'—I wish ye a very good afternoon.'

A second time the gate clanged. They waited till Colonel Dabney had returned to the house, and fell into one another's arms, crowing for breath.

'Oh, my Soul! Oh, my King! Oh, my Heffy! Oh, my Foxy! Zeal, all zeal, Mr. Easy.' Stalky wiped his eyes. 'Oh! Oh! Oh!—"I did boil the exciseman!" We must get out of this or we'll be late for tea.'

'Ge—ge—get the badger and make little Hartopp happy. Ma—ma—make 'em all happy,' sobbed M'-Turk, groping for the door and kicking the prostrate Beetle before him.

They found the beast in an evil-smelling box, left two half-crowns for payment, and staggered home. Only the badger grunted most marvellous like Colonel Dabney, and they dropped him twice or thrice with shrieks of helpless laughter. They were but imperfectly recovered when Foxy met them by the Fives Court with word that they were to go up to their dormitory and wait till sent for.

'Well, take this box to Mr. Hartopp's rooms, then. We've done something for the Natural History Society, at any rate,' said Beetle.

24

''Fraid that won't save you, young gen'elmen,' Foxy answered, in an awful voice. He was sorely ruffled in his mind.

'All sereno, Foxibus.' Stalky had reached the extreme stage of hiccups. 'We—we'll never desert you, Foxy. Hounds choppin' foxes in cover is more a proof of vice, ain't it? . . . No, you're right. I'm—I'm not quite well.'

'They've gone a bit too far this time,' Foxy thought to himself. 'Very far gone, I'd say, excep' there was no smell of liquor. An' yet it isn't like 'em—somehow. King and Prout they'ad their dressin'-down same as me. That's one comfort.'

'Now, we must pull up,' said Stalky, rising from the bed on which he had thrown himself. 'We're injured innocence—as usual. We don't know what we've been sent up here for, do we?'

'No explanation. Deprived of tea. Public disgrace before the house,' said M'Turk, whose eyes were running over. 'It's dam' serious.'

'Well, hold on, till King loses his temper,' said Beetle. 'He's a libellous old rip, an' he'll be in a ravin' paddy-wack. Prout's too beastly cautious. Keep your eye on King, and, if he gives us a chance, appeal to the Head. That always makes 'em sick.'

They were summoned to their house-master's study, King and Foxy supporting Prout, and Foxy had three canes under his arm. King leered triumphantly, for there were tears, undried tears of mirth, on the boys' cheeks. Then the examination began.

Yes, they had walked along the cliffs. Yes, they had entered Colonel Dabney's grounds. Yes, they had seen the notice-boards (at this point Beetle sputtered hysteri-

25

cally). For what purpose had they entered Colonel Dabney's grounds? 'Well, sir, there was a badger.'

Here King, who loathed the Natural History Society because he did not like Hartopp, could no longer be restrained. He begged them not to add mendacity to open insolence. 'But the badger is in Mr. Hartopp's rooms, sir.' The Sergeant had kindly taken it up for them. That disposed of the badger, and the temporary check brought King's temper to boiling-point. They could hear his foot on the floor while Prout prepared his lumbering inquiries. They had settled into their stride now. Their eyes ceased to sparkle; their faces were blank; their hands hung beside them without a twitch. They were learning, at the expense of a fellow-countryman, the lesson of their race, which is to put away all emotion and entrap the alien at the proper time.

So far good. King was importing himself more freely into the trial, being vengeful where Prout was grieved. They knew the penalties of trespassing? With a fine show of irresolution, Stalky admitted that he had gathered some information vaguely bearing on this head, but he thought— The sentence was dragged out to the uttermost: Stalky did not wish to play his trump with such an opponent. Mr. King desired no buts, nor was he interested in Stalky's evasions. They, on the other hand, might be interested in his poor views. Boys who crept—who sneaked—who lurked—out of bounds, even the generous bounds of the Natural History Society, which they had falsely joined as a cloak for their misdeeds—their vices—their villainies—their immoralities—

'He'll break cover in a minute,' said Stalky to himself. 'Then we'll run into him before he gets away.'

Such boys, scabrous boys, moral lepers—the current of his words was carrying King off his feet—evil-speakers, liars, slow-bellies—yea, incipient drunkards.   .   .   .

He was merely working up to a peroration, and the boys knew it; but M'Turk cut through the frothing sentence, the others echoing:

'I appeal to the Head, sir.'

'I appeal to the Head, sir.'

'I appeal to the Head, sir.'

It was their unquestioned right.   Drunkenness meant expulsion after a public flogging.   They had been accused of it.   The case was the Head's, and the Head's alone.

'Thou hast appealed unto Cæsar: unto Cæsar shalt thou go.'   They had heard that sentence once or twice before in their careers.   'None the less,' said King uneasily, 'you would be better advised to abide by our decision, my young friends.'

'Are we allowed to associate with the rest of the school till we see the Head, sir?' said M'Turk to his housemaster, disregarding King.   This at once lifted the situation to its loftiest plane.   Moreover it meant no work, for moral leprosy was strictly quarantined, and the Head never executed judgment till twenty-four cold hours later.

'Well—er—if you persist in your defiant attitude,' said King, with a loving look at the canes under Foxy's arm, 'there is no alternative.'

Ten minutes later the news was over the whole school. Stalky & Co. had fallen at last—fallen by drink.   They had been drinking.   They had returned blind-drunk from a hut.   They were even now lying hopelessly intoxicated on the dormitory floor.   A few bold spirits crept up to look, and received boots about the head.

27

'We've got him—got him on the Caudine Toasting-fork!' said Stalky, after those hints were taken. 'King'll have to prove his charges up to the giddy hilt.'

'Too much ticklee, him bust,' Beetle quoted from a book of his reading. 'Didn't I say he'd go pop if we lat un bide?'

'No prep., either, O ye incipient drunkards,' said M'Turk, 'and it's trig night, too. Hullo! Here's our dear friend Foxy. More tortures, Foxibus?'

'I've brought you something to eat, young gentlemen,' said the Sergeant from behind a crowded tray. Their wars had ever been waged without malice, and a suspicion floated in Foxy's mind that boys who allowed themselves to be tracked so easily might, perhaps, hold something in reserve. Foxy had served through the Mutiny, when early and accurate information was worth much.

'I—I noticed you 'adn't 'ad anything to eat, an' I spoke to Gumbly, an' he said you wasn't exactly cut off from supplies. So I brought up this. It's your potted 'am tin, ain't it, Mr. Corkran?'

'Why, Foxibus, you're a brick,' said Stalky. 'I didn't think you had this much—what's the word, Beetle?'

'Bowels,' Beetle replied promptly. 'Thank you, Sergeant. That's young Carter's potted ham, though.'

'There was a C on it. I thought it was Mr. Corkran's. This is a very serious business, young gentlemen. That's what it is. I didn't know, perhaps, but there might be something on your side which you hadn't said to Mr. King or Mr. Prout, maybe.'

'There is. Heaps, Foxibus.' This from Stalky through a full mouth.

'Then you see, if that was the case, it seemed to me I

28

might represent it, quiet so to say, to the 'Ead when he asks me about it. I've got to take 'im the charges to-night, an'—it looks bad on the face of it.'

' 'Trocious bad, Foxy. Twenty-seven cuts in the Gym before all the school, and public expulsion. "Wine is a mocker, strong drink is ragin'," ' quoth Beetle.

'It's nothin' to make fun of, young gentlemen. I 'ave to go to the 'Ead with the charges. An'—an' you mayn't be aware, per'aps, that I was followin' you this afternoon; havin' my suspicions.'

'Did ye see the notice-boards?' croaked M'Turk, in the very brogue of Colonel Dabney.

'Ye've eyes in your head. Don't attempt to deny it. Ye did!' said Beetle.

'A sergeant! To run about poachin' on your pension! Damnable! Oh, damnable!' said Stalky, without pity.

'Good Lord!' said the Sergeant, sitting heavily upon a bed. 'Where—where the devil was you? I might ha' known it was a do—somewhere.'

'Oh, you clever maniac!' Stalky resumed. 'We mayn't be aware you were followin' us this afternoon, mayn't we? 'Thought you were stalkin' us, eh? Why, we led you bung into it, of course. Colonel Dabney—don't you think he's a nice man, Foxy?—Colonel Dabney's our pet particular friend. We've been goin' there for weeks and weeks. He invited us. You and your duty! Curse your duty, sir! Your duty was to keep off his covers.'

'You'll never be able to hold up your head again, Foxy. The fags 'll hoot at you,' said Beetle. 'Think of your giddy prestige!'

The Sergeant was thinking—hard.

'Look 'ere, young gentlemen,' he said earnestly. 'You aren't surely ever goin' to tell, are you? Wasn't Mr. Prout and Mr. King in—in it too?'

'Foxibusculus, they was. They was—singular horrid. Caught it worse than you. We heard every word of it. You got off easy, considerin'. If I'd been Dabney I swear I'd ha' quadded you. I think I'll suggest it to him to-morrow.'

'An' it's all goin' up to the 'Ead. Oh, Good Lord!'

'Every giddy word of it, my Chingangook,' said Beetle, dancing. 'Why shouldn't it? We've done nothing wrong. We ain't poachers. We didn't cut about blastin' the characters of poor, innocent boys—saying they were drunk.'

'That I didn't,' said Foxy. 'I—I only said that you be'aved uncommon odd when you come back with that badger. Mr. King may have taken the wrong hint from that.'

''Course he did; an' he'll jolly well shove all the blame on you when he finds out he's wrong. We know King, if you don't. I'm ashamed of you. You ain't fit to be a sergeant,' said M'Turk.

'Not with three thorough-goin' young devils like you, I ain't. I've been had. I've been ambuscaded. Horse, foot, an' guns, I've been had, an'—an' there'll be no holdin' the junior forms after this. M'rover, the 'Ead will send me with a note to Colonel Dabney to ask if what you say about bein' invited was true.'

'Then you'd better go in by the Lodge-gates this time, instead of chasin' your dam' boys—oh, that was the Epistle to King—so it was. We-ell, Foxy?' Stalky put his chin on his hands and regarded the victim with deep delight.

'Ti-ra-la-la-i-tu! I gloat! Hear me!' said M'Turk. 'Foxy brought us tea when we were moral lepers. Foxy has a heart. Foxy has been in the Army, too.'

'I wish I'd ha' had you in my company, young gentlemen,' said the Sergeant from the depths of his heart; 'I'd ha' given you something.'

'Silence at drum-head court-martial,' M'Turk went on. 'I'm advocate for the prisoner; and, besides, this is much too good to tell all the other brutes in the Coll. They'd never understand. They play cricket, and say, "Yes, sir," and "Oh, sir," and "No, sir."'

'Never mind that. Go ahead,' said Stalky.

'Well, Foxy's a good little chap when he does not esteem himself so as to be clever.'

'"Take not out your 'ounds on a werry windy day,"' Stalky struck in. 'I don't care if you let him off.'

'Nor me,' said Beetle. 'Heffy is my only joy—Heffy and King.'

'I 'ad to do it,' said the Sergeant plaintively.

'Right O! Led away by bad companions in the execution of his duty, or—or words to that effect. You're dismissed with a reprimand, Foxy. We won't tell about you. I swear we won't,' M'Turk concluded. 'Bad for the discipline of the school. Horrid bad.'

'Well,' said the Sergeant, gathering up the tea-things, 'knowin' what I know o' the young dev—gentlemen of the College, I'm very glad to 'ear it. But what am I to tell the 'Ead?'

'Anything you jolly well please, Foxy. We aren't the criminals.'

To say that the Head was annoyed when the Sergeant appeared after dinner with the day's crime-sheet would be putting it mildly.

'Corkran, M'Turk, & Co., I see. Bounds as usual. Hullo! What the deuce is this? Suspicion of drinking. Whose charge?'

'Mr. King's, sir. I caught 'em out of bounds, sir: at least that was 'ow it looked. But there's a lot be'ind, sir.' The Sergeant was evidently troubled.

'Go on,' said the Head. 'Let us have your version.'

He and the Sergeant had dealt with each other for some seven years; while the Head knew that Mr. King's statements depended very largely on Mr. King's temper.

'I thought they were out of bounds along the cliffs. But it come out they wasn't, sir. I saw them go into Colonel Dabney's woods, and—Mr. King and Mr. Prout come along—and—the fact was, sir, we was mistook for poachers by Colonel Dabney's people—Mr. King and Mr. Prout and me. There were some words, sir, on both sides. The young gentlemen slipped 'ome somehow, and they seemed 'ighly humorous, sir. Mr. King was mistook by Colonel Dabney himself—Colonel Dabney bein' strict. Then they preferred to come straight to you, sir, on account of what—what Mr. King may 'ave said about their 'abits afterwards in Mr. Prout's study. I only said they was 'ighly humorous, laughin' an' gigglin', an' a bit above 'emselves. They've since told me, sir, in a humorous way, that they was invited by Colonel Dabney to go into 'is woods.'

'I see. They didn't tell their house-master that, of course.'

'They took up Mr. King on appeal just as soon as he spoke about their—'abits. Put in the appeal at once, sir, an' asked to be sent to the dormitory waitin' for you. I've since gathered, sir, in their humorous way, sir, that some'ow or other they've 'eard about every word Colonel

Dabney said to Mr. King and Mr. Prout when he mistook 'em for poachers. I—I might ha' known when they led me on so that they 'eld the inner line of communications. It's—it's a plain do, sir, if you ask me; an' they're gloatin' over it in the dormitory.'

The Head saw—saw even to the uttermost farthing—and his mouth twitched a little under his moustache.

'Send them to me at once, Sergeant. This case needn't wait over.'

'Good-evening,' said he when the three appeared under escort. 'I want your undivided attention for a few minutes. You've known me for five years, and I've known you for—twenty-five. I think we understand one another perfectly. I am now going to pay you a tremendous compliment. (The brown one, please, Sergeant. Thanks. You needn't wait.) I'm going to execute you without rhyme, Beetle, or reason. I know you went to Colonel Dabney's covers because you were invited. I'm not even going to send the Sergeant with a note to ask if your statement is true; because I am convinced that, on this occasion, you have adhered strictly to the truth. I know, too, that you were not drinking. (You can take off that virtuous expression, M'Turk, or I shall begin to fear you don't understand me.) There is not a flaw in any of your characters. And that is why I am going to perpetrate a howling injustice. Your reputations have been injured, haven't they? You have been disgraced before the house, haven't you? You have a peculiarly keen regard for the honour of your house, haven't you? Well, now I am going to lick you.'

Six apiece was their portion upon that word.

'And this, I think'—the Head replaced the cane, and

flung the written charge into the waste-paper basket—
'covers the situation.   When you find a variation from
the normal—this will be useful to you in later life—
always meet him in an abnormal way.   And that reminds me.   There are a pile of paper-backs on that shelf.
You can borrow them if you put them back.   I don't
think they'll take any harm from being read in the open.
They smell of tobacco rather.   You will go to prep. this
evening as usual.   Good-night,' said that amazing man.

'Good-night, and thank you, sir.'

'I swear I'll pray for the Head to-night,' said Beetle.
'Those last two cuts were just flicks on my collar.
There's a "Monte Cristo" in that lower shelf.   I saw it.
Bags I, next time we go to Aves!'

'Dearr man!' said M'Turk.   'No gating.   No impots.   No beastly questions.   All settled.   Hullo!
what's King goin' in to him for—King and Prout?'

Whatever the nature of that interview, it did not im-
prove either King's or Prout's ruffled plumes, for, when
they came out of the Head's house, six eyes noted that
the one was red and blue with emotion as to his nose,
and that the other was sweating profusely.   That sight
compensated them amply for the Imperial Jaw with
which they were favoured by the two.   It seems—and
who so astonished as they?—that they had held back
material facts; that they were guilty both of 'suppressio
veri' and 'suggestio falsi' (well-known gods against
whom they often offended); further, that they were
malignant in their dispositions, untrustworthy in their
characters, pernicious and revolutionary in their influences, abandoned to the devils of wilfulness, pride, and a
most intolerable conceit.   Ninthly, and lastly, they were
to have a care and to be very careful.

They were careful, as only boys can be when there is a
hurt to be inflicted. They waited through one suffocat-
ing week till Prout and King were their royal selves
again; waited till there was a house-match—their own
house, too—in which Prout was taking part; waited,
further, till he had buckled on his pads in the pavilion
and stood ready to go forth. King was scoring at the
window, and the three sat on a bench without.

Said Stalky to Beetle: 'I say, Beetle, "Quis custodiet
ipsos custodes?"'

'Don't ask me,' said Beetle. 'I'll have nothin' private with you. Ye can be as private as ye please the
other end of the bench; and I wish ye a very good afternoon.'

M'Turk yawned.

'Well, ye should ha' come up to the lodge like Christians instead o' chasin' your—a-hem—boys through the
length an' breadth of my covers. I think these house-
matches are all rot. Let's go over to Colonel Dabney's
an' see if he's collared any more poachers.'

That afternoon there was joy in Aves.

SLAVES OF THE LAMP

(1897)

PART I

THE music-room on the top floor of Number Five was filled with the 'Aladdin' company at rehearsal. Dickson Quartus, commonly known as Dick Four, was Aladdin, stage-manager, ballet-master, half the orchestra, and largely librettist, for the 'book' had been rewritten and filled with local allusions. The pantomime was to be given next week, in the downstairs study occupied by Aladdin, Abanazar, and the Emperor of China. The Slave of the Lamp, with the Princess Badroulbadour and the Widow Twankey, owned Number Five study across the same landing, so that the company could be easily assembled. The floor shook to the stamp-and-go of the ballet, while Aladdin, in pink cotton tights, a blue and tinsel jacket, and a plumed hat, banged alternately on the piano and his banjo. He was the moving spirit of the game, as befitted a senior who had passed his Army Preliminary and hoped to enter Sandhurst next spring.

Aladdin came to his own at last, Abanazar lay poisoned on the floor, the Widow Twankey danced her dance, and the company decided it would 'come all right on the night.'

36

'What about the last song, though?' said the Emperor, a tallish, fair-headed boy with a ghost of a moustache, at which he pulled manfully. 'We need a rousing old tune.'

' "John Peel"? "Drink, Puppy, Drink"?' suggested Abanazar, smoothing his baggy lilac pyjamas. 'Pussy' Abanazar never looked more than one-half awake, but he owned a soft, slow smile which well suited the part of the Wicked Uncle.

'Stale,' said Aladdin. 'Might as well have "Grandfather's Clock." What's that thing you were humming at prep. last night, Stalky?'

Stalky, The Slave of the Lamp, in black tights and doublet, a black silk half-mask on his forehead, whistled lazily where he lay on the top of the piano. It was a catchy music-hall tune.

Dick Four cocked his head critically, and squinted down a large red nose.

'Once more, and I can pick it up,' he said, strumming. 'Sing the words.'

'Arrah, Patsy, mind the baby! Arrah, Patsy, mind the
    child!
Wrap him up in an overcoat, he's surely goin' wild!
Arrah, Patsy, mind the baby; just ye mind the child
    awhile!
He'll kick an' bite an' cry all night! Arrah, Patsy,
    mind the child!'

'Rippin'! Oh, rippin'!' said Dick Four. 'Only we shan't have any piano on the night. We must work it with the banjos—play an' dance at the same time. You try, Tertius.'

37

The Emperor pushed aside his pea-green sleeves of state, and followed Dick Four on a heavy nickel-plated banjo.

'Yes, but I'm dead all this time. Bung in the middle of the stage, too,' said Abanazar.

'Oh, that's Beetle's biznai,' said Dick Four. 'Vamp it up, Beetle. Don't keep us waiting all night. You've got to get Pussy out of the light somehow, and bring us all in dancin' at the end.'

'All right. You two play it again,' said Beetle, who, in a gray skirt and a wig of chestnut sausage-curls, set slantwise above a pair of spectacles mended with an old boot-lace, represented the Widow Twankey. He waved one leg in time to the hammered refrain, and the banjos grew louder.

'Um! Ah! Er—"Aladdin now has won his wife,"' he sang, and Dick Four repeated it.

'"Your Emperor is appeased."' Tertius flung out his chest as he delivered his line.

'Now jump up, Pussy! Say, "I think I'd better come to life!" Then we all take hands and come forward: "We hope you've all been pleased." Twiggez-vous?'

'Nous twiggons. Good enough. What's the chorus for the final ballet? It's four kicks and a turn,' said Dick Four.

'Oh! Er!

> 'John Short will ring the curtain down,
>   And ring the prompter's bell;
> We hope you know before you go,
>   That we all wish you well.'

'Rippin'! Rippin'! Now for the Widow's scene with the Princess. Hurry up, Turkey.'

M'Turk, in a violet silk skirt and a coquettish blue turban, slouched forward as one thoroughly ashamed of himself. The Slave of the Lamp climbed down from the piano, and dispassionately kicked him. 'Play up, Turkey,' he said; 'this is serious.' But there fell on the door the knock of authority. It happened to be King, in gown and mortar-board, enjoying a Saturday evening prowl before dinner.

'Locked doors! Locked doors!' he snapped with a scowl. 'What's the meaning of this; and what, may I ask, is the intention of this—this epicene attire?'

'Pantomime, sir. The Head gave us leave,' said Abanazar, as the only member of the Sixth concerned. Dick Four stood firm in the confidence born of well-fitting tights, but the Beetle strove to efface himself behind the piano. A gray princess-skirt borrowed from a day-boy's mother and a spotted cotton bodice unsystematically padded with imposition-paper made one ridiculous. And in other regards Beetle had a bad conscience.

'As usual!' sneered King. 'Futile foolery just when your careers, such as they may be, are hanging in the balance. I see! Ah, I see! The old gang of criminals —allied forces of disorder—Corkran'—the Slave of the Lamp smiled politely—'M'Turk'—the Irishman scowled —'and, of course, the unspeakable Beetle, our friend Gigadibs.' Abanazar, the Emperor, and Aladdin had more or less of characters, and King passed them over. 'Come forth, my inky buffoon, from behind yonder instrument of music! You supply, I presume, the doggerel for this entertainment. Esteem yourself to be, as it were, a poet?'

'He's found one of 'em,' thought Beetle, noting the flush on King's cheek-bone.

'I have just had the pleasure of reading an effusion of yours to my address, I believe—an effusion intended to rhyme. So—so you despise me, Master Gigadibs, do you? I am quite aware—you need not explain—that it was ostensibly not intended for my edification. I read it with laughter—yes, with laughter. These paper pellets of inky boys—still a boy we are, Master Gigadibs —do not disturb my equanimity.'

''Wonder which it was,' thought Beetle. He had launched many lampoons on an appreciative public ever since he discovered that it was possible to convey reproof in rhyme.

In sign of his unruffled calm, King proceeded to tear Beetle, whom he called Gigadibs, slowly asunder. From his untied shoe-strings to his mended spectacles (the life of a poet at a big school is hard) he held him up to the derision of his associates—with the usual result. His wild flowers of speech—King had an unpleasant tongue—restored him to good humour at the last. He drew a lurid picture of Beetle's latter end as a scurrilous pamphleteer dying in an attic, scattered a few compliments over M'Turk and Corkran, and, reminding Beetle that he must come up for judgment when called upon, went to Common-room, where he triumphed anew over his victims.

'And the worst of it,' he explained in a loud voice over his soup, 'is that I waste such gems of sarcasm on their thick heads. It's miles above them, I'm certain.'

'We-ell,' said the school chaplain slowly, 'I don't know what Corkran's appreciation of your style may be, but young M'Turk reads Ruskin for his amusement.'

'Nonsense! He does it to show off. I mistrust the dark Celt.'

'He does nothing of the kind. I went into their study the other night, unofficially, and M'Turk was gluing up the back of four odd numbers of "Fors Clavigera."'

'I don't know anything about their private lives,' said a mathematical master hotly, 'but I've learned by bitter experience that Number Five study are best left alone. They are utterly soulless young devils.' He blushed as the others laughed.

But in the music-room there was wrath and bad language. Only Stalky, Slave of the Lamp, lay on the piano unmoved.

'That little swine Manders minor must have shown him your stuff. He's always suckin' up to King. Go and kill him,' he drawled. 'Which one was it, Beetle?'

'Dunno,' said Beetle, struggling out of the skirt. 'There was one about his hunting for popularity with the small boys, and the other one was one about him in hell, tellin' the Devil he was a Balliol man. I swear both of 'em rhymed all right. By gum! P'raps Manders minor showed him both! I'll correct his cæsuras for him.'

He disappeared down two flights of stairs, flushed a small pink-and-white boy in a form-room next door to King's study, which, again, was immediately below his own, and chased him up the corridor into a form-room sacred to the revels of the Lower Third. Thence he came back, greatly disordered, to find M'Turk, Stalky, and the others of the company in his study enjoying an unlimited 'brew'—coffee, cocoa, buns, new bread hot and steaming, sardine, sausage, ham-and-tongue paste, pilchards, three jams, and at least as many pounds of Devonshire cream.

'My Hat!' said he, throwing himself upon the banquet. 'Who stumped up for this, Stalky?' It was within a month of term end, and blank starvation had reigned in the studies for weeks.

'You,' said Stalky serenely.

'Confound you! You haven't been popping my Sunday bags, then?'

'Keep your hair on. It's only your watch.'

'Watch! I lost it—weeks ago. Out on the Burrows, when we tried to shoot the old ram—the day our pistol burst.'

'It dropped out of your pocket (you're so beastly careless, Beetle), and M'Turk and I kept it for you. I've been wearing it for a week, and you never noticed. 'Took it into Bideford after dinner to-day. 'Got thirteen and sevenpence. Here's the ticket.'

'Well, that's pretty average cool,' said Abanazar behind a slab of cream and jam, as Beetle, reassured upon the safety of his Sunday trousers, showed not even surprise, much less resentment. Indeed, it was M'Turk who grew angry, saying:

'You gave him the ticket, Stalky? You pawned it? You unmitigated beast! Why, last month you and Beetle sold mine! 'Never got a sniff of any ticket.'

'Ah, that was because you locked your trunk and we wasted half the afternoon hammering it open. We might have pawned it if you'd behaved like a Christian, Turkey.'

'My Aunt!' said Abanazar, 'you chaps are communists. Vote of thanks to Beetle, though.'

'That's beastly unfair,' said Stalky, 'when I took all the trouble to pawn it. Beetle never knew he had a watch. Oh, I say, Rabbits-Eggs gave me a lift into Bideford this afternoon.'

Rabbits-Eggs was the local carrier—an outcrop of the
early Devonian formation. It was Stalky who had
invented his unlovely name. 'He was pretty average
drunk, or he wouldn't have done it. Rabbits-Eggs is a
little shy of me, somehow. But I swore it was pax
between us, and gave him a bob. He stopped at two
pubs on the way in, so he'll be howling drunk to-night.
Oh, don't begin reading, Beetle; there's a council of
war on. What the deuce is the matter with your
collar?'

' 'Chivied Manders minor into the Lower Third box-
room. 'Had all his beastly little friends on top of me,'
said Beetle, from behind a jar of pilchards and a book.

'You ass! Any fool could have told you where Manders would bunk to,' said M'Turk.

'I didn't think,' said Beetle meekly, scooping out pilchards with a spoon.

' 'Course you didn't. You never do.' M'Turk adjusted Beetle's collar with a savage tug. 'Don't drop
oil all over my "Fors," or I'll scrag you!'

'Shut up, you—you Irish Biddy! 'Tisn't your beastly
"Fors." It's one of mine.'

The book was a fat, brown-backed volume of the later
Sixties, which King had once thrown at Beetle's head
that Beetle might see whence the name Gigadibs came.
Beetle had quietly annexed the book, and had seen—
several things. The quarter-comprehended verses lived
and ate with him, as the be-dropped pages showed. He
removed himself from all that world, drifting at large
with wondrous Men and Women, till M'Turk hammered the pilchard spoon on his head and he snarled.

'Beetle! You're oppressed and insulted and bullied
by King. Don't you feel it?'

43

'Let me alone! I can write some more poetry about him if I am, I suppose.'

'Mad! Quite mad!' said Stalky to the visitors, as one exhibiting strange beasts. 'Beetle reads an ass called Brownin', and M'Turk reads an ass called Ruskin; and—'

'Ruskin isn't an ass,' said M'Turk. 'He's almost as good as the Opium-Eater. He says "we're children of noble races trained by surrounding art." That means me, and the way I decorated the study when you two badgers would have stuck up brackets and Christmas cards. Child of a noble race, trained by surrounding art, stop reading, or I'll shove a pilchard down your neck!'

'It's two to one,' said Stalky warningly, and Beetle closed the book, in obedience to the law under which he and his companions had lived for six checkered years.

The visitors looked on delighted. Number Five study had a reputation for more variegated insanity than the rest of the school put together; and, so far as its code allowed friendship with outsiders, it was polite and open-hearted to its neighbours on the same landing.

'What rot do you want now?' said Beetle.

'King! War!' said M'Turk, jerking his head toward the wall, where hung a small wooden West-African war-drum, a gift to M'Turk from a naval uncle.

'Then we shall be turned out of the study again,' said Beetle, who loved his flesh-pots. 'Mason turned us out for—just warbling on it.' Mason was that mathematical master who had testified in Common-room.

'Warbling?—Oh, Lord!' said Abanazar. 'We couldn't hear ourselves speak in our study when you played the infernal thing. What's the good of getting turned out of your study, anyhow?'

'We lived in the form-rooms for a week, too,' said Beetle tragically. 'And it was beastly cold.'

'Ye-es; but Mason's rooms were filled with rats every day we were out. It took him a week to draw the inference,' said M'Turk. 'He loathes rats. 'Minute he let us go back the rats stopped. Mason's a little shy of us now, but there was no evidence.'

'Jolly well there wasn't,' said Stalky, 'when I got out on the roof and dropped the beastly things down his chimney. But, look here—question is, are our characters good enough just now to stand a study row?'

'Never mind mine,' said Beetle. 'King swears I haven't any.'

'I'm not thinking of you,' Stalky returned scornfully. 'You aren't going up for the Army, you old bat. I don't want to be expelled—and the Head's getting rather shy of us, too.'

'Rot!' said M'Turk. 'The Head never expels except for beastliness or stealing. But I forgot; you and Stalky are thieves—regular burglars.'

The visitors gasped, but Stalky interpreted the parable with large grins.

'Well, you know, that little beast Manders minor saw Beetle and me hammerin' M'Turk's trunk open in the dormitory when we took his watch last month. Of course Manders sneaked to Mason, and Mason solemnly took it up as a case of theft, to get even with us about the rats.'

'That just put Mason into our giddy hands,' said M'Turk blandly. 'We were nice to him, 'cause he was a new master and wanted to win the confidence of the

45

boys. 'Pity he draws inferences, though. Stalky went to his study and pretended to blub, and told Mason he'd lead a new life if Mason would let him off this time, but Mason wouldn't. 'Said it was his duty to report him to the Head.'

'Vindictive swine!' said Beetle. 'It was all those rats! Then I blubbed, too, and Stalky confessed that he'd been a thief in regular practice for six years, ever since he came to the school; and that I'd taught him—a la Fagin. Mason turned white with joy. He thought he had us on toast.'

'Gorgeous! Oh, fids!' said Dick Four. 'We never heard of this.'

''Course not. Mason kept it jolly quiet. He wrote down all our statements on impot-paper. There wasn't anything he wouldn't believe,' said Stalky.

'And handed it all up to the Head, with an extempore prayer. It took about forty pages,' said Beetle. 'I helped him a lot.'

'And then, you crazy idiots?' said Abanazar.

'Oh, we were sent for; and Stalky asked to have the "depositions" read out, and the Head knocked him spinning into a waste-paper basket. Then he gave us eight cuts apiece—welters—for—for—takin' unheard-of liberties with a new master. I saw his shoulders shaking when we went out. Do you know,' said Beetle pensively, 'that Mason can't look at us now in second lesson without blushing? We three stare at him sometimes till he regularly trickles. He's an awfully sensitive beast.'

'He read "Eric; or, Little by Little,"' said M'Turk; 'so we gave him "St. Winifred's; or, The World of School." They spent all their spare time stealing at

St. Winifred's, when they weren't praying or getting drunk at pubs. Well, that was only a week ago, and the Head's a little bit shy of us. He called it constructive deviltry. Stalky invented it all.'

' 'Not the least good having a row with a master unless you can make an ass of him,' said Stalky, extended at ease on the hearth-rug. 'If Mason didn't know Number Five—well, he's learnt, that's all. Now, my dearly beloved 'earers'—Stalky curled his legs under him and addressed the company—'we've got that strong, perseverin' man King on our hands. He went miles out of his way to provoke a conflict.' (Here Stalky snapped down the black silk domino and assumed the air of a judge.) 'He has oppressed Beetle, M'Turk, and me, "privatim et seriatim," one by one, as he could catch us. But now he has insulted Number Five up in the music-room, and in the presence of these —these ossifers of the Ninety-third, wot look like hairdressers. Binjimin, we must make him cry "Capivi!"'

Stalky's reading did not include Browning or Ruskin.

'And, besides,' said M'Turk, 'he's a Philistine, a basket-hanger. He wears a tartan tie. Ruskin says that any man who wears a tartan tie will, without doubt, be damned everlastingly.'

'Bravo, M'Turk,' cried Tertius; 'I thought he was only a beast.'

'He's that, too, of course, but he's worse. He has a china basket with blue ribbons and a pink kitten on it, hung up in his window to grow musk in. You know when I got all that old oak carvin' out of Bideford Church, when they were restoring it (Ruskin says that any man who'll restore a church is an unmitigated sweep), and stuck it up here with glue? Well, King

47

came in and wanted to know whether we'd done it with
a fret-saw! Yah! He is the King of basket-hangers!'

Down went M'Turk's inky thumb over an imaginary
arena full of bleeding Kings. 'Placetne, child of a
generous race!' he cried to Beetle.

'Well,' began Beetle doubtfully, 'he comes from
Balliol, but I'm going to give the beast a chance. You
see I can always make him hop with some more poetry.
He can't report me to the Head, because it makes him
ridiculous. (Stalky's quite right.) But he shall have
his chance.'

Beetle opened the book on the table, ran his finger
down a page, and began at random:

> 'Or who in Moscow toward the Czar
> With the demurest of footfalls,
> Over the Kremlin's pavement white
> With serpentine and syenite,
> Steps with five other generals—'

'That's no good. Try another,' said Stalky.

'Hold on a shake; I know what's coming.' M'Turk
was reading over Beetle's shoulder—

> 'That simultaneously take snuff,
> For each to have pretext enough,
> And kerchiefwise unfold his sash,
> Which—softness' self—is yet the stuff

(Gummy! What a sentence!)

> To hold fast where a steel chain snaps
> And leave the grand white neck no gash.

48

(Full stop.)'

' 'Don't understand a word of it,' said Stalky.

'More fool you! Construe,' said M'Turk. 'Those six bargees scragged the Czar and left no evidence. "Actum est" with King.'

'He gave me that book, too,' said Beetle, licking his lips:

> 'There's a great text in Galatians,
>   Once you trip on it entails
> Twenty-nine distinct damnations,
>   One sure if another fails.'

Then irrelevantly:

> 'Setebos! Setebos! and Setebos!
>   Thinketh he liveth in the cold of the moon.'

'He's just come in from dinner,' said Dick Four, looking through the window. 'Manders minor is with him.'

' 'Safest place for Manders minor just now,' said Beetle.

'Then you chaps had better clear out,' said Stalky politely to the visitors. ' 'Tisn't fair to mix you up in a study row. Besides, we can't afford to have evidence.'

'Are you going to begin at once?' said Aladdin.

'Immediately, if not sooner,' said Stalky, and turned out the gas. 'Strong, perseverin' man—King. Make him cry "Capivi." G'way, Binjimin.'

The company retreated to their neat and spacious study with expectant souls.

'When Stalky blows out his nostrils like a horse,' said

Aladdin to the Emperor of China, 'he's on the war-path. 'Wonder what King will get.'

'Beans,' said the Emperor. 'Number Five generally pays in full.'

''Wonder if I ought to take any notice of it officially,' said Abanazar, who had just remembered that he was a prefect.

'It's none of your business, Pussy. Besides, if you did, we'd have them hostile to us; and we shouldn't be able to do any work,' said Aladdin. 'They've begun already.'

Now that West-African war-drum had been made to signal across estuaries and deltas. Number Five was forbidden to wake the engine within ear-shot of the school. But a deep devastating drone filled the passages as M'Turk and Beetle scientifically rubbed its top. Anon it changed to the blare of trumpets—of savage pursuing trumpets. Then, as M'Turk slapped one side, smooth with the blood of ancient sacrifice, the roar broke into short coughing howls such as the wounded gorilla throws in his native forest. These were followed by the wrath of King—three steps at a time, up the staircase, with a dry whirr of the gown. Aladdin and company, listening, squeaked with excitement as the door crashed open. King stumbled into the darkness, and cursed those performers by the gods of Balliol and quiet repose.

'Turned out for a week,' said Aladdin, holding the study door on the crack. 'Key to be brought down to his study in five minutes. "Brutes! Barbarians! Savages! Children!" He's rather agitated. "Arrah, Patsy, mind the baby,"' he sang in a whisper as he clung to the door-knob, dancing a noiseless war-dance.

King went downstairs again, and Beetle and M'Turk

lit the gas to confer with Stalky. But Stalky had vanished.

''Looks like no end of a mess,' said Beetle, collecting his books and mathematical-instrument case. 'A week in the form-rooms isn't any advantage to us.'

'Yes, but don't you see that Stalky isn't here, you owl?' said M'Turk. 'Take down the key, and look sorrowful. King 'll only jaw you for half an hour. I'm going to read in the lower form-room.'

'But it's always me,' mourned Beetle.

'Wait till we see,' said M'Turk hopefully; 'I don't know any more than you do what Stalky means, but it's something. Go down and draw King's fire. You're used to it.'

No sooner had the key turned in the door than the lid of the coal-box, which was also the window-seat, lifted cautiously. It had been a tight fit, even for the lithe Stalky, his head between his knees, and his stomach under his right ear. From a drawer in the table he took a well-worn catapult, a handful of buckshot, and a duplicate key of the study; noiselessly he raised the window and kneeled by it, his face turned to the road, the wind-sloped trees, the dark levels of the Burrows, and the white line of breakers falling nine-deep along the Pebbleridge. Far down the steep-banked Devonshire lane he heard the husky hoot of the carrier's horn. There was a ghost of melody in it, as it might have been the wind in a gin-bottle essaying to sing 'It's a way we have in the Army.'

Stalky smiled a tight-lipped smile, and at extreme range opened fire: the old horse half wheeled in the shafts.

'Where be gwaine tu?' hiccoughed Rabbits-Eggs.

51

Another buckshot tore through the rotten canvas tilt with a vicious zipp.

'Habet!' murmured Stalky, as Rabbits-Eggs swore into the patient night, protesting that he saw the 'dommed colleger' who was assaulting him.

.   .   .   .

'And so,' King was saying in a high head voice to Beetle, whom he had kept to play with before Manders minor, well knowing that it hurts a Fifth-form boy to be held up to a fag's derision,—'and so, Master Beetle, in spite of all our verses, of which we are so proud, when we presume to come into direct conflict with even so humble a representative of authority as myself, for instance, we are turned out of our studies, are we not?'

'Yes, sir,' said Beetle, with a sheepish grin on his lips and murder in his heart. Hope had nearly left him, but he clung to a well-established faith that never was Stalky so dangerous as when he was invisible.

'You are not required to criticise, thank you. Turned out of our studies, are we, just as if we were no better than little Manders minor. Only inky schoolboys we are, and must be treated as such.'

Beetle pricked up his ears, for Rabbits-Eggs was swearing savagely on the road, and some of the language entered at the upper sash. King believed in ventilation. He strode to the window, gowned and majestic, very visible in the gaslight.

'I zee 'un! I zee 'un!' roared Rabbits-Eggs, now that he had found a visible foe—another shot from the darkness above. 'Yiss, yeou, yeou long-nosed, fower-eyed, gingy-whiskered beggar! Yeou'm tu old for such goin's on. Aie! Poultice yeour nose, I tall 'ee! Poultice yeour long nose!'

SLAVES OF THE LAMP

Beetle's heart leapt up within him. Somewhere, somehow, he knew, Stalky moved behind these manifestations. There was hope and the prospect of revenge. He would embody the suggestion about the nose in deathless verse. King threw up the window, and sternly rebuked Rabbits-Eggs. But the carrier was beyond fear or fawning. He had descended from the cart, and was stooping by the roadside.

It all fell swiftly as a dream. Manders minor raised his hand to his head with a cry, as a jagged flint cannoned on to some rich tree-calf bindings in the bookshelf. Another quoited along the writing-table. Beetle made zealous feint to stop it, and in that endeavour overturned a student's lamp, which dripped, via King's papers and some choice books, greasily on to a Persian rug. There was much broken glass on the window-seat; the china basket—M'Turk's aversion—cracked to flinders, had dropped her musk plant and its earth over the red rep cushions; Manders minor was bleeding profusely from a cut on the cheek-bone; and King, using strange words, every one of which Beetle treasured, ran forth to find the school-sergeant, that Rabbits-Eggs might be instantly cast into jail.

'Poor chap!' said Beetle, with a false, feigned sympathy. 'Let it bleed a little. That'll prevent apoplexy,' and he held the blind head skilfully over the table, and the papers on the table, as he guided the howling Manders to the door.

Then did Beetle, alone with the wreckage, return good for evil. How, in that office, a complete set of 'Gibbon' was scarred all along the back as by a flint; how so much black and copying ink chanced to mingle with Manders's gore on the table-cloth; why the big gum-bottle, unstoppered, had rolled semicircularly across the floor; and in what manner the white china door-knob grew to be painted with yet more of Manders's young blood, were matters which Beetle did not explain when the rabid King returned to find him standing politely over the reeking hearth-rug.

'You never told me to go, sir,' he said, with the air of Casabianca, and King consigned him to the outer darkness.

But it was to a boot-cupboard under the staircase on the ground floor that he hastened, to loose the mirth that was destroying him. He had not drawn breath for a first whoop of triumph when two hands choked him dumb.

'Go to the dormitory and get me my things. Bring 'em to Number Five lavatory. I'm still in tights,' hissed Stalky, sitting on his head. 'Don't run. Walk.'

But Beetle staggered into the form-room next door, and delegated his duty to the yet unenlightened M'Turk, with an hysterical precis of the campaign thus far. So it was M'Turk, of the wooden visage, who brought the clothes from the dormitory while Beetle panted on a form. Then the three buried themselves in Number Five lavatory, turned on all the taps, filled the place with steam, and dropped weeping into the baths, where they pieced out the war.

'Moi! Je! Ich! Ego!' gasped Stalky. 'I waited till I couldn't hear myself think, while you played the drum! Hid in the coal-locker—and tweaked Rabbits-Eggs—and Rabbits-Eggs rocked King. Wasn't it beautiful? Did you hear the glass?'

'Why, he—he—he,' shrieked M'Turk, one trembling finger pointed at Beetle.

54

'Why, I—I—I was through it all,' Beetle howled; 'in his study, being jawed.'

'Oh, my soul!' said Stalky with a yell, disappearing under water.

'The—the glass was nothing. Manders minor's head's cut open. La-la-lamp upset all over the rug. Blood on the books and papers. The gum! The gum! The gum! The ink! The ink! The ink! Oh, Lord!'

Then Stalky leaped out, all pink as he was, and shook Beetle into some sort of coherence; but his tale prostrated them afresh.

'I bunked for the boot-cupboard the second I heard King go downstairs. Beetle tumbled in on top of me. The spare key's hid behind the loose board. There isn't a shadow of evidence,' said Stalky. They were all chanting together.

'And he turned us out himself—himself—himself!' This from M'Turk. 'He can't begin to suspect us. Oh, Stalky, it's the loveliest thing we've ever done.'

'Gum! Gum! Dollops of gum!' shouted Beetle, his spectacles gleaming through a sea of lather. 'Ink and blood all mixed. I held the little beast's head all over the Latin proses for Monday. Golly, how the oil stunk! And Rabbits-Eggs told King to poultice his nose! Did you hit Rabbits-Eggs, Stalky?'

'Did I jolly well not? Tweaked him all over. Did you hear him curse? Oh, I shall be sick in a minute if I don't stop.'

But dressing was a slow process, because M'Turk was obliged to dance when he heard that the musk basket was broken, and, moreover, Beetle retailed all King's language with emendations and purple insets.

'Shockin'!' said Stalky, collapsing in a helpless welter
55

of half-hitched trousers. 'So dam' bad, too, for innocent boys like us! Wonder what they'd say at "St.
Winifred's, or The World of School." By gum! That
reminds me we owe the Lower Third one for assaultin'
Beetle when he chivied Manders minor. Come on! It's
an alibi, Samivel; and besides, if we let 'em off they'll
be worse next time.'

The Lower Third had set a guard upon their form-
room for the space of a full hour, which to a boy is a
lifetime. Now they were busy with their Saturday evening businesses—cooking sparrows over the gas with
rusty nibs; brewing unholy drinks in gallipots; skinning
moles with pocket-knives; attending to paper trays full
of silkworms, or discussing the iniquities of their elders
with a freedom, fluency, and point that would have
amazed their parents. The blow fell without warning.
Stalky upset a crowded form of small boys among their
own cooking utensils; M'Turk raided the untidy lockers
as a terrier digs at a rabbit-hole; while Beetle poured ink
upon such heads as he could not appeal to with a Smith's
Classical Dictionary. Three brisk minutes accounted
for many silkworms, pet larvæ, French exercises, school
caps, half-prepared bones and skulls, and a dozen pots
of home-made sloe jam. It was a great wreckage, and
the form-room looked as though three conflicting tem-
pests had smitten it.

'Phew!' said Stalky, drawing breath outside the door
(amid groans of 'Oh, you beastly ca-ads! You think
yourselves awful funny,' and so forth). 'That's all
right. Never let the sun go down upon your wrath.
Rummy little devils, fags. 'Got no notion o' combinin'.'

'Six of 'em sat on my head when I went in after Manders minor,' said Beetle. 'I warned 'em what they'd get, though.'

'Everybody paid in full—beautiful feelin',' said M'Turk absently, as they strolled along the corridor. ''Don't think we'd better say much about King, though, do you, Stalky?'

'Not much. Our line is injured innocence, of course —same as when old Foxibus reported us on suspicion of smoking in the Bunkers. If I hadn't thought of buyin' the pepper and spillin' it all over our clothes, he'd have smelt us. King was gha-astly facetious about that. 'Called us bird-stuffers in form for a week.'

'Ah, King hates the Natural History Society because little Hartopp is president. 'Mustn't do anything in the Coll. without glorifyin' King,' said M'Turk. 'But he must be a putrid ass, you know, to suppose at our time o' life we'd go out and stuff birds like fags.'

'Poor old King!' said Beetle. 'He's awf'ly unpopular in Common-room, and they'll chaff his head off about Rabbits-Eggs. Golly! How lovely! How beautiful! How holy! But you should have seen his face when the first rock came in! And the earth from the basket!'

So they were all stricken helpless for five minutes.

They repaired at last to Abanazar's study, and were received reverently.

'What's the matter?' said Stalky, quick to realise new atmospheres.

'You know jolly well,' said Abanazar. 'You'll be expelled if you get caught. King is a gibbering maniac.'

'Who? Which? What? Expelled for how? We only played the war-drum. We've got turned out for that already.'

'Do you chaps mean to say you didn't make Rabbits-Eggs drunk and bribe him to rock King's rooms?'

'Bribe him? No, that I'll swear we didn't,' said Stalky, with a relieved heart, for he loved not to tell lies. 'What a low mind you've got, Pussy! We've been down having a bath. Did Rabbits-Eggs rock King? Strong, perseverin' man King? Shockin'!'

'Awf'ly. King's frothing at the mouth. There's bell for prayers. Come on.'

'Wait a sec,' said Stalky, continuing the conversation in a loud and cheerful voice, as they descended the stairs. 'What did Rabbits-Eggs rock King for?'

'I know,' said Beetle, as they passed King's open door. 'I was in his study.'

'Hush, you ass!' hissed the Emperor of China.

'Oh, he's gone down to prayers,' said Beetle, watching the shadow of the house-master on the wall. 'Rabbits-Eggs was only a bit drunk, swearin' at his horse, and King jawed him through the window, and then, of course, he rocked King.'

'Do you mean to say,' said Stalky, 'that King began it?'

King was behind them, and every well-weighed word went up the staircase like an arrow. 'I can only swear,' said Beetle, 'that King cursed like a bargee. Simply disgustin'. I'm goin' to write to my father about it.'

'Better report it to Mason,' suggested Stalky. 'He knows our tender consciences. Hold on a shake. I've got to tie my bootlace.'

The other study hurried forward. They did not wish to be dragged into stage asides of this nature. So it was left to M'Turk to sum up the situation beneath the guns of the enemy.

'You see,' said the Irishman, hanging on the banister, 'he begins by bullying little chaps; then he bullies the big chaps; then he bullies some one who isn't connected with the College, and then he catches it. Serves him jolly well right. . . . I beg your pardon, sir. I didn't see you were coming down the staircase.'

The black gown tore past like a thunder-storm, and in its wake, three abreast, arms linked, the Aladdin Company rolled up the big corridor to prayers, singing with most innocent intention:

'Arrah, Patsy, mind the baby! Arrah, Patsy, mind the
    child!
Wrap him up in an overcoat, he's surely goin' wild!
Arrah, Patsy, mind the baby; just ye mind the child
    awhile!
He'll kick an' bite an' cry all night! Arrah, Patsy,
    mind the child!'

AN UNSAVOURY INTERLUDE

(1898)

IT was a maiden aunt of Stalky who sent him both
books, with the inscription, 'To dearest Artie, on his
sixteenth birthday'; it was M'Turk who ordered
their hypothecation; and it was Beetle, returned from
Bideford, who flung them on the window-sill of Number
Five study with news that Bastable would advance but
ninepence on the two; 'Eric; or, Little by Little,' being
almost as great a drug as 'St. Winifred's.' 'An' I don't
think much of your aunt. We're nearly out of cartridges, too—Artie, dear.'

Whereupon Stalky rose up to grapple with him, but
M'Turk sat on Stalky's head, calling him a 'pure-minded
boy' till peace was declared. As they were grievously
in arrears with a Latin prose, as it was a blazing July
afternoon, and as they ought to have been at a house
cricket-match, they began to renew their acquaintance,
intimate and unholy, with the volumes.

'Here we are!' said M'Turk. '"Corporal punishment
produced on Eric the worst effects. He burned not with
remorse or regret"—make a note o' that, Beetle—"but
with shame and violent indignation. He glared"—oh,
naughty Eric! Let's get to where he goes in for drink.'

'Hold on half a shake. Here's another sample.
"The Sixth," he says, "is the palladium of all public

60

schools." But this lot'—Stalky rapped the gilded book —'can't prevent fellows from drinkin' and stealin', an' lettin' fags out of window at night, an'—an' doin' what they please. Golly, what we've missed—not goin' to St. Winifred's! . . .'

'I'm sorry to see any boys of my house taking so little interest in their matches.'

Mr. Prout could move very silently if he pleased, though that is no merit in a boy's eyes. He had flung open the study-door without knocking—another sin— and looked at them suspiciously. 'Very sorry, indeed, I am to see you frowsting in your studies.'

'We've been out ever since dinner, sir,' said M'Turk wearily. One house-match is just like another, and their 'ploy' of that week happened to be rabbit-shooting with saloon-pistols.

'I can't see a ball when it's coming, sir,' said Beetle. 'I've had my gig-lamps smashed at the Nets till I got excused. I wasn't any good even as a fag, then, sir.'

'Tuck is probably your form. Tuck and brewing. Why can't you three take any interest in the honour of your house?'

They had heard that phrase till they were wearied. The 'honour of the house' was Prout's weak point, and they knew well how to flick him on the raw.

'If you order us to go down, sir, of course we'll go,' said Stalky, with maddening politeness. But Prout knew better than that. He had tried the experiment once at a big match, when the three, self-isolated, stood to attention for half an hour in full view of all the visitors, to whom fags, subsidised for that end, pointed them out as victims of Prout's tyranny. And Prout was a sensitive man.

In the infinitely petty confederacies of the Common-room, King and Macrea, fellow house-masters, had borne it in upon him that by games, and games alone, was salvation wrought. Boys neglected were boys lost. They must be disciplined. Left to himself, Prout would have made a sympathetic house-master; but he was never so left, and, with the devilish insight of youth, the boys knew to whom they were indebted for his zeal.

'Must we go down, sir?' said M'Turk.

'I don't want to order you to do what a right-thinking boy should do gladly. I'm sorry.' And he lurched out with some hazy impression that he had sown good seed on poor ground.

'Now what does he suppose is the use of that?' said Beetle.

'Oh, he's cracked. King jaws him in Common-room about not keepin' us up to the mark, and Macrea burbles about "dithcipline," an' old Heffy sits between 'em sweatin' big drops. I heard Oke [the Common-room butler] talking to Richards [Prout's house-servant] about it down in the basement the other day when I went down to bag some bread,' said Stalky.

'What did Oke say?' demanded M'Turk, throwing 'Eric' into a corner.

' "Oh," he said, "they make more nise nor a nest full o' jackdaws, an' half of it like we'd no ears to our heads that waited on 'em. They talks over old Prout—what he've done an' left undone about his boys. An' how their boys be fine boys, an' his'n be dom bad." Well, Oke talked like that, you know, and Richards got awf'ly wrathy. He has a down on King for something or other. 'Wonder why?'

'Why, King talks about Prout in form-room—makes

allusions, an' all that—only half the chaps are such asses they can't see what he's drivin' at. And d'you remember what he said about the "casual house" last Tuesday? He meant us. They say he says perfectly beastly things to his own house, making fun of Prout's,' said Beetle.

'Well, we didn't come here to mix up in their rows," M'Turk said wrathfully. 'Who'll bathe after call-over?' King's takin' it on the cricket-field. Come on.' Turkey seized his straw and led the way.

They reached the sun-blistered pavilion over against the gray Pebbleridge just before roll-call, and, asking no questions, gathered from King's voice and manner that his house was on the road to victory.

'Ah, ha!' said he, turning to show the light of his countenance. 'Here we have the ornaments of the Casual House at last. You consider cricket beneath you, I believe'—the flannelled crowd sniggered— 'and from what I have seen this afternoon, I fancy many others of your house hold the same view. And may I ask what you purpose to do with your noble selves till tea-time?'

'Going down to bathe, sir,' said Stalky.

'And whence this sudden zeal for cleanliness? There is nothing about you that particularly suggests it. Indeed, so far as I remember—I may be at fault—but a short time ago—'

'Five years, sir,' said Beetle hotly.

King scowled. 'One of you was that thing called a water-funk. Yes, a water-funk. So now you wish to wash? It is well. Cleanliness never injured a boy or— a house. We will proceed to business,' and he addressed himself to the call-over board.

'What the deuce did you say anything to him for, Beetle?' said M'Turk angrily, as they strolled towards the big, open sea-baths.

''Twasn't fair—remindin' one of bein' a water-funk. My first term, too. Heaps of chaps are—when they can't swim.'

'Yes, you ass; but he saw he'd fetched you. You ought never to answer King.'

'But it wasn't fair, Stalky.'

'My Hat! You've been here six years, and you expect fairness. Well, you are a dithering idiot.'

A knot of King's boys, also bound for the baths, hailed them, beseeching them to wash—for the honour of their house.

'That's what comes of King's jawin' and messin'. Those young animals wouldn't have thought of it unless he'd put it into their heads. Now they'll be funny about it for weeks,' said Stalky. 'Don't take any notice.'

The boys came nearer, shouting an opprobrious word. At last they moved to windward, ostentatiously holding their noses.

'That's pretty,' said Beetle. 'They'll be sayin' our house stinks next.'

When they returned from the baths, damp-headed, languid, at peace with the world, Beetle's forecast came only too true. They were met in the corridor by a fag—a common, Lower-Second fag—who at arm's length handed them a carefully wrapped piece of soap 'with the compliments of King's house.'

'Hold on,' said Stalky, checking immediate attack. 'Who put you up to this, Nixon? Rattray and White? [Those were two leaders in King's house.] Thank you. There's no answer.'

'Oh, it's too sickening to have this kind o' rot shoved on to a chap. What's the sense of it? What's the fun of it?' said M'Turk.

'It will go on to the end of the term, though.' Beetle wagged his head sorrowfully. He had worn many jests threadbare on his own account.

In a few days it became an established legend of the school that Prout's house did not wash and were therefore noisome. Mr. King was pleased to smile succulently in form when one of his boys drew aside from Beetle with certain gestures.

'There seems to be some disability attaching to you, my Beetle, or else why should Burton major withdraw, so to speak, the hem of his garments? I confess I am still in the dark. Will some one be good enough to enlighten me?'

Naturally, he was enlightened by half the form.

'Extraordinary! Most extraordinary! However, each house has its traditions, with which I would not for the world interfere. We have a prejudice in favour of washing. Go on, Beetle—from "Jugurtha tamen"—and, if you can, avoid the more flagrant forms of guessing.'

Prout's house was furious because Macrea's and Hartopp's houses joined King's to insult them. They called a house-meeting after dinner—an excited and angry meeting of all save the prefects, whose dignity, though they sympathised, did not allow them to attend. They read ungrammatical resolutions, and made speeches beginning, 'Gentlemen, we have met on this occasion,' and ending with, 'It's a beastly shame,' precisely as houses have done since time and schools began.

Number Five study attended, with its usual air of

bland patronage. At last M'Turk, of the lanthorn jaws, delivered himself:

'You jabber and jaw and burble, and that's about all you can do. What's the good of it? King's house 'll only gloat because they've drawn you, and King will gloat, too. Besides, that resolution of Orrin's is chock-full of bad grammar, and King 'll gloat over that.'

'I thought you an' Beetle would put it right, an'—an' we'd post it in the corridor,' said the composer meekly.

'Pas si je le connai. I'm not goin' to meddle with the biznai,' said Beetle. 'It's a gloat for King's house. Turkey's quite right.'

'Well, won't Stalky, then?'

But Stalky puffed out his cheeks and squinted down his nose in the style of Panurge, and all he said was, 'Oh, you abject burblers!'

'You're three beastly scabs!' was the instant retort of the democracy, and they went out amid execrations.

'This is piffling,' said M'Turk. 'Let's get our sallies, and go shoot bunnies.'

Three saloon-pistols, with a supply of bulleted breech-caps, were stored in Stalky's trunk, and this trunk was in their dormitory, and their dormitory was a three-bed attic one, opening out of a ten-bed establishment, which, in turn, communicated with the great range of dormitories that ran practically from one end of the College to the other. Macrea's house lay next to Prout's, King's next to Macrea's, and Hartopp's beyond that again. Carefully locked doors divided house from house, but each house, in its internal arrangements—the College had originally been a terrace of twelve large houses—was a replica of the next; one straight roof covering all.

They found Stalky's bed drawn out from the wall to

the left of the dormer window, and the latter end of Richards protruding from a two-foot-square cupboard in the wall.

'What's all this? I've never noticed it before. What are you tryin' to do, Fatty?'

'Fillin' basins, Muster Corkran.' Richards's voice was hollow and muffled. 'They've been savin' me trouble. Yiss.'

''Looks like it,' said M'Turk. 'Hi! You'll stick if you don't take care.'

Richards backed puffing.

'I can't rache un. Yiss, 'tess a turncock, Muster M'Turk. They've took an' runned all the watter-pipes a storey higher in the houses—runned 'em all along under the 'ang of the heaves, like. Runned 'em in last holidays. I can't rache the turncock.'

'Let me try,' said Stalky, diving into the aperture.

'Slip 'ee to the left, then, Muster Corkran. Slip 'ee to the left, an' feel in the dark.'

To the left Stalky wriggled, and saw a long line of lead-pipe disappearing up a triangular tunnel, whose roof was the rafters and boarding of the College roof, whose floor was sharp-edged joists, and whose side was the rough studding of the lath and plaster wall under the dormer.

''Rummy show. How far does it go?'

'Right along, Muster Corkran—right along from end to end. Her runs under the 'ang of the heaves. Have 'ee rached the stopcock yet? Mr. King got un put in to save us carryin' watter from downstairs to fill the basins. No place for a lusty man like old Richards. I'm tu thickabout to go ferritin'. Thank 'ee, Muster Corkran.'

The water squirted through the tap just inside the cupboard, and, having filled the basins, the grateful Richards waddled away.

The boys sat round-eyed on their beds considering the possibilities of this trove. Two floors below them they could hear the hum of the angry house; for nothing is so still as a dormitory in mid-afternoon of a midsummer term.

'It has been papered over till now.' M'Turk examined the little door. 'If we'd only known before!'

'I vote we go down and explore. No one will come up this time o' day. We needn't keep cave.'

They crawled in, Stalky leading, drew the door behind them, and on all fours embarked on a dark and dirty road full of plaster, odd shavings, and all the raffle that builders leave in the waste-room of a house. The passage was perhaps three feet wide, and, except for the straggling light round the edges of the cupboards (there was one to each dormer), almost pitchy dark.

'Here's Macrea's house,' said Stalky, his eye at the crack of the third cupboard. 'I can see Barnes's name on his trunk. Don't make such a row, Beetle! We can get right to the end of the Coll. Come on! . . . We're in King's house now—I can see a bit of Rattray's trunk. How these beastly boards hurt one's knees!' They heard his nails scraping on plaster.

'That's the ceiling below. Look out! If we smashed that the plaster 'ud fall down in the lower dormitory,' said Beetle.

'Let's,' whispered M'Turk.

'An' be collared first thing? Not much. Why, I can shove my hand ever so far up between these boards.'

Stalky thrust an arm to the elbow between the joists.

'No good stayin' here. I vote we go back and talk it over. It's a crummy place. 'Must say I'm grateful to King for his waterworks.'

They crawled out, brushed one another clean, slid the saloon-pistols down a trouser-leg, and hurried forth to a deep and solitary Devonshire lane in whose flanks a boy might sometimes slay a young rabbit. They threw themselves down under the rank elder bushes, and began to think aloud.

'You know,' said Stalky at last, sighting at a distant sparrow, 'we could hide our sallies in there like anything.'

'Huh!' Beetle snorted, choked, and gurgled. He had been silent since they left the dormitory.

'Did you ever read a book called "The History of a House" or something? I got it out of the library the other day. A Frenchwoman wrote it—Violet somebody. But it's translated, you know; and it's very interestin'. Tells you how a house is built.'

'Well, if you're in a sweat to find that out, you can go down to the new cottages they're building for the coast-guard.'

'My Hat! I will.' He felt in his pockets. 'Give me tuppence, some one.'

'Rot! Stay here, and don't mess about in the sun.'

'Gi' me tuppence.'

'I say, Beetle, you aren't stuffy about anything, are you?' said M'Turk, handing over the coppers. His tone was serious, for though Stalky often, and M'Turk occasionally, manœuvred on his own account, Beetle had never been known to do so in all the history of the confederacy.

'No, I'm not. I'm thinking.'

69

'Well, we'll come, too,' said Stalky, with a general's suspicion of his aides.

''Don't want you.'

'Oh, leave him alone. He's been taken worse with a poem,' said M'Turk. 'He'll go burbling down to the Pebbleridge and spit it all up in the study when he comes back.'

'Then why did he want the tuppence, Turkey? He's gettin' too beastly independent. Hi! There's a bunny. No, it ain't. It's a cat, by Jove! You plug first.'

Twenty minutes later a boy with a straw hat at the back of his head, and his hands in his pockets, was staring at workmen as they moved about a half-finished cottage. He produced some ferocious tobacco, and was passed from the forecourt into the interior, where he asked many questions.

'Well, let's have your beastly epic,' said Turkey, as they burst into the study, to find Beetle deep in Viollet-le-Duc and some drawings. 'We've had no end of a lark.'

'Epic? What epic? I've been down to the coastguard.'

'No epic? Then we will slay you, O Beadle,' said Stalky, moving to the attack. 'You've got something up your sleeve. I know, when you talk in that tone!'

'Your Uncle Beetle'—with an attempt to imitate Stalky's war-voice—'is a Great Man.'

'Oh no; he jolly well isn't anything of the kind. You deceive yourself, Beetle. Scrag him, Turkey!'

'A Great Man,' Beetle gurgled from the floor. 'You are futile—look out for my tie!—futile burblers. I am the Great Man. I gloat. Ouch! Hear me!'

'Beetle, de-ah'—Stalky dropped unreservedly on

70

Beetle's chest—'we love you, an' you're a poet. If I ever said you were a doggaroo, I apologise; but you know as well as we do that you can't do anything by yourself without mucking it.'

'I've got a notion.'

'And you'll spoil the whole show if you don't tell your Uncle Stalky. Cough it up, ducky, and we'll see what we can do. Notion, you fat impostor—I knew you had a notion when you went away! Turkey said it was a poem.'

'I've found out how houses are built. Le' me get up. The floor-joists of one room are the ceiling-joists of the room below.'

'Don't be so filthy technical.'

'Well, the man told me. The floor is laid on top of those joists—those boards on edge that we crawled over —but the floor stops at a partition. Well, if you get behind a partition, same as you did in the attic, don't you see that you can shove anything you please under the floor between the floor-boards and the lath and plaster of the ceiling below? Look here. I've drawn it.'

He produced a rude sketch, sufficient to enlighten the allies. There is no part of the modern school curriculum that deals with architecture, and none of them had yet reflected whether floors and ceilings were hollow or solid. Outside his own immediate interests the boy is as ignorant as the savage he so admires; but he has also the savage's resource.

'I see,' said Stalky. 'I shoved my hand there. An' then?'

'An' then . . . They've been calling us stinkers, you know. We might shove somethin' under—sulphur,

or something that stunk pretty bad—an' stink 'em out.
I know it can be done somehow.' Beetle's eyes turned
to Stalky handling the diagrams.

'Stinks?' said Stalky interrogatively. Then his face
grew luminous with delight. 'By gum! I've got it.
Horrid stinks! Turkey!' He leaped at the Irishman.
'This afternoon—just after Beetle went away! She's
the very thing!'

'Come to my arms, my beamish boy,' carolled M'-
Turk, and they fell into each other's arms dancing. 'Oh,
frabjous day! Calloo, callay! She will! She will!'

'Hold on,' said Beetle. 'I don't understand.'

'Dearr man! It shall, though. Oh, Artie, my pure-
souled youth, let us tell our darling Reggie about Pestif-
erous Stinkadores.'

'Not until after call-over. Come on!'

'I say,' said Orrin stiffly, as they fell into their places
along the walls of the gymnasium. 'The house are
goin' to hold another meeting.'

'Hold away, then.' Stalky's mind was elsewhere.

'It's about you three this time.'

'All right, give 'em my love. . . . Here, sir,' and
he tore down the corridor.

Gambolling like kids at play, with bounds and side-
starts, with caperings and curvetings, they led the
almost bursting Beetle to the rabbit-lane, and from
under a pile of stones drew forth the new-slain corpse of
a cat. Then did Beetle see the inner meaning of what had
gone before, and lifted up his voice in thanksgiving for that
the world held warriors so wise as Stalky and M'Turk.

'Well-nourished old lady, ain't she?' said Stalky.
'How long d'you suppose it'll take her to get a bit whiff
in a confined space?'

'Bit whiff! What a coarse brute you are!' said M'-Turk. 'Can't a poor pussy-cat get under King's dormitory floor to die without your pursuin' her with your foul innuendoes?'

'What did she die under the floor for?' said Beetle, looking to the future.

'Oh, they won't worry about that when they find her,' said Stalky.

'A cat may look at a king.' M'Turk rolled down the bank at his own jest. 'Pussy, you don't know how useful you're goin' to be to three pure-souled, high-minded boys.'

'They'll have to take up the floor for her, same as they did in Number Nine when the rat croaked. Big medicine—heap big medicine! Phew! Oh, Lord, I wish I could stop laughin',' said Beetle.

'Stinks! Hi, stinks! Clammy ones!' M'Turk gasped as he regained his place. 'And'—the exquisite humour of it brought them sliding down together in a tangle—'it's all for the honour of the house, too!'

'An' they're holdin' another meetin'—on us,' Stalky panted, his knees in the ditch and his face in the long grass. 'Well, let's get the bullet out of her and hurry up. The sooner she's bedded out the better.'

Between them they did some grisly work with a pen-knife; between them (ask not who buttoned her to his bosom) they took up the corpse and hastened back, Stalky arranging their plan of action at the full trot.

The afternoon sun, lying in broad patches on the bed-rugs, saw three boys and an umbrella disappear into a dormitory wall. In five minutes they returned, brushed themselves all over, washed their hands, combed their hair, and descended.

'Are you sure you shoved her far enough under?' said M'Turk suddenly.

'Hang it, man, I shoved her the full length of my arm and Beetle's brolly. That must be about six feet. She's bung in the middle of King's big upper ten-bedder. Eligible central situation, I call it. She'll stink out his chaps, and Hartopp's and Macrea's, when she really begins to fume. I swear your Uncle Stalky is a great man. Do you realise what a great man he is, Beetle?'

'Well, I had the notion first, hadn't I, only—'

'You couldn't do it without your Uncle Stalky, could you?'

'They've been calling us stinkers for a week now,' said M'Turk. 'Oh, won't they catch it!'

'Stinker! Yah! Stink-ah!' rang down the corridor.

'And she's there,' said Stalky, a hand on either boy's shoulder. 'She's—is—there, gettin' ready to surprise 'em. Presently she'll begin to whisper to 'em in their dreams. Then she'll whiff. Golly, how she'll whiff! Oblige me by thinkin' of it for two minutes.'

They went to their study in more or less of silence. There they began to laugh—laugh as only boys can. They laughed with their foreheads on the tables, or on the floor; laughed at length, curled over the backs of chairs or clinging to a book-shelf; laughed themselves limp.

And in the middle of it Orrin entered on behalf of the house.

'Don't mind us, Orrin; sit down. You don't know how we respect and admire you. There's something about your pure, high, young forehead, full of the dreams of innocent boyhood, that's no end fetchin'. It is, indeed.'

'The house sent me to give you this.' He laid a folded sheet of paper on the table and retired with an awful front.

'It's the resolution! Oh, read it, some one. I'm too silly-sick with laughin' to see,' said Beetle.

Stalky jerked it open with a precautionary sniff.

'Phew! Phew! Listen. "The House notices with pain and contempt the attitude of indiference"—how many f's in indifference, Beetle?'

'Two for choice.'

'Only one here—"adopted by the occupants of Number Five Study in relation to the insults offered to Mr. Prout's House at the recent meeting in Number Twelve form-room, and the House hereby pass a vote of censure on the said study." That's all.'

'And she bled all down my shirt, too!' said Beetle.

'An' I'm catty all over,' said M'Turk, 'though I washed twice.'

'An' I nearly broke Beetle's brolly plantin' her where she would blossom!'

The situation was beyond speech, but not laughter. There was some attempt that night to demonstrate against the three in their dormitory; so they came forth.

'You see,' Beetle began suavely as he loosened his braces, 'the trouble with you is that you're a set of unthinkin' asses. You've no more brains than spidgers. We've told you that heaps of times, haven't we?'

'We'll give all three of you a dormitory lickin'. You always jaw at us as if you were prefects,' cried one.

'Oh no, you won't,' said Stalky, 'because you know that if you did you'd get the worst of it sooner or later. We aren't in any hurry. We can afford to wait for our little revenges. You've made howlin' asses of your-

75

selves, and just as soon as King gets hold of your precious resolution to-morrow you'll find that out. If you aren't sick an' sorry by to-morrow night, I'll—I'll eat my hat.'

But or ever the dinner-bell rang the next day Prout's were sadly aware of their error. King received stray members of that house with an exaggerated attitude of fear. Did they purpose to cause him to be dismissed from the College by unanimous resolution? What were their views concerning the government of the school, that he might hasten to give effect to them? He would not offend them for worlds; but he feared—he sadly feared—that his own house, who did not pass resolutions (but washed), might somewhat deride.

King was a happy man, and his house, basking in the favour of his smile, made that afternoon a long penance to the misled Prout's. And Prout himself, with a dull and lowering visage, tried to think out the rights and wrongs of it all, only plunging deeper into bewilderment. Why should his house be called 'stinkers'? Truly, it was a small thing, but he had been trained to believe that straws show which way the wind blows, and that there is no smoke without fire. He approached King in Common-room with a sense of injustice, but King was pleased to be full of airy persiflage that tide, and brilliantly danced dialectical rings round Prout.

'Now,' said Stalky at bedtime, making pilgrimage through the dormitories before the prefects came up, 'now what have you got to say for yourselves? Foster, Carton, Finch, Longbridge, Marlin, Brett! I heard you chaps catchin' it from King—he made hay of you—an' all you could do was to wriggle an' grin an' say, "Yes, sir," an' "No, sir," an' "Oh, sir," an' "Please, sir"! You an' your resolution! Urh!'

76

'Oh, shut up, Stalky.'

'Not a bit of it. You're a gaudy lot of resolutionists, you are! You've made a sweet mess of it. Perhaps you'll have the decency to leave us alone next time.'

Here the house grew angry, and in many voices pointed out how this blunder would never have come to pass if Number Five study had helped them from the first.

'But you chaps are so beastly conceited, an'—an' you swaggered into the meetin' as if we were a lot of idiots,' growled Orrin of the resolution.

'That's precisely what you are! That's what we've been tryin' to hammer into your thick heads all this time,' said Stalky. 'Never mind, we'll forgive you. Cheer up. You can't help bein' asses, you know,' and, the enemy's flank deftly turned, Stalky hopped into bed.

That night was the first of sorrow among the jubilant King's. By some accident of under-floor draughts the cat did not vex the dormitory beneath which she lay, but the next one to the right; stealing on the air rather as a pale-blue sensation than as any poignant offence. But the mere adumbration of an odour is enough for the sensitive nose and clean tongue of youth. Decency demands that we draw several carbolised sheets over what the dormitory said to Mr. King and what Mr. King replied. He was genuinely proud of his house and fastidious in all that concerned their well-being. He came; he sniffed; he said things. Next morning a boy in that dormitory confided to his bosom friend, a fag of Macrea's, that there was trouble in their midst which King would fain keep secret.

But Macrea's boy had also a bosom friend in Prout's, a shock-headed fag of malignant disposition, who, when he had wormed out the secret, told—told it in a high-pitched treble that rang along the corridor like a bat's squeak.

'An'—an' they've been calling us "stinkers" all this week. Why, Harland minor says they simply can't sleep in his dormitory for the stink. Come on!'

'With one shout and with one cry' Prout's juniors hurled themselves into the war, and through the interval between first and second lesson some fifty twelve-year-olds were embroiled on the gravel outside King's windows to a tune whose leit-motif was the word 'stinker.'

'Hark to the minute-gun at sea!' said Stalky. They were in their study collecting books for second lesson—Latin, with King. 'I thought his azure brow was a bit cloudy at prayers.

> 'She is comin', sister Mary,
> She is—'

'If they make such a row now, what will they do when she really begins to look up an' take notice?'

'Well, no vulgar repartee, Beetle. All we want is to keep out of this row like gentlemen.'

' " 'Tis but a little faded flower." Where's my Horace? Look here, I don't understand what she means by stinkin' out Rattray's dormitory first. We holed in under White's, didn't we?' asked M'Turk, with a wrinkled brow.

'Skittish little thing. She's rompin' about all over the place, I suppose.'

'My Aunt! King 'll be a cheerful customer at second lesson. I haven't prepared my Horace one little bit, either,' said Beetle. 'Come on!'

They were outside the form-room door now. It was within five minutes of the bell, and King might arrive at any moment.

Turkey elbowed into a cohort of scuffling fags, cut out Thornton tertius (he that had been Harland's bosom friend), and bade him tell his tale.

It was a simple one, interrupted by tears. Many of King's house had already battered him for libel.

'Oh, it's nothing,' M'Turk cried. 'He says that King's house stinks. That's all.'

'Stale!' Stalky shouted. 'We knew that years ago, only we didn't choose to run about shoutin' "Stinker!" We've got some manners, if they haven't. Catch a fag, Turkey, and make sure of it.'

Turkey's long arm closed on a hurried and anxious ornament of the Lower Second.

'Oh, M'Turk, please let me go. I don't stink—I swear I don't!'

'Guilty conscience!' cried Beetle. 'Who said you did?'

'What d' you make of it?' Stalky punted the small boy into Beetle's arms.

'Snf! Snf! He does, though. I think it's leprosy —or thrush. P'raps it's both. Take it away.'

'Indeed, Master Beetle'—King generally came to the house-door for a minute or two as the bell rang—'we are vastly indebted to you for your diagnosis, which seems to reflect almost as much credit on the natural unwholesomeness of your mind as it does upon your pitiful ignorance of the diseases of which you discourse so glibly. We will, however, test your knowledge in other directions.'

That was a merry lesson, but, in his haste to scarify Beetle, King clean neglected to give him an imposition, and since at the same time he supplied him with many priceless adjectives for later use, Beetle was well content, and applied himself most seriously throughout third lesson (algebra with little Hartopp) to composing a poem entitled 'The Lazar-house.'

After dinner King took his house to bathe in the sea off the Pebbleridge. It was an old promise; but he wished he could have evaded it, for all Prout's lined up by the Fives Court and cheered with intention. In his absence not less than half the school invaded the infected dormitory to draw their own conclusions. The cat had gained in the last twelve hours, but a battlefield of the fifth day could not have been so flamboyant as the spies reported.

'My word, she is doin' herself proud,' said Stalky. 'Did you ever smell anything like it? Ah, an' she isn't under White's dormitory at all yet.'

'But she will be. Give her time,' said Beetle. 'She'll twine like a giddy honeysuckle. What howlin' Lazarites they are! No house is justified in makin' itself a stench in the nostrils of decent—'

'High-minded, pure-souled boys. Do you burn with remorse and regret?' said M'Turk, as they hastened to meet the house coming up from the sea. King had deserted it, so speech was unfettered. Round its front played a crowd of skirmishers—all houses mixed—flying, re-forming, shrieking insults. On its tortured flanks marched the Hoplites, seniors hurling jests one after another—simple and primitive jests of the Stone Age. To these the three added themselves, dispassionately, with an air of aloofness, almost sadly.

'And they look all right, too,' said Stalky. 'It can't be Rattray, can it? Rattray?'

AN UNSAVOURY INTERLUDE

No answer.

'Rattray, dear? He seems stuffy about something or other. Look here, old man, we don't bear any malice about your sending that soap to us last week, do we? Be cheerful, Rat. You can live this down all right. I daresay it's only a few fags. Your house is so beastly slack, though.'

'You aren't going back to the house, are you?' said M'Turk. The victims desired nothing better. 'You've simply no conception of the reek up there. Of course, frowzin' as you do, you wouldn't notice it; but, after this nice wash and the clean, fresh air, even you'd be upset. 'Much better camp on the Burrows. We'll get you some straw. Shall we?' The house hurried in to the tune of 'John Brown's body,' sung by loving school-mates, and barricaded themselves in their form-room. Straightway Stalky chalked a large cross, with 'Lord, have mercy upon us,' on the door, and left King to find it.

The wind shifted that night and wafted a carrion-reek into Macrea's dormitories; so that boys in nightgowns pounded on the locked door between the houses, en-treating King's to wash. Number Five study went to second lesson with not more than half a pound of cam-phor apiece in their clothing; and King, too wary to ask for explanations, gibbered awhile and hurled them forth. So Beetle finished yet another poem at peace in the study.

'They're usin' carbolic now. Malpas told me,' said Stalky. 'King thinks it's the drains.'

'She'll need a lot o' carbolic,' said M'Turk. 'No harm tryin', I suppose. It keeps King out of mischief.'

'I swear I thought he was goin' to kill me when I

sniffed just now.   He didn't mind Burton major sniffin'
at me the other day, though.   He never stopped Alexander howlin' "Stinker!" into our form-room before—
before we doctored 'em.   He just grinned,' said Stalky.
'What was he frothing over you for, Beetle?'

'Aha!   That was my subtle jape.   I had him on
toast.   You know he always jaws about the learned
Lipsius.'

' "Who at the age of four"—that chap?' said M'Turk.

'Yes.   Whenever he hears I've written a poem.
Well, just as I was sittin' down, I whispered, "How is
our learned Lipsius?" to Burton major.   Old Butt
grinned like an owl.   He didn't know what I was drivin'
at; but King jolly well did.   That was really why he
hove us out.   Ain't you grateful?   Now shut up.   I'm
goin' to write the "Ballad of the Learned Lipsius."'

'Keep clear of anything coarse, then,' said Stalky.
'I shouldn't like to be coarse on this happy occasion.'

'Not for wo-worlds.   What rhymes to "stenches,"
some one?'

In Common-room at lunch King discoursed acridly to
Prout of boys with prurient minds, who perverted their
few and baleful talents to sap discipline and corrupt their
equals, to deal in foul imagery and destroy reverence.

'But you didn't seem to consider this when your
house called us—ah—stinkers.   If you hadn't assured
me that you never interfere with another man's house, I
should almost believe that it was a few casual remarks of
yours that started all this nonsense.'

Prout had endured much, for King always took his
temper to meals.

'You spoke to Beetle yourself, didn't you?   Something about not bathing, and being a water-funk?' the

school chaplain put in. 'I was scoring in the pavilion that day.'

'I may have—jestingly. I really don't pretend to remember every remark I let fall among small boys; and full well I know the Beetle has no feelings to be hurt.'

'Maybe; but he, or they—it comes to the same thing —have the fiend's own knack of discovering a man's weak place. I confess I rather go out of my way to conciliate Number Five study. It may be soft, but so far, I believe, I am the only man here whom they haven't maddened by their—well—attentions.'

'That is all beside the point. I flatter myself I can deal with them alone as occasion arises. But if they feel themselves morally supported by those who should wield an absolute and open-handed justice, then I say that my lot is indeed a hard one. Of all things I detest, I admit that anything verging on disloyalty among ourselves is the first.'

The Common-room looked at one another out of the corners of their eyes, and Prout blushed.

'I deny it absolutely,' he said. 'Er—in fact, I own that I personally object to all three of them. It is not fair, therefore, to—'

'How long do you propose to allow it?' said King.

'But surely,' said Macrea, deserting his usual ally, 'the blame, if there be any, rests with you, King. You can't hold them responsible for the—you prefer the good old Anglo-Saxon, I believe—stink in your house. My boys are complaining of it now.'

'What can you expect? You know what boys are. Naturally they take advantage of what to them is a heaven-sent opportunity,' said little Hartopp. 'What is the trouble in your dormitories, King?'

Mr. King explained that as he had made it the one rule of his life never to interfere with another man's house, so he expected not to be too patently interfered with. They might be interested to learn—here the chaplain heaved a weary sigh—that he had taken all steps that, in his poor judgment, would meet the needs of the case. Nay, further, he had himself expended, with no thought of reimbursement, sums, the amount of which he would not specify, on disinfectants. This he had done because he knew by bitter—by most bitter —experience that the management of the College was slack, dilatory, and inefficient. He might even add almost as slack as the administration of certain houses which now thought fit to sit in judgment on his actions. With a short summary of his scholastic career, and a precis of his qualifications, including his degrees, he withdrew, slamming the door.

'Heigho!' said the chaplain. 'Ours is a dwarfing life —a belittling life, my brethren. God help all school-masters! They need it.'

'I don't like the boys, I own'—Prout dug viciously with his fork into the table-cloth—'and I don't pretend to be a strong man, as you know. But I confess I can't see any reason why I should take steps against Stalky and the others because King happens to be annoyed by—by—'

'Falling into the pit he has digged,' said little Hartopp. 'Certainly not, Prout. No one accuses you of setting one house against another through sheer idleness.'

'A belittling life—a belittling life.' The chaplain rose. 'I go to correct French exercises. By dinner King will have scored off some unlucky child of thirteen; he will repeat to us every word of his brilliant repartees, and all will be well.'

'But about those three. Are they so prurient-minded?'

'Nonsense,' said little Hartopp. 'If you thought for a minute, Prout, you would see that the "precocious flow of fetid imagery" that King complains of is borrowed wholesale from King. He "nursed the pinion that impelled the steel." Naturally he does not approve. Come into the smoking-room for a minute. It isn't fair to listen to boys; but they should be now rubbing it into King's house outside. Little things please little minds.'

The dingy den off the Common-room was never used for anything except gowns. Its windows were ground glass; one could not see out of it, but one could hear almost every word on the gravel outside. A light and wary footstep came up from Number Five.

'Rattray!' in a subdued voice—Rattray's study fronted that way. 'D'you know if Mr. King's anywhere about? I've got a—' M'Turk discreetly left the end of his sentence open.

'No. He's gone out,' said Rattray unguardedly.

'Ah! The learned Lipsius is airing himself, is he? His Royal Highness has gone to fumigate.' M'Turk climbed on the railings, where he held forth like the never-wearied rook.

'Now in all the Coll. there was no stink like the stink of King's house, for it stank vehemently and none knew what to make of it. Save King. And he washed the fags "privatim et seriatim." In the fishpools of Heshbon washed he them, with an apron about his loins.'

'Shut up, you mad Irishman!' There was the sound of a golf-ball spurting up the gravel.

'It's no good getting wrathy, Rattray. We've come to jape with you. Come on, Beetle. They're all at home. You can wind 'em.'

'Where's the Pomposo Stinkadore? 'Tisn't safe for a pure-souled, high-minded boy to be seen round his house these days. Gone out, has he? Never mind. I'll do the best I can, Rattray. I'm "in loco parentis" just now.'

('One for you, Prout,' whispered Macrea, for this was Mr. Prout's pet phrase.)

'I have a few words to impart to you, my young friend. We will discourse together awhile.'

Here the listening Prout sputtered. Beetle, in a strained voice, had chosen a favourite gambit of King's.

'I repeat, Master Rattray, we will confer, and the matter of our discourse shall not be stinks, for that is a loathsome and obscene word. We will, with your good leave—granted, I trust, Master Rattray, granted, I trust—study this—this scabrous upheaval of latent demoralisation. What impresses me most is not so much the blatant indecency with which you swagger abroad under your load of putrescence' (you must imagine this discourse punctuated with golf-balls, but old Rattray was ever a bad shot) 'as the cynical immorality with which you revel in your abhorrent aromas. Far be it from me to interfere with another's house—'

('Good Lord!' said Prout, 'but this is King.')

'Line for line, letter for letter. Listen,' said little Hartopp.)

'But to say that you stink, as certain lewd fellows of the baser sort aver, is to say nothing—less than nothing. In the absence of your beloved house-master, for whom no one has a higher regard than myself, I will, if you will allow me, explain the grossness—the unparalleled enormity—the appalling fetor of the stenches (I believe in the good old Anglo-Saxon word), stenches, sir, with which you have seen fit to infect your house. . . .

86

Oh, bother! I've forgotten the rest, but it was very beautiful. Aren't you grateful to us for labourin' with you this way, Rattray? Lots of chaps 'ud never have taken the trouble, but we're grateful, Rattray.'

'Yes, we're horrid grateful,' grunted M'Turk. 'We don't forget that soap. We're polite. Why ain't you polite, Rat?'

'Hallo!' Stalky cantered up, his cap over one eye. 'Exhortin' the Whiffers, eh? I'm afraid they're too far gone to repent. Rattray! White! Perowne! Malpas! No answer. This is distressin'. This is truly distressin'. Bring out your dead, you glandered lepers!'

'You think yourself funny, don't you?' said Rattray, stung from his dignity by this last. 'It's only a rat or something under the floor. We're going to have it up to-morrow.'

'Don't try to shuffle it off on a poor dumb animal, and dead, too. I loathe prevarication. 'Pon my soul, Rattray—'

'Hold on. The Hartoffles never said "'Pon my soul" in all his little life,' said Beetle critically.

('Ah!' said Prout to little Hartopp.)

'Upon my word, sir, upon my word, sir, I expected better things of you, Rattray. Why can you not own up to your misdeeds like a man? Have I ever shown any lack of confidence in you?'

('It's not brutality,' murmured little Hartopp, as though answering a question no one had asked. 'It's boy; only boy.')

'And this was the house.' Stalky changed from a pecking, fluttering voice to tragic earnestness. 'This was the—the—open cesspit that dared to call us "stinkers." And now—and now, it tries to shelter itself behind a dead rat. You annoy me, Rattray. You disgust me! You irritate me unspeakably! Thank Heaven, I am a man of equable temper—'

('This is to your address, Macrea,' said Prout.

'I fear so, I fear so.')

'Or I should scarcely be able to contain myself before your mocking visage.'

'Cave!' in an undertone. Beetle had spied King sailing down the corridor.

'And what may you be doing here, my little friends?' the house-master began. 'I had a fleeting notion— correct me if I am wrong (the listeners with one accord choked)—that if I found you outside my house I should visit you with dire pains and penalties.'

'We were just goin' for a walk, sir,' said Beetle.

'And you stopped to speak to Rattray en route?'

'Yes, sir. We've been throwing golf-balls,' said Rattray, coming out of the study.

('Old Rat is more of a diplomat than I thought. So far he is strictly within the truth,' said little Hartopp. 'Observe the ethics of it, Prout.')

'Oh, you were sporting with them, were you? I must say I do not envy you your choice of associates. I fancy they might have been engaged in some of the prurient discourse with which they have been so disgustingly free of late. I should strongly advise you to direct your steps most carefully in the future. Pick up those golf-balls.' He passed on.

.   .   .   .

Next day Richards, who had been a carpenter in the Navy, and to whom odd jobs were confided, was ordered to take up a dormitory floor; for Mr. King held that something must have died there.

'We need not neglect all our work for a trumpery incident of this nature; though I am quite aware that little things please little minds. Yes, I have decreed the boards to be taken up after lunch under Richards's auspices. I have no doubt it will be vastly interesting to a certain type of so-called intellect; but any boy of my house or another's found on the dormitory stairs will "ipso facto" render himself liable to three hundred lines.'

The boys did not collect on the stairs, but most of them waited outside King's. Richards had been bound to cry the news from the attic window, and, if possible, to exhibit the corpse.

''Tis a cat, a dead cat!' Richards's face showed purple at the window. He had been in the chamber of death and on his knees for some time.

'Cat be blowed!' cried M'Turk. 'It's a dead fag left over from last term. Three cheers for King's dead fag!'

They cheered lustily.

'Show it, show it! Let's have a squint at it!' yelled the juniors. 'Give her to the Bug-hunters. [This was the Natural History Society.] The cat looked at the King—and died of it! Hoosh! Yai! Yaow! Maiow! Ftzz!' were some of the cries that followed.

Again Richards appeared.

'She've been'—he checked himself suddenly—'dead a long taime.'

The school roared.

'Well, come on out for a walk,' said Stalky in a well-chosen pause. 'It's all very disgustin', and I do hope that the Lazar-house won't do it again.'

'Do what?' a King's boy cried furiously.

'Kill a poor innocent cat every time you want to get

off washing. It's awfully hard to distinguish between you as it is. I prefer the cat, I must say. She isn't quite so whiff. What are you goin' to do, Beetle?'

'Je vais gloater. Je vais gloater tout le blessed afternoon. Jamais j'ai gloate comme je gloaterai aujourd'hui. Nous bunkerons aux bunkers.'

And it seemed good to them so to do.

.   .   .   .

Down in the basement, where the gas flickers and the boots stand in racks, Richards, amid his blacking-brushes, held forth to Oke of the Common-room, Gumbly of the dining-halls, and fair Lena of the laundry.

'Yiss. Her were in a shockin' staate an' condition. Her nigh made me sick, I tall 'ee. But I rowted un out, and I rowted un out, an' I made all shipshape, though her smelt like to bilges.'

'Her died mousin', I rackon, poor thing,' said Lena.

'Then her moused different to any made cat o' God's world, Lena. I up with the top-board, an' she were lying on her back, an' I turned un ovver with the brume-handle, an' 'twas her back was all covered with the plaster from 'twixt the lathin'. Yiss, I tall 'ee. An' under her head there lay, like, so's to say, a little pillow o' plaster druv up in front of her by raison of her slidin' along on her back. No cat niver went mousin' on her back, Lena. Some one had shoved her along right underneath, so far as they could shove un. Cats don't make theyselves pillows for to die on. Shoved along, she were, when she was settin' for to be cold, laike.'

'Oh, yeou'm too clever to live, Fatty. Yeou go get wed an' taught some sense,' said Lena, the affianced of Gumbly.

'Larned a little 'fore iver some maidens was born.

90

Sarved in the Queen's Navy, I have, where yeou'm taught to use your eyes. Yeou go 'tend your own business, Lena.'

'Do 'ee mean what you'm been tellin' us?' said Oke.

'Ask me no questions, I'll give 'ee no lies. Bullet-hole clane thru from side to side, an' tu heart-ribs broke like withies. I seed un when I turned un ovver. They'm clever, oh, they'm clever, but they'm not too clever for old Richards! 'Twas on the born tip o' my tongue to tell, tu, but . . . he said us niver washed, he did. Let his dom boys call us "stinkers," he did. Sarved un dom well raight, I say!'

Richards spat on a fresh boot and fell to his work, chuckling.

THE IMPRESSIONISTS

(1898)

THEY had dropped into the Chaplain's study for a Saturday night smoke—all four house-masters —and the three briars and the one cigar reeking in amity proved the Rev. John Gillett's good generalship. Since the discovery of the cat, King had been too ready to see affront where none was meant, and the Reverend John, buffer-state and general confidant, had worked for a week to bring about a good understanding. He was fat, clean-shaven, except for a big moustache, of an imperturbable good temper, and, those who loved him least said, a guileful Jesuit. He smiled benignantly upon his handiwork—four sorely-tried men talking without very much malice.

'Now remember,' he said, when the conversation turned that way, 'I impute nothing. But every time that any one has taken direct steps against Number Five study, the issue has been more or less humiliating to the taker.'

'I can't admit that. I pulverise the egregious Beetle daily for his soul's good; and the others with him,' said King.

'Well, take your own case, King, and go back a couple of years. Do you remember when Prout and you were

on their track—for hutting and trespass, wasn't it?
Have you forgotten Colonel Dabney?'

The others laughed. King did not care to be reminded
of his career as a poacher.

'That was one instance. Again, when you had rooms
below them—I always said that that was entering the
lion's den—you turned them out.'

'For making disgusting noises. Surely, Gillett, you
don't excuse—'

'All I say is that you turned them out. That same
evening your study was wrecked.'

'By Rabbits-Eggs—most beastly drunk—from the
road,' said King. 'What has that—?'

The Reverend John went on.

'Lastly, they conceive that aspersions are cast upon
their personal cleanliness—a most delicate matter with
all boys. Ve-ry good. Observe how, in each case, the
punishment fits the crime. A week after your house calls
them "stinkers," King, your house is, not to put too fine
a point on it, stunk out by a dead cat who chooses to die
in the one spot where she can annoy you most. Again
the long arm of coincidence! Summa. You accuse them
of trespass. Through some absurd chain of circumstances—they may or may not be at the other end of it—
you and Prout are made to appear as trespassers. You
evict them. For a time your study is made untenable.
I have drawn the parallel in the last case. Well?'

'She was under the centre of White's dormitory,' said
King. 'There are double floor-boards there to deaden
noise. No boy, even in my own house, could possibly
have pried up the boards without leaving some trace—
and Rabbits-Eggs was phenomenally drunk that other
night.'

'They are singularly favoured by fortune. That is
all I ever said. Personally, I like them immensely, and
I believe I have a little of their confidence. I confess I
like being called "Padre." They are at peace with me;
consequently I am not treated to bogus confessions of
theft.'

'You mean Mason's case?' said Prout heavily. 'That
always struck me as peculiarly scandalous. I thought
the Head should have taken up the matter more thoroughly. Mason may be misguided, but at least he is
thoroughly sincere and means well.'

'I confess I cannot agree with you, Prout,' said the
Reverend John. 'He jumped at some silly tale of theft
on their part; accepted another boy's evidence without,
so far as I can see, any inquiry; and—frankly, I think
he deserved all he got.'

'They deliberately outraged Mason's best feelings,'
said Prout. 'A word to me on their part would have
saved the whole thing. But they preferred to lure him
on; to play on his ignorance of their characters—'

'That may be,' said King, 'but I don't like Mason.
I dislike him for the very reason that Prout advances
to his credit. He means well.'

'Our criminal tradition is not theft—among ourselves,
at least,' said little Hartopp.

'For the head of a house that raided seven head of
cattle from the innocent pot-wallopers of Northam, isn't
that rather a sweeping statement?' said Macrea.

'Precisely so,' said Hartopp, unabashed. 'That, with
gate-lifting, and a little poaching and hawk-hunting on
the cliffs, is our salvation.'

'It does us far more harm as a school—' Prout began.

'Than any hushed-up scandal could? Quite so. Our

94

reputation among the farmers is most unsavoury. But I would much sooner deal with any amount of ingenious crime of that nature than—some other offences.'

'They may be all right, but they are unboylike, abnormal, and, in my opinion, unsound,' Prout insisted. 'The moral effect of their performances must pave the way for greater harm. It makes me doubtful how to deal with them. I might separate them.'

'You might, of course; but they have gone up the school together for six years. I shouldn't care to do it,' said Macrea.

'They use the editorial "we,"' said King irrelevantly. 'It annoys me. "Where's your prose, Corkran?" "Well, sir, we haven't quite done it yet. We'll bring it in a minute," and so on. And the same with the others.'

'There's great virtue in that "we,"' said little Hartopp. 'You know I take them for trig. M'Turk may have some conception of the meaning of it; but Beetle is as the brutes that perish about sines and cosines. He copies serenely from Stalky, who positively rejoices in mathematics.'

'Why don't you stop it?' said Prout.

'It rights itself at the exams. Then Beetle shows up blank sheets, and trusts to his "English" to save him from a fall. I fancy he spends most of his time with me in writing verse.'

'I wish to Heaven he would transfer a little of his energy in that direction to Elegiacs.' King jerked himself upright. 'He is, with the single exception of Stalky, the very vilest manufacturer of "barbarous hexameters" that I have ever dealt with.'

'The work is combined in that study,' said the chaplain. 'Stalky does the mathematics, M'Turk the Latin, and Beetle attends to their English and French.   At least, when he was in the sick-house last month—'

'Malingering,' Prout interjected.

'Quite possibly.   I found a very distinct falling off in their "Roman d'un Jeune Homme Pauvre" translations.'

'I think it is profoundly immoral,' said Prout.   'I've always been opposed to the study system.'

'It would be hard to find any study where the boys don't help each other; but in Number Five the thing has probably been reduced to a system,' said little Hartopp.   'They have a system in most things.'

'They confess as much,' said the Reverend John. 'I've seen M'Turk being hounded up the stairs to elegise the "Elegy in a Churchyard," while Beetle and Stalky went to punt-about.'

'It amounts to systematic cribbing,' said Prout, his voice growing deeper and deeper.

'No such thing,' little Hartopp returned.   'You can't teach a cow the violin.'

'In intention it is cribbing.'

'But we spoke under the seal of the confessional, didn't we?' said the Reverend John.

'You say you've heard them arranging their work in this way, Gillett?' Prout persisted.

'Good Heavens!   Don't make me Queen's evidence, my dear fellow.   Hartopp is equally incriminated.   If they ever found out that I had sneaked, our relations would suffer—and I value them.'

'I think your attitude in this matter is weak,' said Prout, looking round for support.   'It would be really better to break up the study—for a while—wouldn't it?'

'Oh, break it up by all means,' said Macrea. 'We shall see then if Gillett's theory holds water.'

'Be wise, Prout. Leave them alone or calamity will overtake you; and what is much more important, they will be annoyed with me. I am too fat, alas! to be worried by bad boys. Where are you going?'

'Nonsense! They would not dare—but I am going to think this out,' said Prout. 'It needs thought. In intention they cribbed, and I must think out my duty.'

'He's perfectly capable of putting the boys on their honour. It's I that am a fool!' The Reverend John looked round remorsefully. 'Never again will I forget that a master is not a man. Mark my words,' said the Reverend John. 'There will be trouble.'

.   .   .   .

But by the yellow Tiber
Was tumult and affright.

Out of the blue sky (they were still rejoicing over the cat war) Mr. Prout had dropped into Number Five, read them a lecture on the enormity of cribbing, and bidden them return to the form-rooms on Monday. They had raged, solo and chorus, all through the peaceful Sabbath, for their sin was more or less the daily practice of all the studies.

'What's the good of cursing?' said Stalky at last. 'We're all in the same boat. We've got to go back and consort with the house. A locker in the form-room, and a seat at prep. in Number Twelve.' He looked regretfully round the cosy study which M'Turk, their leader in matters of Art, had decorated with a dado, a stencil, and cretonne hangings.

'Yes! Heffy lurchin' into the form-rooms like a

frowzy old retriever, to see if we aren't up to something. You know he never leaves his house alone, these days,' said M'Turk. 'Oh, it will be giddy!'

' "Why aren't you down watchin' cricket? I like a robust, healthy boy. You mustn't frowst in a form-room. Why don't you take an interest in your house?" Yah!' quoted Beetle.

'Yes, why don't we! Let's! We'll take an interest in the house. We'll take no end of interest in the house! He hasn't had us in the form-rooms for a year. We've learned a lot since then. Oh, we'll make it a be-autiful house before we've done! 'Member that chap in "Eric" or "St. Winifred's"—Belial somebody? I'm goin' to be Belial,' said Stalky, with an ensnaring grin.

'Right O!' said Beetle, 'and I'll be Mammon. I'll lend money at usury—that's what they do at all schools accordin' to the B. O. P. 'Penny a week on a shillin'. That'll startle Heffy's weak intellect. You can be Lucifer, Turkey.'

'What have I got to do?' M'Turk also smiled.

'Head conspiracies—and cabal—and boycotts. Go in for that "stealthy intrigue" that Heffy is always talkin' about. Come on!'

The house received them on their fall with the mixture of jest and sympathy always extended to boys turned out of their study. The known aloofness of the three made them more interesting.

'Quite like old times, ain't it?' Stalky selected a locker and flung in his books. 'We've come to sport with you, my young friends, for a while, because our beloved house-master has hove us out of our diggin's.'

' 'Serve you jolly well right,' said Orrin, 'you cribbers!'

'This will never do,' said Stalky. 'We can't maintain our giddy prestige, Orrin, de-ah, if you make these remarks.'

They wrapped themselves lovingly about the boy, thrust him to the opened window, and drew down the sash to the nape of his neck. With an equal swiftness they tied his thumbs together behind his back with a piece of twine, and then, because he kicked furiously, removed his shoes.

There Mr. Prout happened to find him a few minutes later, guillotined and helpless, surrounded by a convulsed crowd who would not assist.

Stalky, in an upper form-room, had gathered himself allies against vengeance. Orrin presently tore up at the head of a boarding-party, and the form-room grew one fog of dust through which boys wrestled, stamped, shouted, and yelled. A desk was carried away in the tumult, a knot of warriors reeled into and split a door-panel, a window was broken, and a gas-jet fell. Under cover of the confusion the three escaped to the corridor, whence they called in and sent up passersby to the fray.

'Rescue, King's! King's! King's! Number Twelve form-room! Rescue, Prout's! Prout's! Rescue, Macrea's! Rescue, Hartopp's!'

The juniors hurried out like bees a-swarm, asking no questions, clattered up the staircase, and added themselves to the embroilment.

'Not bad for the first evening's work,' said Stalky, re-arranging his collar. 'I fancy Prout 'll be somewhat annoyed. We'd better establish an alibi.' So they sat on Mr. King's railings till prep.

'You see,' quoth Stalky, as they strolled up to prep. with the ignoble herd, 'if you get the houses well mixed up an' scufflin', it's even bettin' that some ass will start a real row. Hullo, Orrin, you look rather metagrobolised.'

'It was all your fault, you beast! You started it. We've got two hundred lines apiece, and Heffy's lookin' for you. Just see what that swine Malpas did to my eye!'

'I like your saying we started it. Who called us cribbers? Can't your infant mind connect cause and effect yet? Some day you'll find out that it don't pay to jest with Number Five.'

'Where's that shillin' you owe me?' said Beetle suddenly.

Stalky could not see Prout behind him, but returned the lead without a quaver.

'I only owed you ninepence, you old usurer.'

'You've forgotten the interest,' said M'Turk. 'A halfpenny a week per bob is Beetle's charge. You must be beastly rich, Beetle.'

'Well, Beetle lent me sixpence.' Stalky came to a full stop and made as to work it out on his fingers. 'Sixpence on the nineteenth, didn't he?'

'Yes; but you've forgotten you paid no interest on the other bob—the one I lent you before.'

'But you took my watch as security.' The game was developing itself almost automatically.

'Never mind. Pay me my interest, or I'll charge you interest on interest. Remember I've got your note-of-hand!' shouted Beetle.

'You're a cold-blooded Jew,' Stalky groaned.

'Hush!' said M'Turk very loudly indeed; then started as Prout came upon them.

'I didn't see you in that disgraceful affair in the form-room just now,' said he.

100

'What, sir? We're just come up from Mr. King's,' said Stalky. 'Please, sir, what am I to do about prep.? They've broken the desk you told me to sit at, and the form's just swimming with ink.'

'Find another seat—find another seat. D'you expect me to dry-nurse you? I wish to know whether you are in the habit of advancing money to your associates, Beetle?'

'No, sir; not as a general rule, sir.'

'It is a most reprehensible habit. I thought that my house, at least, would be free from it. Even with my opinion of you, I hardly thought it was one of your vices.'

'There's no harm in lending money, sir, is there?'

'I am not going to bandy words with you on your notions of morality. How much have you lent Corkran?'

'I—don't quite know,' said Beetle. It is difficult to improvise a going concern on the spur of the minute.

'You seemed certain enough just now.'

'I think it's two and fourpence,' said M'Turk, with a glance of cold scorn at Beetle.

In the hopelessly involved finances of the study there was just that sum to which both M'Turk and Beetle laid claim, as their share in the pledging of Stalky's second-best Sunday trousers. But Stalky had maintained for two terms that the money was his commission for effecting the pawn; and had, of course, spent it on a study 'brew.'

'Understand this, then. You are not to continue your operations as a money-lender. Two and fourpence, you said, Corkran?'

Stalky had said nothing, and continued so to do.

'Your influence for evil is quite strong enough without

101

buying a hold over your companions.' He felt in his pockets, and (oh, joy!) produced a florin and fourpence. 'Bring me what you call Corkran's note-of-hand, and be thankful that I do not carry the matter any further. The money is stopped from your pocket-money, Corkran. The receipt to my study, at once.'

Little they cared! Two and fourpence in a lump is worth six weekly sixpences any hungry day of the week.

'But what the dooce is a note-of-hand?' said Beetle. 'I only read about it in a book.'

'Now you've jolly well got to make one,' said Stalky.

'Yes—but our ink don't turn black till next day. 'S'pose he'll spot that?'

'Not him. He's too worried,' said M'Turk. 'Sign your name on a bit of impot-paper, Stalky, and write, "I O U two and fourpence." Aren't you grateful to me for getting that out of Prout? Stalky'd never have paid. . . . Why, you ass!'

Mechanically Beetle had handed over the money to Stalky as treasurer of the study. The custom of years is not lightly broken. In return for the document, Prout explained to Beetle the enormity of money-lending, which, like everything except compulsory cricket, corrupted houses and destroyed good feeling among boys, made youth cold and calculating, and opened the door to all evil. Finally, did Beetle know of any other cases? If so, it was his duty as proof of repentance to let his house-master know. No names need be mentioned.

Beetle did not know—at least, he was not quite sure, sir. How could he give evidence against his friends? The house might, of course—here he feigned an anguished delicacy—be full of it. He was not in a posi-

102

tion to say. He had not met with any open competition in his trade; but if Mr. Prout considered it was a matter that affected the honour of the house (Mr. Prout did consider it precisely that), perhaps the house-prefects would be better . . .

He spun it out till half-way through prep.

'And,' said the amateur Shylock, returning to the form-room and dropping at Stalky's side, 'if he don't think the house is putrid with it, I'm severial Dutchmen —that's all. . . . I've been to Mr. Prout's study, sir.' This to the prep.-master. 'He said I could sit where I liked, sir. . . . Oh, he is just tricklin' with emotion. . . . Yes, sir, I'm only askin' Corkran to let me have a dip in his ink.'

After prayers, on the road to the dormitories, Harrison and Craye, senior house-prefects, zealous in their office, waylaid them with great anger.

'What have you been doing to Heffy this time, Beetle? He's been jawing us all the evening.'

'What has His Serene Transparency been vexin' you for?' said M'Turk.

'About Beetle lendin' money to Stalky,' began Harrison; 'and then Beetle went and told him that there was any amount of money-lendin' in the house.'

'No, you don't,' said Beetle, sitting on a boot-basket. 'That's just what I didn't tell him. I spoke the giddy truth. He asked me if there was much of it in the house; and I said I didn't know.'

'He thinks you're a set of filthy Shylocks,' said M'-Turk. 'It's just as well for you he don't think you're burglars. You know he never gets a notion out of his conscientious old head.'

'Well-meanin' man. Did it all for the best.' Stalky

curled gracefully round the stair-rail. 'Head in a drain-pipe. Full confession in the left boot. Bad for the honour of the house—very.'

'Shut up,' said Harrison. 'You chaps always behave as if you were jawin' us when we come to jaw you.'

'You're a lot too cheeky,' said Craye.

'I don't quite see where the cheek comes in, except on your part, in interferin' with a private matter between me an' Beetle after it has been settled by Prout.' Stalky winked cheerfully at the others.

'That's the worst of clever little swots,' said M'Turk, addressing the gas. 'They get made prefects before they have any tact, and then they annoy chaps who could really help 'em to look after the honour of the house.'

'We won't trouble you to do that!' said Craye hotly.

'Then what are you badgerin' us for?' said Beetle. 'On your own showing, you've been so beastly slack, looking after the house, that Prout believes it's a nest of money-lenders. I've told him that I've lent money to Stalky, and no one else. I don't know whether he believes me, but that finishes my case. The rest is your business.'

'Now we find out'—Stalky's voice rose—'that there is apparently an organised conspiracy throughout the house. For aught we know, the fags may be lendin' and borrowin' far beyond their means. We aren't responsible for it. We're only the rank and file.'

'Are you surprised we don't wish to associate with the house?' said M'Turk, with dignity. 'We've kept ourselves to ourselves in our study till we were turned out, and now we find ourselves let in for—for this sort of thing. It's simply disgraceful.'

THE IMPRESSIONISTS

'Then you hector and bullyrag us on the stairs,' said Stalky, 'about matters that are your business entirely. You know we aren't prefects.'

'You threatened us with a prefect's lickin' just now,' said Beetle, boldly inventing as he saw the bewilderment in the faces of the enemy.

'And if you expect you'll gain anything from us by your way of approachin' us, you're jolly well mistaken. That's all. Good-night.'

They clattered upstairs, injured virtue on every inch of their backs.

'But—but what the dickens have we done?' said Harrison, amazedly, to Craye.

'I don't know. Only—it always happens that way when one has anything to do with them. They're so beastly plausible.'

And Mr. Prout called the good boys into his study anew, and succeeded in sinking both his and their innocent minds ten fathoms deeper in blindfolded bedazement. He spoke of steps and measures, of tone and loyalty in the house and to the house, and urged them to take up the matter tactfully.

So they demanded of Beetle whether he had any connection with any other establishment. Beetle promptly went to his house-master, and wished to know by what right Harrison and Craye had reopened a matter already settled between him and his house-master. In injured innocence no boy excelled Beetle.

Then it occurred to Prout that he might have been unfair to the culprit, who had not striven to deny or palliate his offence. He sent for Harrison and Craye, reprehending them very gently for the tone they had adopted to a repentant sinner, and when they returned

105

to their study, they used the language of despair. They then made headlong inquisition through the house, driving the fags to the edge of hysterics, and unearthing, with tremendous pomp and parade, the natural and inevitable system of small loans that prevails among small boys.

'You see, Harrison, Thornton minor lent me a penny last Saturday, because I was fined for breaking the window; and I spent it at Keyte's. I didn't know there was any harm in it. And Wray major borrowed twopence from me when my uncle sent me a post-office order—I cashed it at Keyte's—for five bob; but he'll pay me back before the holidays. We didn't know there was anything wrong in it.'

They waded through hours of this kind of thing, but found no usury, or anything approaching to Beetle's gorgeous scale of interest. The seniors—for the school had no tradition of deference to prefects outside compulsory games—told them succinctly to go about their business. They would not give evidence on any terms. Harrison was one idiot, and Craye was another; but the greatest of all, they said, was their house-master.

When a house is thoroughly upset, however good its conscience, it breaks into knots and coteries—small gatherings in the twilight, box-room committees, and groups in the corridor. And when from group to group, with an immense affectation of secrecy, three wicked boys steal, crying 'Cave' when there is no need of caution, and whispering 'Don't tell!' on the heels of trumpery confidences that instant invented, a very fine air of plot and intrigue can be woven round such a house.

At the end of a few days, it dawned on Prout that he moved in an atmosphere of perpetual ambush. Mysteries hedged him on all sides, warnings ran before his

heavy feet, and countersigns were muttered behind his
attentive back. M'Turk and Stalky invented many
absurd and idle phrases—catch-words that swept
through the house as fire through stubble. It was a
rare jest, and the only practical outcome of the Usury
Commission, that one boy should say to a friend, with
awful gravity, 'Do you think there's much of it going on
in the house?' The other would reply, 'Well, one can't
be too careful, you know.' The effect on a house-
master of humane conscience and good intent may be
imagined. Again, a man who has sincerely devoted himself to gaining the esteem of his charges does not like
to hear himself described, even at a distance, as 'Popularity Prout' by a dark and scowling Celt with a fluent
tongue. A rumour that stories—unusual stories—are
told in the form-rooms, between the lights, by a boy
who does not command his confidence, agitates such a
man; and even elaborate and tender politeness—for the
courtesy that wise grown men offer to a bewildered child
was the courtesy which Stalky wrapped round Prout—
restores not his peace of mind.

'The tone of the house seems changed—changed for
the worse,' said Prout to Harrison and Craye. 'Have
you noticed it? I don't for an instant impute—'

He never imputed anything; but, on the other hand,
he never did anything else, and, with the best intentions
in the world, he had reduced the house-prefects to a
state as nearly bordering on nervous irritation as healthy
boys can know. Worst of all, they began at times to
wonder whether Stalky & Co. had not some truth in
their often-repeated assertions that Prout was 'a gloomy
ass.'

'As you know, I am not the kind of man who puts

himself out for every little thing he hears.   I believe in letting the house work out their own salvation—with a light guiding hand on the reins, of course.   But there is a perceptible lack of reverence—a lower tone in matters that touch the honour of the house, a sort of hardness.'

'Oh, Prout he is a nobleman, a nobleman, a nobleman!
  Our Heffy is a nobleman—
  He does an awful lot!
Because his popularity—
Oh, pop-u-pop-u-larity—
His giddy popularity
  Would suffer did he not!'

The study door stood ajar; and the song, borne by twenty clear voices, came faint from a form-room.   The fags rather liked the tune; the words were Beetle's.

'That's a thing no sensible man objects to,' said Prout, with a lop-sided smile; 'but, you know, straws show which way the wind blows.   Can you trace it to any direct influence?   I am speaking to you now as heads of the house.'

'There isn't the least doubt of it,' said Harrison angrily.   'I know what you mean, sir.   It all began when Number Five study came to the form-rooms.   There's no use blinkin' it, Craye.   You know that, too.'

'They make things rather difficult for us, sometimes,' said Craye.   'It's more their manner than anything else, that Harrison means.'

'Do they hamper you in the discharge of your duties, then?'

'Well, no, sir.   They only look on and grin—and turn up their noses generally.'

'Ah,' said Prout sympathetically.

'I think, sir,' said Craye, plunging into the business boldly, 'it would be a great deal better if they were sent back to their studies—better for the house. They are rather old to be knocking about the form-rooms.'

'They are younger than Orrin, or Flint, and a dozen others that I can think of.'

'Yes, sir; but that's different, somehow. They're rather influential. They have a knack of upsettin' things in a quiet way that one can't take hold of. At least, if one does—'

'And you think they would be better in their own studies again?'

Emphatically Harrison and Craye were of that opinion. As Harrison said to Craye, afterwards, 'They've weakened our authority. They're too big to lick; they've made an exhibition of us over this usury business, and we're a laughing-stock to the rest of the school. I'm going up ['for Sandhurst' understood] next term. They've managed to knock me out of half my work already, with their—their lunacy. If they go back to their studies we may have a little peace.'

'Hullo, Harrison.' M'Turk ambled round the corner, with a roving eye on all possible horizons. 'Bearin' up, old man? That's right. Live it down! Live it down!'

'What d'you mean?'

'You look a little pensive,' said M'Turk. 'Exhaustin' job superintendin' the honour of the house, ain't it? By the way, how are you off for mares'-nests?'

'Look here,' said Harrison, hoping for instant reward. 'We've recommended Prout to let you go back to your study.'

'The dooce you have! And who under the sun are

you, to interfere between us and our house-master? Upon my Sam, you two try us very hard—you do, indeed.   Of course we don't know how far you abuse your position to prejudice us with Mr. Prout; but when you deliberately stop me to tell me you've been makin' arrangements behind our back—in secret—with Prout— I—I don't know really what we ought to do.'

'That's beastly unfair!' cried Craye.

'It is.'   M'Turk had adopted a ghastly solemnity that sat well on his long, lean face.   'Hang it all!   A prefect's one thing and an usher's another; but you seem to combine 'em.   You recommend this—you recommend that!   You say how and when we go back to our studies!'

'But—but—we thought you'd like it, Turkey.   We did, indeed.   You know you'll be ever so much more comfortable there.'   Harrison's voice was almost tearful.

M'Turk turned away as if to hide his emotions.

'They're broke!'   He hunted up Stalky and Beetle in a box-room.   'They're sick!   They've been beggin' Heffy to let us go back to Number Five.   Poor devils! Poor little devils!'

'It's the olive branch,' was Stalky's comment.   'It's the giddy white flag, by gum!   Come to think of it, we have metagrobolised 'em.'

Just after tea that day, Mr. Prout sent for them to say that if they chose to ruin their future by neglecting their work, it was entirely their own affair.   He wished them, however, to understand that their presence in the form-rooms could not be tolerated one hour longer.   He personally did not care to think of the time he must spend in eliminating the traces of their evil influences.   How far Beetle had pandered to the baser side of youthful imagination he would ascertain later; and Beetle might be sure that if Mr. Prout came across any soul-corrupting consequences—

'Consequences of what, sir?' said Beetle, genuinely bewildered this time; and M'Turk quietly kicked him on the ankle for being 'fetched' by Prout.

Beetle, the house-master continued, knew very well what was intended. Evil and brief had been their careers under his eye; and as one standing 'in loco parentis' to their yet uncontaminated associates, he was bound to take his precautions. The return of the study key closed the sermon.

'But what was the baser-side-of-imagination business?' said Beetle on the stairs.

'I never knew such an ass as you are for justifyin' yourself,' said M'Turk. 'I hope I jolly well skinned your ankle. Why do you let yourself be drawn by everybody?'

'Draws be blowed! I must have tickled him up in some way I didn't know about. If I'd had a notion of that before, of course I could have rubbed it in better. It's too late now. What a pity! "Baser side." What was he drivin' at?'

'Never mind,' said Stalky. 'I knew we could make a happy little house. I said so, remember—but I swear I didn't think we'd do it so soon.'

.   .   .   .

'No,' said Prout most firmly in Common-room. 'I maintain that Gillett is wrong. True, I let them return to their study.'

'With your known views on cribbing, too?' purred little Hartopp. 'What an immoral compromise!'

'One moment,' said the Reverend John. 'I—we—all of us have exercised an absolutely heart-breaking discretion for the last ten days. Now we want to know. Confess—have you known a happy minute since—'

'As regards my house, I have not,' said Prout. 'But you are entirely wrong in your estimate of those boys. In justice to the others—in self-defence—'

'Ha! I said it would come to that,' murmured the Reverend John.

'—I was forced to send them back. Their moral influence was unspeakable—simply unspeakable.'

And bit by bit he told his tale, beginning with Beetle's usury, and ending with the house-prefect's appeal.

'Beetle in the role of Shylock is new to me,' said King, with twitching lips. 'I heard rumours of it—'

'Before!' said Prout.

'No, after you had dealt with them; but I was careful not to inquire. I never interfere with—'

'I myself,' said Hartopp, 'would cheerfully give him five shillings if he could work out one simple sum in compound interest without three gross errors.'

'Why—why—why!' Mason, the mathematical master, stuttered, a fierce joy on his face. 'You've been had—precisely the same as me!'

'And so you held an inquiry?' Little Hartopp's voice drowned Mason's ere Prout caught the import of the sentence.

'The boy himself hinted at the existence of a good deal of it in the house,' said Prout.

'He is past master in that line,' said the chaplain. 'But, as regards the honour of the house—'

'They lowered it in a week. I have striven to build it up for years. My own house-prefects—and boys do not willingly complain of each other—besought me to get rid of them. You say you have their confidence, Gillett: they may tell you another tale. As far as I am concerned, they may go to the devil in their own way. I'm sick and tired of them,' said Prout bitterly.

But it was the Reverend John, with a smiling countenance, who went to the devil just after Number Five had cleared away a very pleasant little brew (it cost them two and fourpence) and was settling down to prep.

'Come in, Padre, come in,' said Stalky, thrusting forward the best chair. 'We've only met you official-like these last ten days.'

'You were under sentence,' said the Reverend John. 'I do not consort with malefactors.'

'Ah, but we're restored again,' said M'Turk. 'Mr. Prout has relented.'

'Without a stain on our characters,' said Beetle. 'It was a painful episode, Padre, most painful.'

'Now, consider for a while, and perpend, mes enfants. It is about your characters that I've called to-night. In the language of the schools, what the dooce have you been up to in Mr. Prout's house? It isn't anything to laugh over. He says that you so lowered the tone of the house he had to pack you back to your studies. Is that true?'

'Every word of it, Padre.'

'Don't be flippant, Turkey. Listen to me. I've told you very often that no boys in the school have a greater influence for good or evil than you have. You know I don't talk about ethics and moral codes, because I don't believe that the young of the human animal realises what they mean for some years to come. All

113

the same, I don't want to think you've been perverting the juniors. Don't interrupt, Beetle. Listen to me! Mr. Prout has a notion that you have been corrupting our associates somehow or other.'

'Mr. Prout has so many notions, Padre,' said Beetle wearily. 'Which one is this?'

'Well, he tells me that he heard you telling a story in the twilight in the form-room, in a whisper. And Orrin said, just as he opened the door, "Shut up, Beetle; it's too beastly." Now then?'

'You remember Mrs. Oliphant's "Beleaguered City" that you lent me last term?' said Beetle.

The Padre nodded.

'I got the notion out of that. Only, instead of a city, I made it the Coll. in a fog—besieged by ghosts of dead boys, who hauled chaps out of their beds in the dormitory. All the names are quite real. You tell it in a whisper, you know—with the names. Orrin didn't like it one little bit. None of 'em have ever let me finish it. It gets just awful at the end.'

'But why in the world didn't you explain to Mr. Prout, instead of leaving him under the impression—'

'Padre Sahib,' said M'Turk, 'it isn't the least good explainin' to Mr. Prout. If he hasn't one impression, he's bound to have another.'

'He'd do it with the best o' motives. He's "in loco parentis,"' purred Stalky.

'You young demons!' the Reverend John replied. 'And am I to understand that the—the usury business was another of your house-master's impressions?'

'Well—we helped a little in that,' said Stalky. 'I did owe Beetle two and fourpence—at least, Beetle says I did, but I never intended to pay him. Then we started a bit of an argument on the stairs, and—and Mr. Prout dropped into it accidental. That was how it was, Padre. He paid me cash down like a giddy Dook (stopped it out of my pocket-money just the same), and Beetle gave him my note-of-hand all correct. I don't know what happened after that.'

'I was too truthful,' said Beetle. 'I always am. You see, he was under an impression, Padre, and I suppose I ought to have corrected that impression; but of course I couldn't be quite certain that his house wasn't given over to money-lendin', could I? I thought the house-prefects might know more about it than I did. They ought to. They're giddy palladiums of public schools.'

'They did, too—by the time they'd finished,' said M'Turk. 'As nice a pair of conscientious, well-meanin', upright, pure-souled boys as you'd ever want to meet, Padre. They turned the house upside down—Harrison and Craye—with the best motives in the world.'

'They said so.

> 'They said it very loud and clear,
>   They went and shouted in our ear,'

said Stalky.

'My own private impression is that all three of you will infallibly be hanged,' said the Reverend John.

'Why, we didn't do anything,' replied M'Turk. 'It was all Mr. Prout. Did you ever read a book about Japanese wrestlers? My uncle—he's in the Navy—gave me a beauty once.'

'Don't try to change the subject, Turkey.'

'I'm not, sir. I'm givin' an illustration—same as a

115

sermon. These wrestler-chaps have got some sort of trick that lets the other chap do all the work. Then they give a little wriggle, and he upsets himself. It's called shibbuwichee or tokonoma, or somethin'. Mr. Prout's a shibbuwicher. It isn't our fault.'

'Did you suppose we went round corruptin' the minds of the fags?' said Beetle. 'They haven't any, to begin with; and if they had, they're corrupted long ago. I've been a fag, Padre.'

'Well, I fancied I knew the normal range of your iniquities; but if you take so much trouble to pile up circumstantial evidence against yourselves, you can't blame any one if—'

'We don't blame any one, Padre. We haven't said a word against Mr. Prout, have we?' Stalky looked at the others. 'We love him. He hasn't a notion how we love him.'

'H'm! You dissemble your love very well. Have you ever thought who got you turned out of your study, in the first place?'

'It was Mr. Prout turned us out,' said Stalky, with significance.

'Well, I was that man. I didn't mean it; but some words of mine, I'm afraid, gave Mr. Prout the impression—'

Number Five laughed aloud.

'You see it's just the same thing with you, Padre,' said M'Turk. 'He is quick to get an impression, ain't he? But you mustn't think we don't love him, 'cause we do. There isn't an ounce of vice about him.'

A double knock fell on the door.

'The Head to see Number Five study in his study at once,' said the voice of Foxy, the school-sergeant.

'Whew!' said the Reverend John. 'It seems to me that there is a great deal of trouble coming for some people.'

'My word! Mr. Prout's gone and told the Head,' said Stalky. 'He's a moral double-ender. Not fair, luggin' the Head into a house-row.'

'I should recommend a copy-book on a—h'm—safe and certain part,' said the Reverend John disinterestedly.

'Huh! He licks across the shoulders, an' it would slam like a beastly barn-door,' said Beetle. 'Goodnight, Padre. We're in for it.'

Once more they stood in the presence of the Head— Belial, Mammon, and Lucifer. But they had to deal with a man more subtle than them all. Mr. Prout had talked to him, heavily and sadly, for half an hour; and the Head had seen all that was hidden from the housemaster.

'You've been bothering Mr. Prout,' he said pensively. 'House-masters aren't here to be bothered by boys more than is necessary. I don't like being bothered by these things. You are bothering me. That is a very serious offence. You see it?'

'Yes, sir.'

'Well, now, I purpose to bother you, on personal and private grounds, because you have broken into my time. You are much too big to lick, so I suppose I shall have to mark my displeasure in some other way. Say, a thousand lines apiece, a week's gating, and a few things of that kind. Much too big to lick, aren't you?'

'Oh no, sir,' said Stalky cheerfully; for a week's gating in the summer term is serious.

'Ve-ry good. Then we will do what we can. I wish you wouldn't bother me.'

It was a fair, sustained, equable stroke, with a little draw to it, but what they felt most was his unfairness in stopping to talk between executions. Thus:

'Among the—lower classes this would lay me open to a charge of—assault. You should be more grateful for your—privileges than you are. There is a limit—one finds it by experience, Beetle—beyond which it is never safe to pursue private vendettas, because—don't move —sooner or later one comes—into collision with the— higher authority, who has studied the animal. "Et ego"—M'Turk, please—"in Arcadia vixi." There's a certain flagrant injustice about this that ought to appeal to—your temperament. And that's all! You will tell your house-master that you have been formally caned by me.'

'My word!' said M'Turk, wriggling his shoulder-blades all down the corridor. 'That was business! The Prooshian Bates has an infernal straight eye.'

'Wasn't it wily of me to ask for the lickin',' said Stalky, 'instead of those impots?'

'Rot! We were in for it from the first. I knew the cock of his old eye,' said Beetle. 'I was within an inch of blubbing.'

'Well, I didn't exactly smile,' Stalky confessed.

'Let's go down to the lavatory and have a look at the damage. One of us can hold the glass and t'others can squint.'

They proceeded on these lines for some ten minutes. The wales were very red and very level. There was not a penny to choose between any of them for thoroughness, efficiency, and a certain clarity of outline that stamps the work of the artist.

'What are you doing down there?' Mr. Prout was

at the head of the lavatory stairs, attracted by the noise of splashing.

'We've only been caned by the Head, sir, and we're washing off the blood. The Head said we were to tell you. We were coming to report ourselves in a minute, sir. (Sotto voce.) That's a score for Heffy!'

'Well, he deserves to score something, poor devil,' said M'Turk, putting on his shirt. 'We've sweated a stone and a half off him since we began.'

'But look here, why aren't we wrathy with the Head? He said it was a flagrant injustice. So it is!' said Beetle.

'Dearr man,' said M'Turk, and vouchsafed no further answer.

It was Stalky who laughed till he had to hold on by the edge of a basin.

'You are a funny ass! What's that for?' said Beetle.

'I'm—I'm thinking of the flagrant injustice of it!'

THE MORAL REFORMERS

(1898)

THERE was no disguising the defeat. The victory was to Prout, but they grudged it not. If he had broken the rules of the game by calling in the Head, they had had a good run for their money.

The Reverend John sought the earliest opportunity of talking things over. Members of a bachelor Common-room, in a school where masters' studies are designedly dotted among studies and form-rooms, can, if they choose, see a great deal of their charges. Number Five had spent some cautious years in testing the Reverend John. He was emphatically a gentleman. He knocked at a study door before entering; he comported himself as a visitor and not a strayed lictor; he never prosed, and he never carried over into official life the confidences of idle hours. Prout was ever an unmitigated nuisance; King came solely as the avenger of blood; even little Hartopp, talking natural history, seldom forgot his office; but the Reverend John was a guest desired and beloved by Number Five.

Behold him, then, in their only armchair, a bent briar between his teeth, chin down in three folds on his clerical collar, and blowing like an amiable whale, while Number Five discoursed of life as it appeared to them, and specially of that last interview with the Head—in the matter of usury.

'One licking once a week would do you an immense amount of good,' he said, twinkling and shaking all over; 'and, as you say, you were entirely in the right.'

'Ra-ather, Padre! We could have proved it if he'd let us talk,' said Stalky; 'but he didn't. The Head's a downy bird.'

'He understands you perfectly. Ho! ho! Well, you worked hard enough for it.'

'But he's awfully fair. He doesn't lick a chap in the morning an' preach at him in the afternoon,' said Beetle.

'He can't; he ain't in Orders, thank goodness,' said M'Turk. Number Five held the very strongest views on clerical head-masters, and were ever ready to meet their pastor in argument.

'Almost all other schools have clerical Heads,' said the Reverend John gently.

'It isn't fair on the chaps,' Stalky replied. 'Makes 'em sulky. Of course it's different with you, sir. You belong to the school—same as we do. I mean ordinary clergymen.'

'Well, I am a most ordinary clergyman; and Mr. Hartopp's in Orders too.'

'Ye—es, but he took 'em after he came to the Coll. We saw him go up for his exam. That's all right,' said Beetle. 'But just think if the Head went and got ordained!'

'What would happen, Beetle?'

'Oh, the Coll. 'ud go to pieces in a year, sir. There's no doubt o' that.'

'How d'you know?' The Reverend John was smiling.

'We've been here nearly six years now. There are

121

precious few things about the Coll. we don't know,' Stalky replied. 'Why, even you came the term after I did, sir. I remember your asking our names in form your first lesson. Mr. King, Mr. Prout, and the Head, of course, are the only masters senior to us—in that way.'

'Yes, we've changed a good deal—in Common-room.'

'Huh!' said Beetle, with a grunt. 'They came here, an' they went away to get married. Jolly good riddance, too!'

'Doesn't our Beetle hold with matrimony?'

'No, Padre; don't make fun of me. I've met chaps in the holidays who've got married house-masters. It's perfectly awful! They have babies and teething and measles and all that sort of thing, right bung in the school; and the masters' wives give tea-parties—tea-parties, Padre!—and ask the chaps to breakfast.'

'That don't matter so much,' said Stalky. 'But the house-masters let their houses alone, and they leave everything to the prefects. Why, in one school, a chap told me, there were big baize doors and a passage about a mile long between the house and the master's house. They could do just what they pleased.'

'Satan rebuking sin with a vengeance.'

'Oh, larks are right enough; but you know what we mean, Padre. After a bit it gets worse an' worse. Then there's a big bust-up and a row that gets into the papers, and a lot of chaps are expelled, you know.'

'Always the wrong uns; don't forget that. Have a cup of cocoa, Padre?' said M'Turk, with the kettle.

'No, thanks; I'm smoking. Always the wrong uns? Proceed, my Stalky.'

'And then'—Stalky warmed to the work—'everybody says, "Who'd ha' thought it? Shockin' boys!

Wicked little kids!" It all comes of havin' married house-masters, I think.'

'A Daniel come to judgment!'

'But it does,' M'Turk interrupted. 'I've met chaps in the holidays, an' they've told me the same thing. It looks awfully pretty for one's people to see—a nice separate house with a nice lady in charge an' all that. But it isn't. It takes the house-masters off their work, and it gives the prefects a heap too much power, an'—an'—it rots up everything. You see it isn't as if we were just an ordinary school. We take crammers' rejections as well as good little boys like Stalky. We've got to do that to make our name, of course, and we get 'em into Sandhurst somehow or other, don't we?'

'True, O Turk. Like a book thou talkest, Turkey.'

'And so we want rather different masters, don't you think so, to other places? We aren't like the rest of the schools.'

'It leads to all sorts of bullyin', too, a chap told me,' said Beetle.

'Well, you do need most of a single man's time, I must say.' The Reverend John considered his hosts critically. 'But do you never feel that the world—the Common-room—is too much with you sometimes?'

'Not exactly—in summer, anyhow.' Stalky's eye roved contentedly to the window. 'Our bounds are pretty big, too, and they leave us to ourselves a good deal.'

'For example, here am I sitting in your study, very much in your way, eh?'

'Indeed you aren't, Padre. Sit down. Don't go, sir. You know we're glad whenever you come.'

There was no doubting the sincerity of the voices.

The Reverend John flushed a little with pleasure and refilled his briar.

'And we generally know where the Common-room are,' said Beetle triumphantly. 'Didn't you come through our lower dormitories last night after ten, sir?'

'I went to smoke a pipe with your house-master. No, I didn't give him any impressions. ⌐I took a short cut through your dormitories.'

'I sniffed a whiff of 'baccy this mornin'. Yours is stronger than Mr. Prout's. I knew,' said Beetle, wagging his head.

'Good heavens!' said the Reverend John absently. It was some years before Beetle perceived that this was rather a tribute to innocence than observation. The long, light, blindless dormitories, devoid of inner doors, were crossed at all hours of the night by masters visiting one another; for bachelors sit up later than married folk. Beetle had never dreamed that there might be a purpose in this steady policing.

'Talking about bullying,' the Reverend John resumed, 'you all caught it pretty hot when you were fags, didn't you?'

'Well, we must have been rather awful little beasts,' said Beetle, looking serenely over the gulf between eleven and sixteen. 'My Hat, what bullies they were then—Fairburn, "Gobby" Maunsell, and all that gang!'

''Member when "Gobby" called us the Three Blind Mice, and we had to get up on the lockers and sing while he buzzed inkpots at us?' said Stalky. 'They were bullies if you like!'

'But there isn't any of it now,' said M'Turk soothingly.

'That's where you make a mistake. We're all inclined to say that everything is all right as long as we ourselves aren't hurt.   I sometimes wonder if it is extinct—bullying,' the Reverend John mused.

'Fags bully each other horrid; but the upper forms are supposed to be swottin' for exams.   They've got something else to think about,' said Beetle.

'Why?   What do you think?'   Stalky was watching the chaplain's face.

'I have my doubts.'   Then, explosively, 'On my word, for three moderately intelligent boys you aren't very observant.   I suppose you were too busy making things warm for your house-master to see what lay under your noses when you were in the form-rooms last week?'

'What, sir?   I—I swear we didn't see anything,' said Beetle.

'Then I'd advise you to look.   When a little chap is whimpering in a corner and wears his clothes like rags, and never does any work, and is notoriously the dirtiest little "corridor-caution" in the Coll., something's wrong somewhere.'

'That's Clewer,' said M'Turk under his breath.

'Yes, Clewer.   He comes to me for his French.   It's his first term, and he's almost as complete a wreck as you were, Beetle.   He's not naturally clever, but he has been hammered till he's nearly an idiot.'

'Oh no.   They sham silly to get off more lickings,' said Beetle.   'I know that.'

'I've never actually seen him knocked about,' said the Reverend John.

'The genuine article don't do that in public,' said Beetle.   'Fairburn never touched me when any one was looking on.'

'You needn't swagger about it, Beetle,' said M' Turk. 'We all caught it in our time.'

125

'But I got it worse than any one,' said Beetle. 'If you want an authority on bullyin', Padre, come to me. Corkscrews—brush-drill—keys—head-knucklin'—arm-twistin'—rockin'—Ag Ags—and all the rest of it.'

'Yes. I do want you as an authority, or rather I want your authority to stop it—all of you.'

'What about Abana and Pharpar, Padre—Harrison and Craye? They are Mr. Prout's pets,' said M'Turk a little bitterly. 'We aren't even sub-prefects.'

'I've considered that, but, on the other hand, since most bullying is mere thoughtlessness—'

'Not one little bit of it, Padre,' said M'Turk. 'Bullies like bullyin'. They mean it. They think it up in lesson and practise it in the quarters.'

'Never mind. If the thing goes up to the prefects it may make another house-row. You've had one already. Don't laugh. Listen to me. I ask you—my own Tenth Legion—to take the thing up quietly. I want little Clewer made fairly clean and decent—'

'Blowed if I wash him!' whispered Stalky.

'Decent and self-respecting. As for the other boy, whoever he is, you can use your influence'—a purely secular light flickered in the chaplain's eye—'in any way you please to—to dissuade him. That's all. I'll leave it to you. Good-night, mes enfants.'

.   .   .   .

'Well, what are we goin' to do?' Number Five stared at each other.

'Young Clewer would give his eyes for a place to be quiet in. I know that,' said Beetle. 'If we made him a study-fag, eh?'

'No!' said M'Turk firmly. 'He's a dirty little brute, and he'd mess up everything. Besides, we ain't goin'

126

to have any beastly Erickin'. D'you want to walk about with your arm round his neck?'

'He'd clean out the jam-pots, anyhow; an' the burnt-porridge saucepan—it's filthy now.'

'Not good enough,' said Stalky, bringing up both heels with a crash on the table. 'If we find the merry jester who's been bullyin' him an' make him happy, that 'll be all right. Why didn't we spot him when we were in the form-rooms, though?'

'Maybe a lot of fags have made a dead set at Clewer. They do that sometimes.'

'Then we'll have to kick the whole of the lower school in our house—on spec. Come on,' said M'Turk.

'Keep your hair on! We mustn't make a fuss about the biznai. Whoever it is, he's kept quiet or we'd have seen him,' said Stalky. 'We'll walk round and sniff about till we're sure.'

They drew the house form-rooms, accounting for every junior and senior against whom they had suspicions—investigated, at Beetle's suggestion, the lavatories and box-rooms, but without result. Everybody seemed to be present save Clewer.

'Rum!' said Stalky, pausing outside a study door. 'Golly!'

A thin piping mixed with tears came muffled through the panels.

'As beautiful Kitty one morning was tripping—'

'Louder, you young devil, or I'll buzz a book at you!'

'With a pitcher of milk—

Oh, Campbell, please don't!

To the fair of—'

A book crashed on something soft, and squeals arose.

'Well, I never thought it was a study-chap, anyhow. That accounts for our not spotting him,' said Beetle. 'Sefton and Campbell are rather hefty chaps to tackle. Besides, one can't go into their study like a form-room.'

'What swine!' M'Turk listened. 'Where's the fun of it? I suppose Clewer's faggin' for them.'

'They aren't prefects. That's one good job,' said Stalky, with his war-grin. 'Sefton and Campbell! Um! Campbell and Sefton! Ah! One of 'em's a crammer's pup.'

The two were precocious hairy youths between seventeen and eighteen, sent to the school in despair by parents who hoped that six months' steady cram might, perhaps, jockey them into Sandhurst. Nominally they were in Mr. Prout's house; actually they were under the Head's eye; and since he was very careful never to promote strange new boys to prefectships, they considered they had a grievance against the school. Sefton had spent three months with a London crammer, and the tale of his adventures there lost nothing in the telling. Campbell, who had a fine taste in clothes and a fluent vocabulary, followed his lead in looking down loftily on the rest of the world. This was only their second term, and the school, used to what it profanely called 'crammers' pups,' had treated them with rather galling reserve. But their whiskers—Sefton owned a real razor—and their moustaches were beyond question impressive.

'Shall we go in an' dissuade 'em?' M'Turk asked. 'I've never had much to do with 'em, but I'll bet my hat Campbell's a funk.'

'No-o! That's "oratio directa,"' said Stalky, shak-

ing his head. 'I like "oratio obliqua." 'Sides, where'd
our moral influence be then? Think o' that!'

'Rot! What are you goin' to do?' Beetle turned into
Lower Number Nine form-room, next door to the study.

'Me?' The lights of war flickered over Stalky's face.
'Oh, I want to jape with 'em. Shut up a bit!'

He drove his hands into his pockets and stared out of
window at the sea, whistling between his teeth. Then
a foot tapped the floor; one shoulder lifted; he wheeled,
and began the short quick double-shuffle—the war-
dance of Stalky in meditation. Thrice he crossed the
empty form-room, with compressed lips and expanded
nostrils, swaying to the quick-step. Then he halted
before the dumb Beetle and softly knuckled his head,
Beetle bowing to the strokes. M'Turk nursed one knee
and rocked to and fro. They could hear Clewer howling as though his heart would break.

'Beetle is the sacrifice,' Stalky said at last. 'I'm
sorry for you, Beetle. 'Member Galton's "Art of
Travel" [one of the forms had been studying that
pleasant work] an' the kid whose bleatin' excited the
tiger?'

'Oh, curse!' said Beetle uneasily. It was not his first
season as a sacrifice. 'Can't you get on without me?'

''Fraid not, Beetle, dear. You've got to be bullied
by Turkey an' me. The more you howl, o' course, the
better it'll be. Turkey, go an' covet a stump and a box-
rope from somewhere. We'll tie him up for a kill—a la
Galton. 'Member when "Molly" Fairburn made us
cock-fight with our shoes off, an' tied up our knees?'

'But that hurt like sin.'

''Course it did. What a clever chap you are, Beetle!
Turkey'll knock you all over the place. 'Member we've

129

had a big row all round, an' I've trapped you into doin' this. Lend us your wipe.'

Beetle was trussed for cock-fighting; but, in addition to the transverse stump between elbow and knee, his knees were bound with a box-rope. In this posture, at a push from Stalky he rolled over sideways, covering himself with dust.

'Ruffle his hair, Turkey. Now you get down, too. "The bleatin' of the kid excites the tiger." You two are in such a sweatin' wax with me that you only curse. 'Member that. I'll tickle you up with a stump. You'll have to blub, Beetle.'

'Right O! I'll work up to it in half a shake,' said Beetle.

'Now begin—and remember the bleatin' o' the kid.'

'Shut up, you brutes! Let me up! You've nearly cut my knees off. Oh, you are beastly cads! Do shut up. 'Tisn't a joke!' Beetle's protest was, in tone, a work of art.

'Give it to him, Turkey! Kick him! Roll him over! Kill him! Don't funk, Beetle, you brute. Kick him again, Turkey.'

'He's not blubbin' really. Roll up, Beetle, or I'll kick you into the fender,' roared M'Turk.

They made a hideous noise among them, and the bait allured their quarry.

'Hullo! What's the giddy jest?' Sefton and Campbell entered to find Beetle on his side, his head against the fender, weeping copiously, while M'Turk prodded him in the back with his toes.

'It's only Beetle,' Stalky explained. 'He's shammin' hurt, I can't get Turkey to go for him properly.'

Sefton promptly kicked both boys, and his face

lighted. 'All right, I'll attend to 'em. Get up an' cock-fight, you two. Give me the stump. I'll tickle 'em. Here's a giddy jest! Come on, Campbell. Let's cook 'em.'

Then M'Turk turned on Stalky and called him very evil names.

'You said you were goin' to cock-fight too, Stalky. Come on!'

'More ass you for believin' me, then!' shrieked Stalky.

'Have you chaps had a row?' said Campbell.

'Row?' said Stalky. 'Huh! I'm only educatin' them. D'you know anythin' about cock-fighting, Seffy?'

'Do I know? Why, at Maclagan's, where I was crammin' in town, we used to cock-fight in his drawing-room, and little Maclagan daren't say anything. But we were just the same as men there, of course. Do I know? I'll show you.'

'Can't I get up?' moaned Beetle, as Stalky sat on his shoulder.

'Don't jaw, you fat piffler. You're going to fight Seffy.'

'He'll slay me!'

'Oh, lug 'em into our study,' said Campbell. 'It's nice an' quiet in there. I'll cock-fight Turkey. This is an improvement on young Clewer.'

'Right O! I move it's shoes-off for them an' shoes-on for us,' said Sefton joyously, and the two were flung down on the study floor. Stalky rolled them behind an armchair.

'Now I'll tie you two up an' direct the bull-fight. Golly, what wrists you have, Seffy. They're too thick for a wipe. Got a box-rope?' said he.

'Lots in the corner,' Sefton replied. 'Hurry up! Stop blubbin', you brute, Beetle. We're goin' to have a giddy campaign. Losers have to sing for the winners —sing odes in honour of the conqueror. You call yourself a beastly poet, don't you, Beetle? I'll poet you.' He wriggled into position by Campbell's side.

Swiftly and scientifically the stumps were thrust through the natural crooks, and the wrists tied with well-stretched box-ropes to an accompaniment of insults from M'Turk, bound, betrayed, and voluble behind the chair.

Stalky set away Campbell and Sefton, and strode over to his allies, locking the door on the way.

'And that's all right,' said he in a changed voice.

'What the devil—?' Sefton began. Beetle's false tears had ceased; M'Turk, smiling, was on his feet. Together they bound the knees and ankles of the enemy even more straitly.

Stalky took the armchair and contemplated the scene with his blandest smile. The man trussed for cock-fighting is, perhaps, the most helpless thing in the world.

'The bleatin' of the kid excites the tiger. Oh, you frabjous asses!' He lay back and laughed till he could no more. The victims took in the situation but slowly.

'We'll give you the finest lickin' you ever had in your young lives when we get up!' thundered Sefton from the floor. 'You'll laugh the other side of your mouth before you've done. What the deuce d'you mean by this?'

'You'll see in two shakes,' said M'Turk. 'Don't swear like that. What we want to know is, why you two hulkin' swine have been bullyin' Clewer?'

'It's none of your business.'

'What did you bully Clewer for?' The question was repeated with maddening iteration by each in turn. They knew their work.

132

'Because we jolly well chose,' was the answer at last. 'Let's get up.' Even then they could not realise the game.

'Well, now we're goin' to bully you because we jolly well choose. We're goin' to be just as fair to you as you were to Clewer. He couldn't do anything against you. You can't do anything to us. Odd, ain't it?'

'Can't we? You wait an' see.'

'Ah,' said Beetle reflectively, 'that shows you've never been properly jested with. A public lickin' ain't in it with a gentle jape. Bet a bob you'll weep an' promise anything.'

'Look here, young Beetle, we'll half kill you when we get up. I'll promise you that, at any rate.'

'You're going to be half killed first, though. Did you give Clewer Head-knuckles?'

'Did you give Clewer Head-knuckles?' M'Turk echoed. At the twentieth repetition—no boy can stand the torture of one unvarying query, which is the essence of bullying—came confession.

'We did, confound you!'

'Then you'll be knuckled'; and knuckled they were, according to ancient experience. Head-knuckling is no trifle; 'Molly' Fairburn of the old days could not have done better.

'Did you give Clewer Brush-drill?'

This time the question was answered sooner, and Brush-drill was dealt out for the space of five minutes by Stalky's watch. They could not even writhe in their bonds. No brush is employed in Brush-drill.

'Did you give Clewer the Key?'

'No; we didn't. I swear we didn't!' from Campbell, rolling in agony.

133

'Then we'll give it to you, so you can see what it would be like if you had.'

The torture of the Key—which has no key at all—hurts excessively. They endured several minutes of it, and their language necessitated the gag.

'Did you give Clewer Corkscrews?'

'Yes. Oh, curse your silly souls! Let us alone, you cads.'

They were corkscrewed, and the torture of the Corkscrew—this has nothing to do with corkscrews—is keener than the torture of the Key.

The method and silence of the attacks was breaking their nerves. Between each new torture came the pitiless, dazing rain of questions, and when they did not answer to the point, Isabella-coloured handkerchiefs were thrust into their mouths.

'Now are those all the things you did to Clewer? Take out the gag, Turkey, and let 'em answer.'

'Yes, I swear that was all. Oh, you're killing us, Stalky!' cried Campbell.

'Pre-cisely what Clewer said to you. I heard him. Now we're goin' to show you what real bullyin' is. What I don't like about you, Sefton, is, you come to the Coll. with your stick-up collars an' patent-leather boots, an' you think you can teach us something about bullying. Do you think you can teach us anything about bullying? Take out the gag and let him answer.'

'No!'—ferociously.

'He says no. Rock him to sleep. Campbell can watch.'

It needs three boys and two boxing-gloves to rock a boy to sleep. Again the operation has nothing to do with its name. Sefton was 'rocked' till his eyes set in

his head and he gasped and crowed for breath, sick and
dizzy.

'My Aunt!' said Campbell, appalled, from his corner,
and turned white.

'Put him away,' said Stalky. 'Bring on Campbell.
Now this is bullyin'. Oh, I forgot! I say, Campbell,
what did you bully Clewer for? Take out his gag and
let him answer.'

'I—I don't know. Oh, let me off! I swear I'll make
it pax. Don't "rock" me!'

' "The bleatin' of the kid excites the tiger." He says
he don't know. Set him up, Beetle. Give me the
glove an' put in the gag.'

In silence Campbell was 'rocked' sixty-four times.

'I believe I'm goin' to die!' he gasped.

'He says he is goin' to die. Put him away. Now,
Sefton! Oh, I forgot! Sefton, what did you bully
Clewer for?'

The answer is unprintable; but it brought not the
faintest flush to Stalky's downy cheek.

'Make him an Ag Ag, Turkey!'

And an Ag Ag was he made, forthwith. The hard-
bought experience of nearly eighteen years was at his
disposal, but he did not seem to appreciate it.

'He says we are sweeps. Put him away! Now,
Campbell! Oh, I forgot! I say, Campbell, what did
you bully Clewer for?'

Then came the tears—scalding tears; appeals for
mercy and abject promises of peace. Let them cease
the tortures and Campbell would never lift hand against
them. The questions began again—to an accompaniment of keen persuasions.

'You seem hurt, Campbell. Are you hurt?'

'Yes. Awfully!'

'He says he is hurt. Are you broke?'

'Yes, yes! I swear I am. Oh, stop!'

'He says he is broke. Are you humble?'

'Yes!'

'He says he is humble. Are you devilish humble?'

'Yes!'

'He says he is devilish humble. Will you bully Clewer any more?'

'No. No—ooh!'

'He says he won't bully Clewer. Or any one else?'

'No. I swear I won't!'

'Or any one else. What about that lickin' you and Sefton were goin' to give us?'

'I won't! I won't! I swear I won't!'

'He says he won't lick us. Do you esteem yourself to know anything about bullyin'?'

'No, I don't!'

'He says he doesn't know anything about bullyin'. Haven't we taught you a lot?'

'Yes—yes!'

'He says we've taught him a lot. Aren't you grateful?'

'Yes!'

'He says he is grateful. Put him away. Oh, I forgot! I say, Campbell, what did you bully Clewer for?'

He wept anew; his nerves being raw. 'Because I was a bully. I suppose that's what you want me to say?'

'He says he is a bully. Right he is. Put him in the corner. No more japes for Campbell. Now, Sefton!'

'You devils! You young devils!' This and much more as Sefton was punted across the carpet by skilful knees.

' "The bleatin' of the kid excites the tiger." We're

goin' to make you beautiful. Where does he keep his shaving-things? [Campbell told.] Beetle, get some water. Turkey, make the lather. We're goin' to shave you, Seffy, so you'd better lie jolly still, or you'll get cut. I've never shaved any one before.'

'Don't! Oh, don't! Please don't!'

'Gettin' polite, eh? I'm only goin' to take off one ducky little whisker—'

'I'll—I'll make it pax, if you don't. I swear I'll let you off your lickin' when I get up!'

'And half that moustache we're so proud of. He says he'll let us off our lickin'. Isn't he kind?'

M'Turk laughed into the nickel-plated shaving-cup, and settled Sefton's head between Stalky's vice-like knees.

'Hold on a shake,' said Beetle, 'you can't shave long hairs. You've got to cut all that moustache short first, an' then scrope him.'

'Well, I'm not goin' to hunt about for scissors. Won't a match do? Chuck us the match-box. He is a hog, you know; we might as well singe him. Lie still!'

He lit a vesta, but checked his hand. 'I only want to take off half, though.'

'That's all right.' Beetle waved the brush. 'I'll lather up to the middle—see? and you can burn off the rest.'

The thin-haired first moustache of youth fluffed off in flame to the lather-line in the centre of the lip, and Stalky rubbed away the burnt stumpage with his thumb. It was not a very gentle shave, but it abundantly accomplished its purpose.

'Now the whisker on the other side. Turn him over!' Between match and razor this, too, was removed. 'Give him his shaving-glass. Take the gag out. I want to hear what he'll say.'

But there were no words. Sefton gazed at the lop-sided wreck in horror and despair. Two fat tears rolled down his cheek.

'Oh, I forgot! I say, Sefton, what did you bully Clewer for?'

'Leave me alone! Oh, you infernal bullies, leave me alone! Haven't I had enough!'

'He says we must leave him alone,' said M'Turk.

'He says we are bullies, an' we haven't even begun yet,' said Beetle. 'You're ungrateful, Seffy. Golly! You do look an atrocity and a half!'

'He says he has had enough,' said Stalky. 'He errs!'

'Well, to work, to work!' chanted M'Turk, waving a stump. 'Come on, my giddy Narcissus. Don't fall in love with your own reflection!'

'Oh, let him off,' said Campbell from his corner; 'he's blubbing, too.'

Sefton cried like a twelve-year-old with pain, shame, wounded vanity, and utter helplessness.

'You'll make it pax, Sefton, won't you? You can't stand up to those young devils—'

'Don't be rude, Campbell, de-ah,' said M'Turk, 'or you'll catch it again!'

'You are devils, you know,' said Campbell.

'What? for a little bullyin'—same as you've been givin' Clewer! How long have you been jestin' with him?' said Stalky. 'All this term?'

'We didn't always knock him about, though!'

'You did when you could catch him,' said Beetle, cross-legged on the floor, dropping a stump from time to time across Sefton's instep. 'Don't I know it!'

'I—perhaps we did.'

'And you went out of your way to catch him? Don't I know it! Because he was an awful little beast, eh? Don't I know it! Now, you see you're awful beasts, and you're gettin' what he got—for bein' a beast. Just because we choose.'

'We never really bullied him—like you've done us.'

'Yah!' said Beetle. 'They never really bully—"Molly" Fairburn didn't. Only knock 'em about a little bit. That's what they say. Only kick their souls out of 'em, and they go and blub in the box-rooms. Shove their heads into the ulsters an' blub. Write home three times a day—yes, you brute, I've done that —askin' to be taken away. You've never been bullied properly, Campbell. I'm sorry you made pax.'

'I'm not!' said Campbell, who was a humorist in a way. 'Look out, you're slaying Sefton!'

In his excitement Beetle had used the stump unreflectingly, and Sefton was now shouting for mercy.

'An' you!' he cried, wheeling where he sat. 'You've never been bullied, either. Where were you before you came here?'

'I—I had a tutor.'

'Yah! You would. You never blubbed in your life. But you're blubbin' now, by gum. Aren't you blubbin'?'

'Can't you see, you blind beast?' Sefton fell over sideways, tear-tracks furrowing the dried lather. Crack came the cricket-stump on the curved latter-end of him.

'Blind am I,' said Beetle, 'and a beast? Shut up, Stalky. I'm goin' to jape a bit with our friend, a la "Molly" Fairburn. I think I can see. Can't I see, Sefton?'

'The point is well taken,' said M'Turk, watching the stump at work. 'You'd better say that he sees, Seffy.'

'You do—you can! I swear you do!' yelled Sefton, for strong arguments were coercing him.

'Aren't my eyes lovely?' The stump rose and fell steadily throughout this catechism.

'Yes.'

'A gentle hazel, aren't they?'

'Yes—oh yes!'

'What a liar you are! They're sky-blue. Ain't they sky-blue?'

'Yes—oh yes!'

'You don't know your mind from one minute to another. You must learn—you must learn.'

'What a bait you're in!' said Stalky. 'Keep your hair on, Beetle.'

'I've had it done to me,' said Beetle. 'Now—about my being a beast.'

'Pax—oh, pax!' cried Sefton; 'make it pax. I'll give up! Let me off! I'm broke! I can't stand it!'

'Ugh! Just when we were gettin' our hand in!' grunted M'Turk. 'They didn't let Clewer off, I'll swear.'

'Confess—apologise—quick!' said Stalky.

From the floor Sefton made unconditional surrender, more abjectly even than Campbell. He would never touch any one again. He would go softly all the days of his life.

'We've got to take it, I suppose?' said Stalky. 'All right, Sefton. You're broke? Very good. Shut up, Beetle! But before we let you up, you an' Campbell will kindly oblige us with "Kitty of Coleraine"—a la Clewer.'

'That's not fair,' said Campbell; 'we've surrendered.'

''Course you have. Now you're goin' to do what we tell you—same as Clewer would. If you hadn't surrendered you'd ha' been really bullied. Havin' surrendered—do you follow, Seffy?—you sing odes in honour of the conquerors. Hurry up!'

They dropped into chairs luxuriously. Campbell and Sefton looked at each other, and, neither taking comfort from that view, struck up 'Kitty of Coleraine.'

'Vile bad,' said Stalky, as the miserable wailing ended. 'If you hadn't surrendered it would have been our painful duty to buzz books at you for singin' out o' tune. Now then.'

He freed them from their bonds, but for several minutes they could not rise. Campbell was first on his feet, smiling uneasily. Sefton staggered to the table, buried his head in his arms, and shook with sobs. There was no shadow of fight in either—only amazement, distress, and shame.

'Ca—can't he shave clean before tea, please?' said Campbell. 'It's ten minutes to bell.'

Stalky shook his head. He meant to escort the half-shaved one to that meal.

M'Turk yawned in his chair and Beetle mopped his face. They were all dripping with excitement and exertion.

'If I knew anything about it, I swear I'd give you a moral lecture,' said Stalky severely.

'Don't jaw; they've surrendered,' said M'Turk. 'This moral suasion biznai takes it out of a chap.'

'Don't you see how gentle we've been? We might have called Clewer in to look at you,' said Stalky. 'The bleatin' of the tiger excites the kid. But we didn't.

We've only got to tell a few chaps in Coll. about this
and you'd be hooted all over the shop. Your life
wouldn.'t be worth havin'. But we aren't goin' to do
that, either. We're strictly moral suasers, Campbell;
so, unless you or Seffy split about this, no one will.'

'I swear you're a brick,' said Campbell. 'I suppose
I was rather a brute to Clewer.'

'It looked like it,' said Stalky. 'But I don't think
Seffy need come into hall with cock-eye whiskers. Hor-
rid bad for the fags if they saw him. He can shave.
Ain't you grateful, Sefton?'

The head did not lift. Sefton was deeply asleep.

'That's rummy,' said M'Turk, as a snore mixed with
a sob. ''Cheek, I think; or else he's shammin'.'

'No, 'tisn't,' said Beetle. 'When "Molly" Fairburn
had attended to me for an hour or so I used to go bung
off to sleep on a form sometimes. Poor devil! But he
called me a beastly poet, though.'

'Well, come on.' Stalky lowered his voice. 'Good-
bye, Campbell. 'Member, if you don't talk, nobody
will.'

There should have been a war-dance, but that all
three were so utterly tired that they almost went to
sleep above the tea-cups in their study, and slept till
prep.

.   .   .   .

'A most extraordinary letter. Are all parents in-
curably mad? What do you make of it?' said the
Head, handing a closely-written eight pages to the
Reverend John.

' "The only son of his mother, and she a widow."
That is the least reasonable sort.' The chaplain read
with pursed lips.

142

'If half those charges are true he should be in the sick-house; whereas he is disgustingly well. Certainly he has shaved. I noticed that.'

'Under compulsion, as his mother points out. How delicious! How salutary!'

'You haven't to answer her. It isn't often I don't know what has happened in the school; but this is beyond me.'

'If you asked me I should say seek not to propitiate. When one is forced to take crammers' pups—'

'He was perfectly well at extra-tuition—with me—this morning,' said the Head absently. 'Unusually well-behaved, too.'

'—they either educate the school, or the school, as in this case, educates them. I prefer our own methods,' the chaplain concluded.

'You think it was that?' A lift of the Head's eyebrow.

'I'm sure of it! And nothing excuses his trying to give the College a bad name.'

'That's the line I mean to take with him,' the Head answered.

The Augurs winked.

.   .   .   .

A few days later the Reverend John called on Number Five. 'Why haven't we seen you before, Padre?' said they.

'I've been watching times and seasons and events and men—and boys,' he replied. 'I am pleased with my Tenth Legion. I make them my compliments. Clewer was throwing ink-balls in form this morning, instead of doing his work. He is now doing fifty lines for—unheard-of audacity.'

143

'You can't blame us, sir,' said Beetle. 'You told us to remove the—er—pressure. That's the worst of a fag.'

'I've known boys five years his senior throw ink-balls, Beetle. To such an one have I given two hundred lines —not so long ago. And now I come to think of it, were those lines ever shown up?'

'Were they, Turkey?' said Beetle unblushingly.

'Don't you think Clewer looks a little cleaner, Padre?' Stalky interrupted.

'We're no end of moral reformers,' said M'Turk.

'It was all Stalky, but it was a lark,' said Beetle.

'I have noticed the moral reform in several quarters. Didn't I tell you you had more influence than any boys in the Coll. if you cared to use it?'

'It's a trifle exhaustin' to use frequent—our kind of moral suasion. Besides, you see, it only makes Clewer cheeky.'

'I wasn't thinking of Clewer; I was thinking of—the other people, Stalky.'

'Oh, we didn't bother much about the other people,' said M'Turk. 'Did we?'

'But I did—from the beginning.'

'Then you knew, sir?'

A downward puff of smoke.

'Boys educate each other, they say, more than we can or dare. If I had used one half of the moral suasion you may or may not have employed—'

'With the best motives in the world. Don't forget our pious motives, Padre,' said M'Turk.

'I suppose I should be now languishing in Bideford jail, shouldn't I? Well, to quote the Head, in a little business which we have agreed to forget, that strikes me

144

as flagrant injustice. . . . What are you laughing at, you young sinners? Isn't it true? I will not stay to be shouted at. What I looked into this den of iniquity for was to find out if any one cared to come down for a bathe off the Ridge. But I see you won't.'

'Won't we, though! Half a shake, Padre sahib, till we get our towels, and nous sommes avec vous!'

A LITTLE PREP.

(1898)

' "Qui procul hinc"—the legend's writ,
The frontier grave is far away;
"Qui ante diem periit,
Sed miles, sed pro patria."'

Newbolt.

THE Easter term was but a month old when Stettson major, a day-boy, contracted diphtheria, and the Head was very angry. He decreed a new and narrower set of bounds—the infection had been traced to an outlying farm-house—urged the prefects severely to lick all trespassers, and promised extra attentions from his own hand. There were no words bad enough for Stettson major, quarantined at his mother's house, who had lowered the school-average of health. This he said in the gymnasium after prayers. Then he wrote some two hundred letters to as many anxious parents and guardians, and bade the school carry on. The trouble did not spread, but, one night, a dog-cart drove to the Head's door, and in the morning the Head had gone, leaving all things in charge of Mr. King, senior house-master. The Head often ran up to town, where the school devoutly believed he bribed officials for early proofs of the Army Examination papers; but this absence was unusually prolonged.

'Downy old bird!' said Stalky to the allies, one wet afternoon, in the study. 'He must have gone on a bend an' been locked up, under a false name.'

'What for?' Beetle entered joyously into the libel.

'Forty shillin's or a month for hackin' the chucker-out of the Pavvy on the shins. Bates always has a spree when he goes to town. 'Wish he was back, though. I'm about sick o' King's "whips an' scorpions" an' lectures on public-school spirit—yah!—and scholar-ship!'

' "Crass an' materialised brutality of the middle-classes—readin' solely for marks. Not a scholar in the whole school." ' M'Turk quoted, pensively boring holes in the mantelpiece with a hot poker.

'That's rather a sickly way of spending an afternoon. 'Stinks, too. Let's come out an' smoke. Here's a treat.' Stalky held up a long Indian cheroot. ' 'Bagged it from my pater last holidays. I'm a bit shy of it, though; it's heftier than a pipe. We'll smoke it palaver-fashion. Hand it round, eh? Let's lie up behind the old harrow on the Monkey-farm Road.'

'Out of bounds. Bounds beastly strict these days, too. Besides, we shall cat.' Beetle sniffed the cheroot critically. 'It's a regular Pomposo Stinkadore.'

'You can. I shan't. What d'you say, Turkey?'

'Oh, may's well, I s'pose.'

'Chuck on your cap, then. It's two to one, Beetle. Hout you come!'

They saw a group of boys by the notice-board in the corridor; little Foxy, the school-sergeant, among them.

'More bounds, I expect,' said Stalky. 'Hullo, Foxibus, who are you in mournin' for?' There was a broad band of crape round Foxy's arm.

'He was in my old regiment,' said Foxy, jerking his head towards the notices, where a newspaper cutting was thumb-tacked between call-over lists.

'By gum!' quoth Stalky, uncovering as he read. 'It's old Duncan—Fat-Sow Duncan—killed on duty at something or other Kotal. "Rallyin' his men with conspicuous gallantry." He would, of course. "The body was recovered." That's all right. They cut 'em up sometimes, don't they, Foxy?'

'Horrid,' said the Sergeant briefly.

'Poor old Fat-Sow! I was a fag when he left. How many does that make to us, Foxy?'

'Mr. Duncan, he is the ninth. He came here when he was no bigger than little Grey tertius. My old regiment, too. Yiss, nine to us, Mr. Corkran, up to date.'

The boys went out into the wet, walking swiftly.

''Wonder how it feels—to be shot and all that,' said Stalky, as they splashed down a lane. 'Where did it happen, Beetle?'

'Oh, out in India somewhere. We're always rowin' there. But look here, Stalky, what is the good o' sittin' under a hedge an' cattin'? It's be-eastly cold. It's be-eastly wet, and we'll be collared as sure as a gun.'

'Shut up! Did you ever know your Uncle Stalky get you into a mess yet?' Like many other leaders, Stalky did not dwell on past defeats.

They pushed through a dripping hedge, landed among water-logged clods, and sat down on a rust-coated harrow. The cheroot burned with sputterings of saltpetre. They smoked it gingerly, each passing to the other between closed forefinger and thumb.

'Good job we hadn't one apiece, ain't it?' said Stalky, shivering through set teeth. To prove his words he immediately laid all before them, and they followed his example. . . .

'I told you,' moaned Beetle, sweating clammy drops. 'Oh, Stalky, you are a fool!'

'Je cat, tu cat, il cat. Nous cattons!' M'Turk handed up his contribution and lay hopelessly on the cold iron.

'Something's wrong with the beastly thing. I say, Beetle, have you been droppin' ink on it?'

But Beetle was in no case to answer. Limp and empty, they sprawled across the harrow, the rust marking their ulsters in red squares and the abandoned cheroot-end reeking under their very cold noses. Then —they had heard nothing—the Head himself stood before them—the Head who should have been in town bribing examiners—the Head fantastically attired in old tweeds and a deerstalker!

'Ah,' he said, fingering his moustache. 'Very good. I might have guessed who it was. You will go back to the College and give my compliments to Mr. King and ask him to give you an extra-special licking. You will then do me five hundred lines. I shall be back to-morrow. Five hundred lines by five o-clock to-morrow. You are also gated for a week. This is not exactly the time for breaking bounds. Extra-special, please.'

He disappeared over the hedge as lightly as he had come. There was a murmur of women's voices in the deep lane.

'Oh, you Prooshian brute!' said M'Turk as the voices died away. 'Stalky, it's all your silly fault.'

'Kill him! Kill him!' gasped Beetle.

'I ca-an't. I'm going to cat again . . . I don't

mind that, but King 'll gloat over us horrid. Extra-special, o-oh!'

Stalky made no answer—not even a soft one. They went to College and received that for which they had been sent. King enjoyed himself most thoroughly, for by virtue of their seniority the boys were exempt from his hand, save under special order. Luckily, he was no expert in the gentle art.

' "Strange, how desire doth outrun performance,"' said Beetle irreverently, quoting from some Shakespeare play that they were cramming that term. They regained their study and settled down to the imposition.

'You're quite right, Beetle.' Stalky spoke in silky and propitiating tones. 'Now if the Head had sent us to a prefect, we'd have got something to remember!'

'Look here,' M'Turk began with cold venom, 'we aren't going to row you about this business, because it's too bad for a row; but we want you to understand you're jolly well excommunicated, Stalky. You're a plain ass.'

'How was I to know that the Head 'ud collar us? What was he doin' in those ghastly clothes, too?'

'Don't try to raise a side-issue,' Beetle grunted severely.

'Well, it was all Stettson major's fault. If he hadn't gone an' got diphtheria 'twouldn't have happened. But don't you think it rather rummy—the Head droppin' on us that way?'

'Shut up! You're dead!' said Beetle. 'We've chopped your spurs off your beastly heels. We've cocked your shield upside down, and—and I don't think you ought to be allowed to brew for a month.'

'Oh, stop jawin' at me. I want—'

'Stop? Why—why, we're gated for a week.' M'Turk

almost howled as the agony of the situation overcame him. 'A lickin' from King, five hundred lines, and a gating. D'you expect us to kiss you, Stalky, you beast?'

'Drop rottin' for a minute. I want to find out about the Head bein' where he was.'

'Well, you have. You found him quite well and fit. 'Found him making love to Stettson major's mother. That was her in the lane—I heard her. And so we were ordered a licking before a day-boy's mother. Bony old widow, too,' said M'Turk. 'Anything else you'd like to find out?'

'I don't care. I swear I'll get even with him some day,' Stalky growled.

''Looks like it,' said M'Turk. 'Extra-special, week's gatin' and five hundred . . . and now you're goin' to row about it! 'Help scrag him, Beetle!' Stalky had thrown his Virgil at them.

The Head returned next day without explanation, to find the lines waiting for him and the school a little relaxed under Mr. King's viceroyalty. Mr. King had been talking at and round and over the boys' heads, in a lofty and promiscuous style, of public-school spirit and the traditions of ancient seats; for he always improved an occasion. Beyond waking in two hundred and fifty young hearts a lively hatred of all other foundations, he accomplished little—so little, indeed, that when, two days after the Head's return, he chanced to come across Stalky & Co., gated but ever resourceful, playing marbles in the corridor, he said that he was not surprised—not in the least surprised. This was what he had expected from persons of their morale.

'But there isn't any rule against marbles, sir. Very

interestin' game,' said Beetle, his knees white with chalk and dust. Then he received two hundred lines for insolence, besides an order to go to the nearest prefect for judgment and slaughter.

This is what happened behind the closed doors of Flint's study, and Flint was then Head of the Games:—

'Oh, I say, Flint. King has sent me to you for playin' marbles in the corridor an' shoutin' "alley tor" an' "knuckle down."'

'What does he suppose I have to do with that?' was the answer.

'Dunno. Well?' Beetle grinned wickedly. 'What am I to tell him?   He's rather wrathy about it.'

'If the Head chooses to put a notice in the corridor forbiddin' marbles, I can do something; but I can't move on a house-master's report.   He knows that as well as I do.'

The sense of this oracle Beetle conveyed, all unsweetened, to King, who hastened to interview Flint.

Now Flint had been seven and a half years at the College, counting six months with a London crammer, from whose roof he had returned, homesick, to the Head for the final Army polish.   There were four or five other seniors who had gone through much the same mill, not to mention boys, rejected by other establishments on account of a certain overwhelmingness, whom the Head had wrought into very fair shape.   It was not a Sixth to be handled without gloves, as King found.

'Am I to understand it is your intention to allow Board-school games under your study windows, Flint? If so, I can only say—'   He said much, and Flint listened politely.

'Well, sir, if the Head sees fit to call a prefects' meeting we are bound to take the matter up.   But the tradition of the school is that the prefects can't move in any matter affecting the whole school without the Head's direct order.'

Much more was then delivered; both sides a little losing their temper.

After tea, at an informal gathering of prefects in his study, Flint related the adventure.

'He's been playin' for this for a week, and now he's got it. You know as well as I do that if he hadn't been gassing at us the way he has, that young devil Beetle wouldn't have dreamed of marbles.'

'We know that,' said Perowne, 'but that isn't the question. On Flint's showin' King has called the prefects names enough to justify a first-class row. Crammers' rejections, ill-regulated hobbledehoys, wasn't it? Now it's impossible for prefects—'

'Rot,' said Flint. 'King's the best classical cram we've got; and 'tisn't fair to bother the Head with a row. He's up to his eyes with extra-tu. and Army work as it is. Besides, as I told King, we aren't a public school. We're a limited liability company payin' four per cent. My father's a shareholder, too.'

'What's that got to do with it?' said Venner, a red-headed boy of nineteen.

'Well, seems to me that we should be interferin' with ourselves. We've got to get into the Army or—get out, haven't we? King's hired by the Council to teach us. All the rest's flumdiddle. Can't you see?'

It might have been because he felt the air was a little thunderous that the Head took his after-dinner cheroot to Flint's study; but he so often began an evening in a prefect's room that nobody suspected when he drifted in politely, after the knocks that etiquette demanded.

153

'Prefects' meeting?' A cock of one wise eyebrow.

'Not exactly, sir; we're just talking things over. Won't you take the easy chair?'

'Thanks. Luxurious infants, you are.' He dropped into Flint's big half-couch and puffed for a while in silence. 'Well, since you're all here, I may confess that I'm the mute with the bowstring.'

The young faces grew serious. The phrase meant that certain of their number would be withdrawn from all further games for extra-tuition. It might also mean future success at Sandhurst; but it was present ruin for the First Fifteen.

'Yes, I've come for my pound of flesh. I ought to have had you out before the Exeter match; but it's our sacred duty to beat Exeter.'

'Isn't the Old Boys' match sacred too, sir?' said Perowne. The Old Boys' match was the event of the Easter term.

'We'll hope they aren't in training. Now for the list. First I want Flint. It's the Euclid that does it. You must work deductions with me. Perowne, extra mechanical drawing. Dawson goes to Mr. King for extra Latin, and Venner to me for German. Have I damaged the First Fifteen much?' He smiled sweetly.

'Ruined it, I'm afraid, sir,' said Flint. 'Can't you let us off till the end of the term?'

'Impossible. It will be a tight squeeze for Sandhurst this year.'

'And all to be cut up by those vile Afghans, too,' said Dawson. ''Wouldn't think there'd be so much competition, would you?'

'Oh, that reminds me. Crandall is coming down with the Old Boys—I've asked twenty of them, but we

shan't get more than a weak team. I don't know
whether he'll be much use, though. He was rather
knocked about, recovering poor old Duncan's body.'

'Crandall major—the Gunner?' Perowne asked.

'No, the minor—"Toffee" Crandall—in a Native
Infantry regiment. He was almost before your time,
Perowne.'

'The papers didn't say anything about him. We
read about Fat-Sow, of course. What's Crandall done,
sir?'

'I've brought over an Indian paper that his mother
sent me. It was rather a—hefty, I think you say—
piece of work. Shall I read it?'

The Head knew how to read. When he had finished
the quarter-column of small type everybody thanked
him politely.

'Good for the old Coll.!' said Perowne. 'Pity he
wasn't in time to save Fat-Sow, though. That's nine
to us, isn't it, in the last three years?'

'Yes . . . And I took old Duncan off all games
for extra-tu. five years ago this term,' said the Head.
'By the way, who do you hand over the Games to,
Flint?'

'Haven't thought yet. Who'd you recommend, sir?'

'No, thank you. I've heard it casually hinted behind
my back that the Prooshian Bates is a downy bird, but
he isn't going to make himself responsible for a new
Head of the Games. Settle it among yourselves. Good-
night.'

'And that's the man,' said Flint, when the door shut,
'that you want to bother with a dame's-school row!'

'I was only pullin' your fat leg,' Perowne returned
hastily. 'You're so easy to draw, Flint.'

'Well, never mind that. The Head's knocked the First Fifteen to bits, and we've got to pick up the pieces, or the Old Boys will have a walk-over. Let's promote all the Second Fifteen and make Big Side play up. There's heaps of talent somewhere that we can polish up between now and the match.'

The case was represented so urgently to the school that even Stalky and M'Turk, who affected to despise football, played one Big-Side game seriously. They were forthwith promoted ere their ardour had time to cool, and the dignity of their Caps demanded that they should keep some show of virtue. The match-team was worked at least four days out of seven, and the school saw hope ahead.

With the last week of the term the Old Boys began to arrive, and their welcome was nicely proportioned to their worth. Gentlemen cadets from Sandhurst and Woolwich, who had only left a year ago, but who carried enormous side, were greeted with a cheerful 'Hullo! What's the Shop like?' from those who had shared their studies. Militia subalterns had more consideration, but it was understood they were not precisely of the true metal. Recreants who, failing for the Army, had gone into business or banks were received for old sake's sake, but in no way made too much of. But when the real subalterns, officers and gentlemen full-blown—who had been to the ends of the earth and back again and so carried no side—came on the scene strolling about with the Head, the school divided right and left in admiring silence. And when one laid hands on Flint, even upon the Head of the Games, crying, 'Good Heavens! What do you mean by growing in this way? You were a beastly little fag when I left,' visible halos encircled

156

Flint. They would walk to and fro in the corridor with the little red school-sergeant, telling news of old regiments; they would burst into form-rooms sniffing the well-remembered smells of ink and whitewash; they would find nephews and cousins in the lower forms and present them with enormous wealth; or they would invade the gymnasium and make Foxy show off the new stock on the bars.

Chiefly, though, they talked with the Head, who was father-confessor and agent-general to them all; for what they shouted in their unthinking youth, they proved in their thoughtless manhood—to wit, that the Prooshian Bates was 'a downy bird.' Young blood who had stumbled into an entanglement with a pastry-cook's daughter at Plymouth; experience who had come into a small legacy but mistrusted lawyers; ambition halting at cross-roads, anxious to take the one that would lead him farthest; extravagance pursued by the money-lender; arrogance in the thick of a regimental row—each carried his trouble to the Head; and Chiron showed him, in language quite unfit for little boys, a quiet and safe way round, out, or under. So they overflowed his house, smoked his cigars, and drank his health as they had drunk it all the earth over when two or three of the old school had forgathered.

'Don't stop smoking for a minute,' said the Head. 'The more you're out of training the better for us. I've demoralised the First Fifteen with extra-tu.'

'Ah, but we're a scratch lot. Have you told 'em we shall need a substitute even if Crandall can play?' said a Lieutenant of Engineers with the D. S. O. to his credit.

'He wrote me he'd play, so he can't have been much hurt. He's coming down to-morrow morning.'

'Crandall minor that was, and brought off poor Duncan's body?' The Head nodded. 'Where are you going to put him? We've turned you out of house and home already, Head Sahib.' This was a Squadron-Commander of Bengal Lancers, home on leave.

'I'm afraid he'll have to go up to his old dormitory. You know old boys can claim that privilege. Yes, I think leetle Crandall minor must bed down there once more.'

'Bates Sahib'—a Gunner flung a heavy arm round the Head's neck—'you've got something up your sleeve. Confess! I know that twinkle.'

'Can't you see, you cuckoo?' a Submarine Miner interrupted. 'Crandall goes up to the dormitory as an object-lesson, for moral effect and so forth. Isn't that true, Head Sahib?'

'It is. You know too much, Purvis. I licked you for that in '79.'

'You did, sir, and it's my private belief you chalked the cane.'

'N-no. But I've a very straight eye. Perhaps that misled you.'

That opened the flood-gates of fresh memories, and they all told tales out of school.

When Crandall minor that was—Lieutenant R. Crandall of an ordinary Indian regiment—arrived from Exeter on the morning of the match, he was cheered along the whole front of the College, for the prefects had repeated the sense of that which the Head had read them in Flint's study. When Prout's house understood that he would claim his Old Boy's right to a bed for one night, Beetle ran into King's house next door and executed a public 'gloat' up and down the enemy's big form-room; departing in a haze of ink-pots.

A LITTLE PREP.

'What d'you take any notice of those rotters for?'
said Stalky, playing substitute for the Old Boys, magnificent in black jersey, white knickers, and black stock-
ings. 'I talked to him up in the dormitory when he
was changin'. Pulled his sweater down for him. He's
cut about all over the arms—horrid purply ones. He's
goin' to tell us about it to-night. I asked him to when
I was lacin' his boots.'

'Well, you have got cheek,' said Beetle enviously.

'Slipped out before I thought. But he wasn't a bit
angry. He's no end of a chap. I swear I'm goin' to
play up like beans. Tell Turkey!'

The technique of that match belongs to a bygone age.
Scrimmages were tight and enduring; hacking was direct and to the purpose; and round the scrimmage stood
the school crying, 'Put down your heads and shove!'
Toward the end everybody lost all sense of decency, and
mothers of day-boys too close to the touch-line heard
language not included in the bills. No one was actually
carried off the field, but both sides felt happier when
time was called, and Beetle helped Stalky and M'Turk
into their overcoats. The two had met in the many-
legged heart of things, and as Stalky said, had 'done
each other proud.' As they swaggered woodenly behind the teams—substitutes do not rank as equals of
hairy men—they passed a pony-carriage near the wall,
and a husky voice cried, 'Well played. Oh, played
indeed!' It was Stettson major, white-cheeked and
hollow-eyed, who had fought his way to the ground
under escort of an impatient coachman.

'Hullo, Stettson,' said Stalky, checking. 'Is it safe
to come near you yet?'

'Oh yes. I'm all right. They wouldn't let me out

before, but I had to come to the match. Your mouth looks pretty plummy.'

'Turkey trod on it accidental-done-a-purpose. Well, I'm glad you're better, because we owe you something. You and your membranes got us into a sweet mess, young man.'

'I heard of that,' said the boy, giggling. 'The Head told me.'

'Dooce he did! When?'

'Oh, come on up to Coll. My shin'll stiffen if we stay jawin' here.'

'Shut up, Turkey. I want to find out about this. Well?'

'He was stayin' at our house all the time I was ill.'

'What for? Neglectin' the Coll. that way? 'Thought he was in town.'

'I was off my head, you know, and they said I kept on callin' for him.'

'Cheek! You're only a day-boy.'

'He came just the same, and he about saved my life. I was all bunged up one night—just goin' to croak, the doctor said—and they stuck a tube or somethin' in my throat, and the Head sucked out the stuff.'

'Ugh! 'Shot if I would!'

'He ought to have got diphtheria himself, the doctor said. So he stayed on at our house instead of going back. I'd ha' croaked in another twenty minutes, the doctor says.'

Here the coachman, being under orders, whipped up and nearly ran over the three.

'My Hat!' said Beetle. 'That's pretty average heroic.'

'Pretty average!' M'Turk's knee in the small of his

160

back cannoned him into Stalky, who punted him back. 'You ought to be hung!'

'And the Head ought to get the V. C.,' said Stalky. 'Why, he might have been dead and buried by now. But he wasn't. But he didn't. Ho! ho! He just nipped through the hedge like a lusty old blackbird. Extra-special, five hundred lines, an' gated for a week—all sereno!'

'I've read o' something like that in a book,' said Beetle. 'Gummy, what a chap! Just think of it!'

'I'm thinking,' said M'Turk; and he delivered a wild Irish yell that made the team turn round.

'Shut your fat mouth,' said Stalky, dancing with impatience. 'Leave it to your Uncle Stalky, and he'll have the Head on toast. If you say a word, Beetle, till I give you leave, I swear I'll slay you. "Habeo Capitem crinibus minimis." I've got him by the short hairs! Now look as if nothing had happened.'

There was no need of guile. The school was too busy cheering the drawn match. It hung round the lavatories regardless of muddy boots while the team washed. It cheered Crandall minor whenever it caught sight of him, and it cheered more wildly than ever after prayers, because the Old Boys in evening dress, openly twirling their moustaches, attended, and instead of standing with the masters, ranged themselves along the wall immediately before the prefects; and the Head called them over, too—majors, minors, and tertiuses, after their old names.

'Yes, it's all very fine,' he said to his guests after dinner, 'but the boys are getting a little out of hand. There will be trouble and sorrow later, I'm afraid. You'd better turn in early, Crandall. The dormitory

161

will be sitting up for you. I don't know to what dizzy heights you may climb in your profession, but I do know you'll never get such absolute adoration as you're getting now.'

'Confound the adoration. I want to finish my cigar, sir.'

'It's all pure gold. Go where glory waits, Crandall—minor.'

The setting of that apotheosis was a ten-bed attic dormitory, communicating through doorless openings with three others. The gas flickered over the raw pine wash-stands. There was an incessant whistling of draughts, and outside the naked windows the sea beat on the Pebbleridge.

'Same old bed—same old mattress, I believe,' said Crandall, yawning. 'Same old everything. Oh, but I'm lame! I'd no notion you chaps could play like this.' He caressed a battered shin. 'You've given us all something to remember you by.'

It needed a few minutes to put them at their ease; and, in some way they could not understand, they were more easy when Crandall turned round and said his prayers—a ceremony he had neglected for some years.

'Oh, I am sorry. I've forgotten to put out the gas.'

'Please don't bother,' said the prefect of the dormitory. 'Worthington does that.'

A nightgowned twelve-year-old, who had been waiting to show off, leaped from his bed to the bracket and back again, by way of a wash-stand.

'How d'you manage when he's asleep?' said Crandall, chuckling.

'Shove a cold cleek down his neck.'

162

'It was a wet sponge when I was junior in the dormitory. . . . Hullo! What's happening?'

The darkness had filled with whispers, the sound of trailing rugs, bare feet on bare boards, protests, giggles, and threats such as:

'Be quiet, you ass! . . . Squattez-vous on the floor, then! . . . I swear you aren't going to sit on my bed! . . . Mind the tooth-glass,' and so forth.

'Sta—Corkran said,' the prefect began, his tone showing his sense of Stalky's insolence, 'that perhaps you'd tell us about that business with Duncan's body.'

'Yes—yes—yes,' ran the keen whispers. 'Tell us.'

'There's nothing to tell. What on earth are you chaps hoppin' about in the cold for?'

'Never mind us,' said the voices. 'Tell about Fat-Sow.'

So Crandall turned on his pillow and spoke to the generation he could not see.

'Well, about three months ago he was commanding a treasure-guard—a cart full of rupees to pay troops with —five thousand rupees in silver. He was comin' to a place called Fort Pearson, near Kalabagh.'

'I was born there,' squeaked a small fag. 'It was called after my uncle.'

'Shut up—you and your uncle! Never mind him, Crandall.'

'Well, ne'er mind. The Afridis found out that this treasure was on the move, and they ambushed the whole show a couple of miles before he got to the fort, and cut up the escort. Duncan was wounded, and the escort hooked it. There weren't more than twenty Sepoys all told, and there were any amount of Afridis. As things turned out, I was in charge at Fort Pearson. Fact was,

I'd heard the firing and was just going to see about it, when Duncan's men came up. So we all turned back together. They told me something about an officer, but I couldn't get the hang of things till I saw a chap under the wheels of the cart out in the open, propped up on one arm, blazing away with a revolver. You see, the escort had abandoned the cart, and the Afridis—they're an awfully suspicious gang—thought the retreat was a trap —sort of draw, you know—and the cart was the bait. So they had left poor old Duncan alone. 'Minute they spotted how few we were, it was a race across the flat who should reach old Duncan first. We ran, and they ran, and we won, and after a little hackin' about they pulled off. I never knew it was one of us till I was right on top of him. There are heaps of Duncans in the service, and of course the name didn't remind me. He wasn't changed at all hardly. He'd been shot through the lungs, poor old man, and he was pretty thirsty. I gave him a drink and sat down beside him, and—funny thing, too—he said, "Hullo, Toffee!" and I said, "Hullo, Fat-Sow! hope you aren't hurt," or something of the kind. But he died in a minute or two—never lifted his head off my knees. . . . I say, you chaps out there will get your death of cold. Better go to bed.'

'All right. In a minute. But your cuts—your cuts. How did you get wounded?'

'That was when we were taking the body back to the Fort. They came on again, and there was a bit of a scrimmage.'

'Did you kill any one?'

'Yes. Shouldn't wonder. Good-night.'

'Good-night. Thank you, Crandall. Thanks awf'ly, Crandall. Good-night.'

A LITTLE PREP.

The unseen crowds withdrew. His own dormitory rustled into bed and lay silent for a while.

'I say, Crandall'—Stalky's voice was tuned to a wholly foreign reverence.

'Well, what?'

'Suppose a chap found another chap croaking with diphtheria—all bunged up with it—and they stuck a tube in his throat and the chap sucked the stuff out, what would you say?'

'Um,' said Crandall reflectively. 'I've only heard of one case, and that was a doctor. He did it for a woman.'

'Oh, this wasn't a woman. It was only a boy.'

'Makes it all the finer, then. It's about the bravest thing a man can do. Why?'

'Oh, I heard of a chap doin' it. That's all.'

'Then he's a brave man.'

'Would you funk it?'

'Ra-ather. Anybody would. Fancy dying of diphtheria in cold blood.'

'Well—ah! Er! Look here!' That sentence ended in a grunt, for Stalky had leaped out of bed and with M'Turk was sitting on the head of Beetle, who would have sprung the mine there and then.

Next day, which was the last of the term and given up to a few wholly unimportant examinations, began with wrath and war. Mr. King had discovered that nearly all his house—it lay, as you know, next door but one to Prout's in the long range of buildings—had unlocked the doors between the dormitories and had gone in to listen to a story told by Crandall. He went to the Head, clamorous, injured, appealing; for he never approved of allowing so-called young men of the world to

165

contaminate the morals of boyhood. 'Very good,' said
the Head. He would attend to it.

'Well, I'm awf'ly sorry,' said Crandall guiltily. 'I
don't think I told 'em anything they oughtn't to hear.
Don't let them get into trouble on my account.'

'Tck!' the Head answered, with the ghost of a wink.
'It isn't the boys that make trouble; it's the masters.
However, Prout and King don't approve of dormitory
gatherings on this scale, and one must back up the house-
masters. Moreover, it's hopeless to punish two houses
only, so late in the term. We must be fair and include
everybody. Let's see. They have a holiday task for
the Easters, which, of course, none of them will ever look
at. We will give the whole school, except prefects and
study-boys, regular prep. to-night; and the Common-
room will have to supply a master to take it. We must
be fair to all.'

'Prep. on the last night of the term. Whew!' said
Crandall, thinking of his own wild youth. 'I fancy
there will be larks.'

The school, frolicking among packed trunks, whoop-
ing down the corridor, and 'gloating' in form-rooms,
received the news with amazement and rage. No school
in the world did prep. on the last night of the term.
This thing was monstrous, tyrannical, subversive of law,
religion, and morality. They would go into the form-
rooms, and they would take their degraded holiday task
with them, but—here they smiled and speculated what
manner of man the Common-room would send up against
them. The lot fell on Mason, credulous and enthusias-
tic, who loved youth. No other master was anxious
to take prep., for the school lacked the steadying influence of tradition; and men accustomed to the ordered

routine of ancient foundations found it occasionally insubordinate. The four long form-rooms, in which all below the rank of study-boys worked, received him with thunders of applause. Ere he had coughed twice they favoured him with a metrical summary of the marriage-laws of Great Britain, as recorded by the High Priest of the Israelites and commented on by the leader of the host. The lower forms reminded him that it was the last day, and that therefore he must 'take it all in play.' When he dashed off to rebuke them, the Lower Fourth and Upper Third began with one accord to be sick, loudly and realistically. Mr. Mason tried, of all vain things under heaven, to argue with them, and a bold soul at a back desk bade him 'take fifty lines for not 'olding up 'is 'and before speaking.' As one who prided himself upon the precision of his English this cut Mason to the quick, and while he was trying to discover the offender, the Upper and Lower Second, three form-rooms away, turned out the gas and threw ink-pots. It was a pleasant and stimulating prep. The study-boys and prefects heard the echoes of it far off, and the Common-room at dessert smiled.

Stalky waited, watch in hand, till half-past eight.

'If it goes on much longer the Head will come up,' said he. 'We'll tell the studies first, and then the form-rooms. Look sharp!'

He allowed no time for Beetle to be dramatic or M'-Turk to drawl. They poured into study after study, told their tale, and went again so soon as they saw they were understood, waiting for no comment; while the noise of that unholy prep. grew and deepened. By the door of Flint's study they met Mason flying towards the corridor.

167

'He's gone to fetch the Head. Hurry up! Come on!'
They broke into Number Twelve form-room abreast
and panting.

'The Head! The Head! The Head!' That call
stilled the tumult for a minute, and Stalky leaping to a
desk shouted, 'He went and sucked the diphtheria stuff
out of Stettson major's throat when we thought he
was in town. Stop rotting, you asses! Stettson major
would have croaked if the Head hadn't done it. The
Head might have died himself. Crandall says it's the
bravest thing any livin' man can do, and'—his voice
cracked—'the Head don't know we know!'

M'Turk and Beetle, jumping from desk to desk, drove
the news home among the junior forms. There was a
pause, and then, Mason behind him, the Head entered.
It was in the established order of things that no boy
should speak or move under his eye. He expected the
hush of awe. He was received with cheers—steady,
ceaseless cheering. Being a wise man he went away,
and the forms were silent and a little frightened.

'It's all right,' said Stalky. 'He can't do much.
'Tisn't as if you'd pulled the desks up like we did when
old Carleton took prep. once. Keep it up! Hear 'em
cheering in the studies!' He rocketed out with a yell,
to find Flint and the prefects lifting the roof off the
corridor.

When the Head of a limited liability company, paying
four per cent, is cheered on his saintly way to prayers,
not only by four form-rooms of boys waiting punishment, but by his trusted prefects, he can either ask for
an explanation or go his road with dignity, while the
senior house-master glares like an excited cat and points
out to a white and trembling mathematical master that

certain methods—not his, thank God—usually produce certain results. Out of delicacy the Old Boys did not attend that call-over; and it was to the school drawn up in the gymnasium that the Head spoke icily.

'It is not often that I do not understand you; but I confess I do not to-night. Some of you, after your idiotic performances at prep., seem to think me a fit person to cheer. I'm going to show you that I am not.'

Crash—crash—crash—came the triple cheer that disproved it, and the Head glowered under the gas.

'That is enough. You will gain nothing. The little boys (the Lower School did not like that form of address), will do me three hundred lines apiece in the holidays. I shall take no further notice of them. The Upper School will do me one thousand lines apiece in the holidays, to be shown up the evening of the day they come back. And further—'

'Gummy, what a glutton!' Stalky whispered.

'For your behaviour towards Mr. Mason I intend to lick the whole of the Upper School to-morrow when I give you your journey-money. This will include the three study-boys I found dancing on the form-room desks when I came up. Prefects will stay after call-over.'

The school filed out in silence, but gathered in groups by the gymnasium door waiting what might befall.

'And now, Flint,' said the Head, 'will you be good enough to give me some explanation of your conduct?'

'Well, sir,' said Flint desperately, 'if you save a chap's life at the risk of your own when he's dyin' of diphtheria, and the Coll. finds it out, wha-what can you expect, sir?'

'Um, I see. Then that noise was not meant for—ah, cheek. I can connive at immorality, but I cannot stand impudence. However, it does not excuse their insolence to Mr. Mason. I'll forgo the lines this once, remember; but the lickings hold good.'

When this news was made public, the school, lost in wonder and admiration, gasped at the Head as he went to his house. Here was a man to be reverenced. On the rare occasions when he caned he did it very scientifically, and the execution of a hundred boys would be epic—immense.

'It's all right, Head Sahib. We know,' said Crandall, as the Head slipped off his gown with a grunt in his smoking-room. 'I found out just now from our substitute. He was gettin' my opinion of your performance last night in the dormitory. I didn't know then that it was you he was talkin' about. Crafty young animal. Freckled chap with eyes—Corkran, I think his name is.'

'Oh, I know him, thank you,' said the Head; and reflectively, 'Ye-es, I should have included them even if I hadn't seen 'em.'

'If the old Coll. weren't a little above themselves already, we'd chair you down the corridor,' said the Engineer. 'Oh, Bates, how could you? You might have caught it yourself, and where would we have been then?'

'I always knew you were worth twenty of us any day. Now I'm sure of it,' said the Squadron-Commander, looking round for contradictions.

'He isn't fit to manage a school, though. Promise you'll never do it again, Bates Sahib. We—we can't go away comfy in our minds if you take these risks,' said the Gunner.

'Bates Sahib, you aren't ever goin' to cane the whole Upper School, are you?' said Crandall.

170

'I can connive at immorality, as I said, but I can't stand impudence. Mason's lot is quite hard enough even when I back him. Besides, the men at the golf-club heard them singing "Aaron and Moses." I shall have complaints about that from the parents of day-boys. Decency must be preserved.'

'We're coming to help,' said all the guests.

.   .   .   .

The Upper School were caned one after the other, their overcoats over their arms, the brakes waiting in the road below to take them to the station, their journey-money on the table. The Head began with Stalky, M'Turk, and Beetle. He dealt faithfully by them.

'And here's your journey-money. Good-bye, and pleasant holidays.'

'Good-bye. Thank you, sir. Good-bye.'

They shook hands.

'Desire don't outrun performance—much—this mornin'. We got the cream of it,' said Stalky. 'Now wait till a few chaps come out, and we'll really cheer him.'

'Don't wait on our account, please,' said Crandall, speaking for the Old Boys. 'We're going to begin now.'

It was very well so long as the cheering was confined to the corridor, but when it spread to the gymnasium, when the boys awaiting their turn cheered, the Head gave it up in despair, and the remnant flung themselves upon him to shake hands.

Then they seriously devoted themselves to cheering till the brakes were hustled off the premises in dumb show.

'Didn't I say I'd get even with him?' said Stalky on the box-seat, as they swung into the narrow Northam

171

street. 'Now all together—takin' time from your
Uncle Stalky:

> 'It's a way we have in the Army,
> It's a way we have in the Navy,
> It's a way we have in the Public Schools,
>   Which nobody can deny!'

THE FLAG OF THEIR COUNTRY

(1899)

IT was winter and bitter cold of mornings. Consequently Stalky and Beetle—M'Turk being of the offensive type that makes ornate toilet under all circumstances—drowsed till the last moment before turning out to call-over in the gas-lit gymnasium. It followed that they were often late; and since every unpunctuality earned them a black mark, and since three black marks a week meant defaulters' drill, equally it followed that they spent hours under the Sergeant's hand. Foxy drilled the defaulters with all the pomp of his old parade-ground.

'Don't think it's any pleasure to me' (his introduction never varied). 'I'd much sooner be smoking a quiet pipe in my own quarters—but I see we 'ave the Old Brigade on our 'ands this afternoon. If I only 'ad you regular, Muster Corkran,' said he, dressing the line.

'You've had me for nearly six weeks, you old glutton. Number off from the right!'

'Not quite so previous, please. I'm taking this drill. Left—half—turn! Slow—march.' Twenty-five sluggards, all old offenders, filed into the gymnasium. 'Quietly provide yourselves with the requisite dumb-bells; returnin' quietly to your place. Number off from the right, in a low voice. Odd numbers one pace to the

173

front. Even numbers stand fast. Now, leanin' forward from the 'ips, takin' your time from me.'

The dumb-bells rose and fell, clashed and were returned as one. The boys were experts at the weary game.

'Ve-ry good. I shall be sorry when any of you resume your 'abits of punctuality. Quietly return dumbbells. We will now try some simple drill.'

'Ugh! I know that simple drill.'

'It would be 'ighly to your discredit if you did not, Muster Corkran. At the same time, it is not so easy as it looks.'

'Bet you a bob, I can drill as well as you, Foxy.'

'We'll see later. Now try to imagine you ain't defaulters at all, but an 'arf company on parade, me bein' your commandin' officer. There's no call to laugh. If you're lucky, most of you will 'ave to take drills 'arf your life. Do me a little credit. You've been at it long enough, goodness knows.'

They were formed into fours, marched, wheeled, and countermarched, the spell of ordered motion strong on them. As Foxy said, they had been at it a long time.

The gymnasium door opened, revealing M'Turk in charge of an old gentleman.

The Sergeant, leading a wheel, did not see. 'Not so bad,' he murmured. 'Not 'arf so bad. The pivotman of the wheel honly marks time, Muster Swayne. Now, Muster Corkran, you say you know the drill? Oblige me by takin' over the command and, reversin' my words step by step, relegate them to their previous formation.'

'What's this? What's this?' cried the visitor authoritatively.

'A—a little drill, sir,' stammered Foxy, saying nothing of first causes.

'Excellent—excellent. I only wish there were more of it,' he chirruped. 'Don't let me interrupt. You were just going to hand over to some one, weren't you?' He sat down, breathing frostily in the chill air.

'I shall muck it. I know I shall,' whispered Stalky uneasily; and his discomfort was not lightened by a murmur from the rear rank that the old gentleman was General Collinson, a member of the College Board of Council.

'Eh—what?' said Foxy.

'Collinson, K. C. B.—He commanded the Pompadours—my father's old regiment,' hissed Swayne major.

'Take your time,' said the visitor. 'I know how it feels. Your first drill—eh?'

'Yes, sir.' He drew an unhappy breath. ' 'Tention. Dress!' The echo of his own voice restored his confidence.

The wheel was faced about, flung back, broken into fours, and restored to line without a falter. The official hour of punishment was long past, but no one thought of that. They were backing up Stalky—Stalky in deadly fear lest his voice should crack.

'He does you credit, Sergeant,' was the visitor's comment. 'A good drill—and good material to drill. Now, it's an extraordinary thing: I've been lunching with your head master and he never told me you had a cadet-corps in the College.'

'We 'aven't, sir. This is only a little drill,' said the Sergeant.

'But aren't they keen on it?' said M'Turk, speaking for the first time, with a twinkle in his deep-set eyes.

175

STALKY & CO.

'Why aren't you in it, though, Willy?'

'Oh, I'm not punctual enough,' said M'Turk. 'The Sergeant only takes the pick of us.'

'Dismiss! Break off!' cried Foxy, fearing an explosion in the ranks. 'I—I ought to have told you, sir, that—'

'But you should have a cadet-corps.' The General pursued his own line of thought. 'You shall have a cadet-corps, too, if my recommendation in Council is any use. I don't know when I've been so pleased. Boys animated by a spirit like yours should set an example to the whole school.'

'They do,' said M'Turk.

'Bless my soul! Can it be so late? I've kept my fly waiting half an hour. Well, I must run away. Nothing like seeing things for oneself. Which end of the building does one get out at? Will you show me, Willy? Who was that boy who took the drill?'

'Corkran, I think his name is.'

'You ought to know him. That's the kind of boy you should cultivate. Evidently an unusual sort. A wonderful sight. Five-and-twenty boys, who, I daresay, would much sooner be playing cricket—' (it was the depth of winter; but grown people, especially those who have lived long in foreign parts, make these little errors, and M'Turk did not correct him)—'drilling for the sheer love of it. A shame to waste so much good stuff; but I think I can carry my point.'

'An' who's your friend with the white whiskers?' demanded Stalky, on M'Turk's return to the study.

'General Collinson. He comes over to shoot with my father sometimes. Rather a decent old bargee, too. He said I ought to cultivate your acquaintance, Stalky.'

176

'Did he tip you?'

M'Turk exhibited a blessed whole sovereign.

'Ah,' said Stalky, annexing it, for he was treasurer. 'We'll have a hefty brew. You'd pretty average cool cheek, Turkey, to jaw about our keenness an' punctuality.'

'Didn't the old boy know we were defaulters?' said Beetle.

'Not him. He came down to lunch with the Head. I found him pokin' about the place on his own hook afterwards, an' I thought I'd show him the giddy drill. When I found he was so pleased, I wasn't goin' to damp his giddy ardour. He mightn't ha' given me the quid if I had.'

'Wasn't old Foxy pleased? Did you see him get pink behind the ears?' said Beetle. 'It was an awful score for him. Didn't we back him up beautifully? Let's go down to Keyte's and get some cocoa and sassingers.'

They overtook Foxy, speeding down to retail the adventure to Keyte, who in his time had been Troop-Sergeant-Major in a cavalry regiment, and now, a war-worn veteran, was local postmaster and confectioner.

'You owe us something,' said Stalky, with meaning.

'I'm 'ighly grateful, Muster Corkran. I've 'ad to run against you pretty hard in the way o' business, now and then, but I will say that outside o' business—bounds an' smokin', an' such like—I don't wish to have a more trustworthy young gentleman to 'elp me out of a hole. The way you 'andled the drill was beautiful, though I say it. Now, if you come regular henceforward—'

'But he'll have to be late three times a week,' said Beetle. 'You can't expect a chap to do that—just to please you, Foxy.'

'Ah, that's true. Still, if you could manage it—and

177

you, Muster Beetle—it would give you a big start when the cadet-corps is formed. I expect the General will recommend it.'

They raided Keyte's very much at their own sweet will, for the old man, who knew them well, was deep in talk with Foxy.

'I make what we've taken seven and six,' Stalky called at last over the counter; 'but you'd better count for yourself.'

'No—no. I'd take your word any day, Muster Corkran.—In the Pompadours, was he, Sergeant? We lay with them once—at Umballa, I think it was.'

'I don't know whether this ham-and-tongue tin is eighteen-pence or one an' four.'

'Say one an' fourpence, Muster Corkran. . . . Of course, Sergeant, if it was any use to give my time, I'd be pleased to do it, but I'm too old. I'd like to see a drill again.'

'Oh, come on, Stalky,' cried M'Turk. 'He isn't listenin' to you. Chuck over the money.'

'I want the quid changed, you ass. Keyte! Private Keyte! Corporal Keyte! Terroop-Sergeant-Major Keyte, will you give me change for a quid?'

'Yes—yes, of course. Seven an' six.' He stared abstractedly, pushed the silver over, and melted away into the darkness of the back room.

'Now those two 'll jaw about the Mutiny till tea-time,' said Beetle.

'Old Keyte was at Sobraon,' said Stalky. 'Hear him talk about that sometimes! Beats Foxy hollow.'

.   .   .   .

The Head's face, inscrutable as ever, was bent over a pile of letters.

178

'What do you think?' he said at last to the Reverend John Gillett.

'It's a good idea.   There's no denying that—an estimable idea.'

'We concede that much.   Well?'

'I have my doubts about it—that's all.   The more I know of boys the less do I profess myself capable of following their moods; but I own I shall be very much surprised if the scheme takes.   It—it isn't the temper of the school.   We prepare for the Army.'

'My business—in this matter—is to carry out the wishes of the Council.   They demand a volunteer cadet-corps.   A volunteer cadet-corps will be furnished.   I have suggested, however, that we need not embark upon the expense of uniforms till we are drilled.   General Collinson is sending us fifty lethal weapons—cut-down Sniders, he calls them—all carefully plugged.'

'Yes, that is necessary in a school that uses loaded saloon-pistols to the extent we do.'   The Reverend John smiled.

'Therefore there will be no outlay except the Sergeant's time.'

'But if he fails you will be blamed.'

'Oh, assuredly.   I shall post a notice in the corridor this afternoon, and—'

'I shall watch the result.'

.   .   .   .

'Kindly keep your 'ands off the new arm-rack.'

Foxy wrestled with a turbulent crowd in the gymnasium.   'Nor it won't do even a condemned Snider any good to be continual snappin' the lock, Mr. Swayne.— Yiss, the uniforms will come later, when we're more proficient; at present we will confine ourselves to drill.

179

I am 'ere for the purpose of takin' the names o' those
willin' to join.—Put down that Snider, Muster Hogan!'

'What are you goin' to do, Beetle?' said a voice.

'I've had all the drill I want, thank you.'

'What! After all you've learned? Come on. Don't
be a scab! They'll make you corporal in a week,' cried
Stalky.

'I'm not goin' up for the Army.' Beetle touched his
spectacles.

'Hold on a shake, Foxy,' said Hogan. 'Where are
you goin' to drill us?'

'Here—in the gym—till you are fit an' capable to be
taken out on the road.' The Sergeant threw a chest.

'For all the Northam cads to look at? Not good
enough, Foxibus.'

'Well, we won't make a point of it. You learn your
drill first, an' later we'll see.'

'Hullo,' said Ansell of Macrea's, shouldering through
the mob. 'What's all this about a giddy cadet-corps?'

'It will save you a lot o' time at Sandhurst,' the Sergeant replied promptly. 'You'll be dismissed your drills
early if you go up with groundin' before'and.'

'Hm! 'Don't mind learnin' my drill, but I'm not
goin' to ass about the country with a toy Snider. Perowne, what are you goin' to do? Hogan's joinin'.'

''Don't know whether I've the time,' said Perowne.
'I've got no end of extra-tu. as it is.'

'Well, call this extra-tu.,' said Ansell. ''Twon't take
us long to mug up the drill.'

'Oh, that's right enough, but what about marchin' in
public?' said Hogan, not foreseeing that three years
later he should die in the Burmese sunlight outside
Minhla Fort.

'Afraid the uniform won't suit your creamy complexion?' M'Turk asked with a villainous sneer.

'Shut up, Turkey. You aren't goin' up for the Army.'

'No, but I'm goin' to send a substitute. Hi! Morrell an' Wake! You two fags by the arm-rack, you've got to volunteer.'

Blushing deeply—they had been too shy to apply before—the youngsters sidled towards the Sergeant.

'But I don't want the little chaps—not at first,' said the Sergeant disgustedly. 'I want—I'd like some o' the Old Brigade—the defaulters—to stiffen 'em a bit.'

'Don't be ungrateful, Sergeant. They're nearly as big as you get 'em in the Army now.' M'Turk read the papers of those years and could be trusted for general information, which he used as he used his 'tweaker.' Yet he did not know that Wake minor would be a bimbashi of the Egyptian Army ere his thirtieth year.

Hogan, Swayne, Stalky, Perowne, and Ansell were deep in consultation by the vaulting-horse, Stalky as usual laying down the law. The Sergeant watched them uneasily, knowing that many waited on their lead.

'Foxy don't like my recruits,' said M'Turk, in a pained tone, to Beetle. 'You get him some.'

Nothing loath, Beetle pinioned two more fags—each no taller than a carbine.

'Here you are, Foxy. Here's food for powder. Strike for your hearths an' homes, you young brutes—an' be jolly quick about it.'

'Still he isn't happy,' said M'Turk.

'For the way we have with our Army
Is the way we have with our Navy.'

STALKY & CO.

Here Beetle joined in. They had found the poem in an old volume of 'Punch,' and it seemed to cover the situation:

> 'An' both of 'em lead to adversity,
>   Which nobody can deny!'

'You be quiet, young gentlemen. If you can't 'elp—don't 'inder.' Foxy's eye was still on the council by the horse. Carter, White, and Tyrrell, all boys of influence, had joined it. The rest fingered the rifles irresolutely.

'Half a shake,' cried Stalky. 'Can't we turn out those rotters before we get to work?'

'Certainly,' said Foxy. 'Any one wishful to join will stay 'ere. Those who do not so intend will go out, quietly closin' the door be'ind 'em.'

Half a dozen of the earnest-minded rushed at M'Turk and Beetle, and they had just time to escape into the corridor.

'Well, why don't you join?' Beetle asked, resettling his collar.

'Why didn't you?'

'What's the good? We aren't goin' up for the Army. Besides, I know the drill—all except the manual, of course. 'Wonder what they're doin' inside?'

'Makin' a treaty with Foxy. Didn't you hear Stalky say: "That's what we'll do—an' if he don't like it he can lump it"? They'll use Foxy for a cram. Can't you see, you idiot? They're goin' up for Sandhurst or the Shop in less than a year. They'll learn their drill an' then they'll drop it like a shot. D'you suppose chaps with their amount of extra-tu. are takin' up volunteerin' for fun?'

182

'Well, I don't know. I thought of doin' a poem about it—rottin' 'em, you know—"The Ballad of the Dog-shooters"—eh?'

'I don't think you can, because King 'll be down on the corps like a cartload o' bricks. He hasn't been consulted. He's sniffin' round the notice-board now. Let's lure him.' They strolled up carelessly towards the house-master—a most meek couple.

'How's this?' said King, with a start of feigned surprise. 'Methought you would be learning to fight for your country.'

'I think the company's full, sir,' said M'Turk.

'It's a great pity,' sighed Beetle.

'Forty valiant defenders, have we, then? How noble! What devotion! I presume that it is possible that a desire to evade their normal responsibilities may be at the bottom of this zeal. Doubtless they will be accorded special privileges, like the Choir and the Natural History Society—one must not say Bug-hunters.'

'Oh, I suppose so, sir,' said M'Turk cheerily. 'The Head hasn't said anything about it yet, but he will, of course.'

'Oh, sure to.'

'It is just possible, my Beetle,' King wheeled on the last speaker, 'that the house-masters—a necessary but somewhat neglected factor in our humble scheme of existence—may have a word to say on the matter. Life, for the young at least, is not all weapons and munitions of war. Education is incidentally one of our aims.'

'What a consistent pig he is,' cooed M'Turk, when they were out of ear-shot. 'One always knows where to have him. Did you see how he rose to that draw about the Head and special privileges?'

'Confound him, he might have had the decency to have backed the scheme. I could do such a lovely ballad, rottin' it; and now I'll have to be a giddy enthusiast. It don't bar our pulling Stalky's leg in the study, does it?'

'Oh no; but in the Coll. we must be pro-cadet-corps like anything. Can't you make up a filthy epigram, a la Catullus, about King objectin' to it?' Beetle was at this noble task when Stalky returned all hot from his first drill.

'Hullo, my ramrod-bunger!' began M'Turk. 'Where's your dead dog? Is it Defence or Defiance?'

'Defiance,' said Stalky, and leaped on him at that word. 'Look here, Turkey, you mustn't rot the corps. We've arranged it beautifully. Foxy swears he won't take us out into the open till we want to go.'

' "Dis-gustin' exhibition of immature infants apin' the idiosyncrasies of their elders. Snff!" '

'Have you drawn King, Beetle?' Stalky asked in a pause of the scuffle.

'Not exactly; but that's his genial style.'

'Well, listen to your Uncle Stalky—who is a Great Man. Moreover and subsequently, Foxy's goin' to let us drill the corps in turn—privatim et seriatim—so that we'll all know how to handle a half company anyhow. Ergo, an' propter hoc, when we go to the Shop we shall be dismissed drill early; thus, my beloved 'earers, combinin' education with wholesome amusement.'

'I knew you'd make a sort of extra-tu. of it, you cold-blooded brute,' said M'Turk. 'Don't you want to die for your giddy country?'

'Not if I can jolly well avoid it. So you mustn't rot the corps.'

'We'd decided on that, years ago,' said Beetle scornfully. 'King 'll do the rottin'.'

'Then you've got to rot King, my giddy poet. Make up a good catchy Limerick, and let the fags sing it.'

'Look here, you stick to volunteerin', and don't jog the table.'

'He won't have anything to take hold of,' said Stalky, with dark significance.

They did not know what that meant till, a few days later, they proposed to watch the corps at drill. They found the gymnasium door locked and a fag on guard.

'This is sweet cheek,' said M'Turk, stooping.

''Mustn't look through the key-hole,' said the sentry.

'I like that. Why, Wake, you little beast, I made you a volunteer.'

'Can't help it. My orders are not to allow any one to look.'

'S'pose we do?' said M'Turk. 'S'pose we jolly well slay you?'

'My orders are, I am to give the name of anybody who interferes with me on my post, to the corps, an' they'd deal with him after drill, accordin' to martial law.'

'What a brute Stalky is!' said Beetle. They never doubted for a moment who had devised that scheme.

'You esteem yourself a giddy centurion, don't you?' said Beetle, listening to the crash and rattle of grounded arms within.

'My orders are, not to talk except to explain my orders—they'll lick me if I do.'

M'Turk looked at Beetle. The two shook their heads and turned away.

185

STALKY & CO.

'I swear Stalky is a great man,' said Beetle after a long pause. 'One consolation is that this sort of secret-society biznai will drive King wild.'

It troubled many more than King, but the members of the corps were muter than oysters. Foxy, being bound by no vow, carried his woes to Keyte.

'I never come across such nonsense in my life. They've tiled the lodge, inner and outer guard all complete, and then they get to work, keen as mustard.'

'But what's it all for?' asked the ex-Troop-Sergeant-Major.

'To learn their drill. You never saw anything like it. They begin after I've dismissed 'em—practisin' tricks; but out into the open they will not come—not for ever so. The 'ole thing is pre-posterous. If you're a cadet-corps, I say, be a cadet-corps, instead o' hidin' be'ind locked doors.'

'And what do the authorities say about it?'

'That beats me again.' The Sergeant spoke fretfully. 'I go to the 'Ead an' 'e gives me no help. There's times when I think he's makin' fun o' me. I've never been a Volunteer-sergeant, thank God—but I've always had the consideration to pity 'em. I'm glad o' that.'

'I'd like to see 'em,' said Keyte. 'From your statements, Sergeant, I can't get at what they're after.'

'Don't ask me, Major! Ask that freckle-faced young Corkran. He's their generalissimo.'

One does not refuse a warrior of Sobraon, or deny the only pastry-cook within bounds. So Keyte came, by invitation, leaning upon a stick, tremulous with old age, to sit in a corner and watch.

'They shape well. They shape uncommon well,' he whispered between evolutions.

186

'Oh, this isn't what they're after. Wait till I dismiss 'em.'

At the 'break-off' the ranks stood fast. Perowne fell out, faced them, and, refreshing his memory by glimpses at a red-bound, metal-clasped book, drilled them for ten minutes. (This is that Perowne who was shot in Equatorial Africa by his own men.)

Ansell followed him, and Hogan followed Ansell. All three were implicitly obeyed.

Then Stalky laid aside his Snider, and, drawing a long breath, favoured the company with a blast of withering invective.

''Old 'ard, Muster Corkran. That ain't in any drill,' cried Foxy.

'All right, Sergeant. You never know what you may have to say to your men.—For pity's sake, try to stand up without leanin' against each other, you blear-eyed, herrin'-gutted gutter-snipes. It's no pleasure to me to comb you out. That ought to have been done before you came here, you—you Militia broom-stealers!'

'The old touch—the old touch. We know it,' said Keyte, wiping his rheumy eyes. 'But where did he pick it up?'

'From his father—or his uncle. Don't ask me! Half of 'em must have been born within ear-shot o' the barracks.' (Foxy was not far wrong in his guess.) 'I've heard more back-talk since this volunteerin' nonsense began than I've heard in a year in the service.'

'There's a rear-rank man lookin' as though his belly were in the pawn-shop. Yes, you, Private Ansell,' and Stalky tongue-lashed the victim for three minutes, in gross and in detail.

'Hullo!' He returned to his normal tone. 'First blood to me. You flushed, Ansell. You wriggled.'

'Couldn't help flushing,' was the answer. 'Don't think I wriggled, though.'

'Well, it's your turn now.' Stalky resumed his place in the ranks.

'Lord, Lord! It's as good as a play,' chuckled the attentive Keyte.

Ansell, too, had been blessed with relatives in the service, and slowly, in a lazy drawl—his style was more reflective than Stalky's—descended the abysmal depths of personality.

'Blood to me!' he shouted triumphantly. 'You couldn't stand it, either.' Stalky was a rich red, and his Snider shook visibly.

'I didn't think I would,' he said, struggling for composure, 'but after a bit I got in no end of a bait. Curious, ain't it?'

'Good for the temper,' said the slow-moving Hogan, as they returned arms to the rack.

'Did you ever?' said Foxy, hopelessly, to Keyte.

'I don't know much about volunteers, but it's the rummiest show I ever saw. I can see what they're gettin' at, though. Lord! how often I've been told off an' dressed down in my day! They shape well—extremely well they shape.'

'If I could get 'em out into the open, there's nothing I couldn't do with 'em, Major. Perhaps when the uniforms come down, they'll change their tune.'

Indeed it was time that the corps made some concession to the curiosity of the school. Thrice had the guard been maltreated and thrice had the corps dealt out martial law to the offender. The school raged.

What was the use, they asked, of a cadet-corps, which none might see? Mr. King congratulated them on their invisible defenders, and they could not parry his thrusts. Foxy was growing sullen and restive. A few of the corps openly expressed doubts as to the wisdom of their course; and the question of uniforms loomed on the near horizon. If those were issued, they would be forced to wear them.

But as so often happens in this life, the matter was suddenly settled from without.

The Head had duly informed the Council that their recommendation had been acted upon, and that, so far as he could learn, the boys were drilling.

He said nothing of the terms on which they drilled. Naturally, General Collinson was delighted and told his friends. One of his friends rejoiced in a friend, a Member of Parliament—a zealous, an intelligent, and, above all, a patriotic person, anxious to do the most good in the shortest possible time. But we cannot answer, alas! for the friends of our friends. If Collinson's friend had introduced him to the General, the latter would have taken his measure and saved much. But the friend merely spoke of his friend; and since no two people in this world see eye to eye, the picture conveyed to Collinson was inaccurate. Moreover, the man was an M. P., an impeccable Conservative, and the General had the English soldier's lurking respect for any member of the Court of Last Appeal. The man was going down into the West country, to spread light in some benighted constituency. Wouldn't it be a good idea if, armed with the General's recommendation, he, taking the admirable and newly-established cadet-corps for his text, spoke a few words—'Just talked to the boys a little—eh? You know the kind of thing that would be acceptable; and he'd be the very man to do it. The sort of talk that boys understand, you know.'

'They didn't talk to 'em much in my time,' said the General suspiciously.

'Ah! but times change—with the spread of education and so on. The boys of to-day are the men of to-morrow. An impression in youth is likely to be permanent. And in these times, you know, with the country going to the dogs!'

'You're quite right.' The island was then entering on five years of Mr. Gladstone's rule; and the General did not like what he had seen of it. He would certainly write to the Head, for it was beyond question that the boys of to-day made the men of to-morrow. That, if he might say so, was uncommonly well put.

In reply, the Head stated that he should be delighted to welcome Mr. Raymond Martin, M. P., of whom he had heard so much; to put him up for the night, and to allow him to address the school on any subject that he conceived would interest them. If Mr. Martin had not yet faced an audience of this particular class of British youth, the Head had no doubt that he would find it an interesting experience.

'And I don't think I am very far wrong in that last,' he confided to the Reverend John. 'Do you happen to know anything of one Raymond Martin?'

'I was at College with a man of that name,' the chaplain replied. 'He was without form and void, so far as I remember, but desperately earnest.'

'He will address the Coll. on "Patriotism" next Saturday.'

'If there is one thing our boys detest more than an-

190

other it is having their Saturday evenings broken into.
Patriotism has no chance beside "brewing."'

'Nor art either. D'you remember our "Evening
with Shakespeare"?' The Head's eyes twinkled. 'Or
the humorous gentleman with the magic-lantern?'

.   .   .   .

'An' who the dooce is this Raymond Martin, M. P.?'
demanded Beetle, when he read the notice of the lecture
in the corridor. 'Why do the brutes always turn up on
a Saturday?'

'"Ouh! Reomeo, Reomeo. Wherefore art thou
Reomeo?"' said M'Turk over his shoulder, quoting the
Shakespeare artiste of last term. 'Well, he won't be as
bad as her, I hope. Stalky, are you properly patriotic?
Because if you ain't, this chap's goin' to make you.'

''Hope he won't take up the whole of the evening. I
suppose we've got to listen to him.'

''Wouldn't miss him for the world,' said M'Turk.
'A lot of chaps thought that Romeo-Romeo woman was
a bore. I didn't. I liked her! 'Member when she
began to hiccough in the middle of it? P'raps he'll
hiccough. Whoever gets into the Gym first, bags seats
for the other two.'

.   .   .   .

There was no nervousness, but a brisk and cheerful
affability about Mr. Raymond Martin, M. P., as he
drove up, watched by many eyes, to the Head's house.

''Looks a bit of a bargee,' was M'Turk's comment.
''Shouldn't be surprised if he was a Radical. He rowed
the driver about the fare. I heard him.'

'That was his giddy patriotism,' Beetle explained.

After tea they joined the rush for seats, secured a
private and invisible corner, and began to criticise.

191

Every gas-jet was lit. On the little dais at the far end stood the Head's official desk, whence Mr. Martin would discourse, and a ring of chairs for the masters.

Entered then Foxy, with official port, and leaned something like a cloth rolled round a stick against the desk. No one in authority was yet present, so the school applauded, crying: 'What's that, Foxy? What are you stealin' the gentleman's brolly for? We don't birch here. We cane! Take away that bauble! Number off from the right'—and so forth, till the entry of the Head and the masters ended all demonstrations.

'One good job—the Common-room hate this as much as we do. Watch King wrigglin' to get out of the draught.'

'Where's the Raymondiferous Martin? Punctuality, my beloved 'earers, is the image o' war—'

'Shut up. Here's the giddy Duke. Golly, what a dewlap!' Mr. Martin, in evening dress, was undeniably throaty—a tall, generously-designed, pink-and-white man. Still, Beetle need not have been coarse.

'Look at his back while he's talkin' to the Head. Vile bad form to turn your back on the audience! He's a Philistine—a Bopper—a Jebusite an' a Hivite.' M'-Turk leaned back and sniffed contemptuously.

In a few colourless words the Head introduced the speaker and sat down amid applause. When Mr. Martin took the applause to himself, they naturally applauded more than ever. It was some time before he could begin. He had no knowledge of the school—its tradition or heritage. He did not know that the last census showed that eighty per cent of the boys had been born abroad—in camp, cantonment, or upon the high seas; or that seventy-five per cent were sons of officers in one or other of the services—Willoughbys, Paulets, De Castros, Maynes, Randalls, after their kind —looking to follow their fathers' profession. The Head might have told him this, and much more; but, after an hour-long dinner in his company, the Head decided to say nothing whatever. Mr. Raymond Martin seemed to know so much already.

He plunged into his speech with a long-drawn, rasping 'Well, boys,' that, though they were not conscious of it, set every young nerve ajar. He supposed they knew—hey?—what he had come down for? It was not often that he had an opportunity to talk to boys. He supposed that boys were very much the same kind of persons—some people thought them rather funny persons—as they had been in his youth.

'This man,' said M'Turk, with conviction, 'is the Gadarene Swine.'

But they must remember that they would not always be boys. They would grow up into men, because the boys of to-day made the men of to-morrow, and upon the men of to-morrow the fair fame of their glorious native land depended.

'If this goes on, my beloved 'earers, it will be my painful duty to rot this bargee.' Stalky drew a long breath through his nose.

'Can't do that,' said M'Turk. 'He ain't chargin' anything for his Romeo.'

And so they ought to think of the duties and responsibilities of the life that was opening before them. Life was not all—he enumerated a few games, and, that nothing might be lacking to the sweep and impact of his fall, added 'marbles.' 'Yes, life was not,' he said, 'all marbles.'

There was one tense gasp—among the juniors almost a shriek—of quivering horror. He was a heathen—an outcast—beyond the extremest pale of toleration—self-damned before all men! Stalky bowed his head in his hands. M'Turk, with a bright and cheerful eye, drank in every word, and Beetle nodded solemn approval.

Some of them, doubtless, expected in a few years to have the honour of a commission from the Queen, and to wear a sword. Now, he himself had had some experience of these duties, as a Major in a volunteer regiment, and he was glad to learn that they had established a volunteer corps in their midst. The establishment of such an establishment conduced to a proper and healthy spirit, which, if fostered, would be of great benefit to the land they loved and were so proud to belong to. Some of those now present expected, he had no doubt—some of them anxiously looked forward to leading their men against the bullets of England's foes; to confronting the stricken field in all the pride of their youthful manhood.

Now the reserve of a boy is tenfold deeper than the reserve of a maid, she being made for one end only by blind Nature, but man for several. With a large and healthy hand, he tore down these veils, and trampled them under the well-intentioned feet of eloquence. In a raucous voice he cried aloud little matters, like the hope of Honour and the dream of Glory, that boys do not discuss even with their most intimate equals; cheerfully assuming that, till he spoke, they had never considered these possibilities. He pointed them to shining goals, with fingers which smudged out all radiance on all horizons. He profaned the most secret places of their souls with outcries and gesticulations. He bade them consider the deeds of their ancestors in such fashion that they were flushed to their tingling ears. Some of them—the rending voice cut a frozen stillness—might have had relatives who perished in defence of their country. [They thought, not a few of them, of an old sword in a passage, or above a breakfast-room table, seen and fingered by stealth since they could walk.] He adjured them to emulate those illustrious examples; and they looked all ways in their extreme discomfort.

Their years forbade them even to shape their thoughts clearly to themselves. They felt savagely that they were being outraged by a fat man who considered marbles a game.

And so he worked towards his peroration—which, by the way, he used later with overwhelming success at a meeting of electors—while they sat, flushed and uneasy, in sour disgust. After many many words, he reached for the cloth-wrapped stick and thrust one hand in his bosom. This—this was the concrete symbol of their land—worthy of all honour and reverence! Let no boy look on this flag who did not purpose to worthily add to its imperishable lustre. He shook it before them—a large calico Union Jack, staring in all three colours, and waited for the thunder of applause that should crown his effort.

They looked in silence. They had certainly seen the thing before—down at the coastguard station, or through a telescope, half-mast high when a brig went ashore on Braunton sands; above the roof of the Golf Club, and in Keyte's window, where a certain kind of striped sweetmeat bore it in paper on each box. But the College never displayed it; it was no part of the scheme of their lives; the Head had never alluded to it; their fathers had not declared it unto them. It was a matter shut up,

195

sacred and apart. What, in the name of everything caddish, was he driving at, who waved that horror before their eyes? Happy thought! Perhaps he was drunk.

The Head saved the situation by rising swiftly to propose a vote of thanks, and at his first motion the school clapped furiously, from a sense of relief.

'And I am sure,' he concluded, the gaslight full on his face, 'that you will all join me in a very hearty vote of thanks to Mr. Raymond Martin for the most enjoyable address he has given us.'

To this day we shall never know the rights of the case. The Head vows that he did no such thing; or that, if he did, it must have been something in his eye; but those who were present are persuaded that he winked, once, openly and solemnly, after the word 'enjoyable.' Mr. Raymond Martin got his applause full tale. As he said, 'Without vanity, I think my few words went to their hearts. I never knew boys could cheer like that.'

He left as the prayer-bell rang, and the boys lined up against the wall. The flag lay still unrolled on the desk, Foxy regarding it with pride, for he had been touched to the quick by Mr. Martin's eloquence. The Head and the Common-room, standing back on the dais, could not see the glaring offence, but a prefect left the line, rolled it up swiftly, and as swiftly tossed it into a glove-and-foil locker.

Then, as though he had touched a spring, broke out the low murmur of content, changing to quick-volleyed hand-clapping.

They discussed the speech in the dormitories. There was not one dissentient voice. Mr. Raymond Martin, beyond question, was born in a gutter, and bred in a

Board-school, where they played marbles. He was further (I give the barest handful from great store) a Flopshus Cad, an Outrageous Stinker, a Jelly-bellied Flag-flapper (this was Stalky's contribution), and several other things which it is not seemly to put down.

The volunteer cadet-corps fell in next Monday, depressedly, with a face of shame. Even then, judicious silence might have turned the corner.

Said Foxy: 'After a fine speech like what you 'eard night before last, you ought to take 'old of your drill with re-newed activity. I don't see how you can avoid comin' out an' marchin' in the open now.'

'Can't we get out of it, then, Foxy?' Stalky's fine old silky tone should have warned him.

'No, not with his giving the flag so generously. He told me before he left this morning that there was no objection to the corps usin' it as their own. It's a handsome flag.'

Stalky returned his rifle to the rack in dead silence, and fell out. His example was followed by Hogan and Ansell.

Perowne hesitated. 'Look here, oughtn't we—?' he began.

'I'll get it out of the locker in a minute,' said the Sergeant, his back turned. 'Then we can—'

'Come on!' shouted Stalky. 'What the devil are you waiting for? Dismiss! Break off.'

'Why—what the—where the—?'

The rattle of Sniders, slammed into the rack, drowned his voice, as boy after boy fell out.

'I—I don't know that I shan't have to report this to the Head,' he stammered.

'Report, then, and be damned to you,' cried Stalky, white to the lips, and ran out.

197

'Rummy thing!' said Beetle to M'Turk. 'I was in the study, doin' a simply lovely poem about the Jelly-bellied Flag-flapper, an' Stalky came in, an' I said "Hullo!" an' he cursed me like a bargee, and then he began to blub like anything. Shoved his head on the table and howled. Hadn't we better do something?'

M'Turk was troubled. 'P'raps he's smashed himself up somehow.'

They found him, with very bright eyes, whistling between his teeth.

'Did I take you in, Beetle? I thought I would. Wasn't it a good draw? Didn't you think I was blubbin'? Didn't I do it well? Oh, you fat old ass!' And he began to pull Beetle's ears and cheeks, in the fashion that was called 'milking.'

'I knew you were blubbin',' Beetle replied composedly. 'Why aren't you at drill?'

'Drill! What drill?'

'Don't try to be a clever fool. Drill in the Gym.'

''Cause there isn't any. The volunteer cadet-corps is broke up—disbanded—dead—putrid—corrupt—stinkin'. An' if you look at me like that, Beetle, I'll slay you too. . . . Oh yes, an' I'm goin' to be reported to the Head for swearin'.'

THE LAST TERM

(1899)

IT was within a few days of the holidays, the term-end examinations, and, more important still, the issue of the College paper which Beetle edited. He had been cajoled into that office by the blandishments of Stalky and M'Turk and the extreme rigour of study law. Once installed, he discovered, as others have done before him, that his duty was to do the work while his friends criticised. Stalky christened it the 'Swillingford Patriot,' in pious memory of Sponge—and M'Turk compared the output unfavourably with Ruskin and De Quincey. Only the Head took an interest in the publication, and his methods were peculiar. He gave Beetle the run of his brown-bound, tobacco-scented library; prohibiting nothing, recommending nothing. There Beetle found a fat armchair, a silver inkstand, and unlimited pens and paper. There were scores and scores of ancient dramatists; there were Hakluyt, his voyages; French translations of Muscovite authors called Pushkin and Lermontoff; little tales of a heady and bewildering nature, interspersed with unusual songs— Peacock was that writer's name; there was Borrow's 'Lavengro'; an odd theme, purporting to be a translation of something called a 'Rubaiyat,' which the Head said was a poem not yet come to its own; there were

199

STALKY & CO.

hundreds of volumes of verse—Crashaw; Dryden;
Alexander Smith; L. E. L.; Lydia Sigourney; Fletcher
and a purple island; Donne; Marlowe's 'Faust'; and—
this made M'Turk (to whom Beetle conveyed it) sheer
drunk for three days—Ossian; 'The Earthly Paradise';
'Atalanta in Calydon'; and Rossetti—to name only a
few. Then the Head, drifting in under pretence of
playing censor to the paper, would read here a verse and
here another of these poets; opening up avenues. And,
slow breathing, with half-shut eyes above his cigar,
would he speak of great men living, and journals, long
dead, founded in their riotous youth; of years when all
the planets were little new-lit stars trying to find their
places in the uncaring void, and he, the Head, knew
them as young men know one another. So the regular
work went to the dogs, Beetle being full of other matters
and metres, hoarded in secret and only told to M'Turk
of an afternoon, on the sands, walking high and dis-
posedly round the wreck of the Armada galleon, shouting and declaiming against the long-ridged seas.

Thanks in large part to their house-master's experi-
enced distrust, the three for three consecutive terms had
been passed over for promotion to the rank of prefect—
an office that went by merit, and carried with it the
honour of the ground-ash, and liberty, under restric-
tions, to use it.

'But,' said Stalky, 'come to think of it, we've done
more giddy jesting with the Sixth since we've been
passed over than any one else in the last seven years.'

He touched his neck proudly. It was encircled by
the stiffest of stick-up collars, which custom decreed
could be worn only by the Sixth. And the Sixth saw
those collars and said no word. 'Pussy,' Abanazar, or

Dick Four of a year ago would have seen them discarded in five minutes or . . .   But the Sixth of that term was made up mostly of young but brilliantly clever boys, pets of the house-masters, too anxious for their dignity to care to come to open odds with the resourceful three. So they crammed their caps at the extreme back of their heads, instead of a trifle over one eye as the Fifth should, and rejoiced in patent-leather boots on week-days and marvellous made-up ties on Sundays—no man rebuking. M'Turk was going up for Cooper's Hill, and Stalky for Sandhurst, in the spring; and the Head had told them both that, unless they absolutely collapsed during the holidays, they were safe. As a trainer of colts, the Head seldom erred in an estimate of form.

He had taken Beetle aside that day and given him much good advice, not one word of which did Beetle remember when he dashed up to the study, white with excitement, and poured out the wondrous tale. It demanded a great belief.

'You begin on a hundred a year?' said M'Turk unsympathetically.   'Rot!'

'And my passage out!   It's all settled.   The Head says he's been breaking me in for this for ever so long, and I never knew—I never knew.   One don't begin with writing straight off, y'know.   Begin by filling in telegrams and cutting things out o' papers with scissors.'

'Oh, Scissors!   What an ungodly mess you'll make of it,' said Stalky.   'But, anyhow, this will be your last term, too.   Seven years, my dearly beloved 'earers— though not prefects.'

'Not half bad years, either,' said M'Turk.   'I shall be sorry to leave the old Coll.; shan't you?'

They looked out over the sea creaming along the

Pebbleridge in the clear winter light. ''Wonder where we shall all be this time next year?' said Stalky absently.

'This time five years,' said M'Turk.

'Oh,' said Beetle, 'my leavin's between ourselves. The Head hasn't told any one. I know he hasn't, because Prout grunted at me to-day that if I were more reasonable—yah!—I might be a prefect next term. I suppose he's hard up for his prefects.'

'Let's finish up with a row with the Sixth,' suggested M'Turk.

'Dirty little schoolboys!' said Stalky, who already saw himself a Sandhurst cadet. 'What's the use?'

'Moral effect,' quoth M'Turk. 'Leave an imperishable tradition, and all the rest of it.'

'Better go into Bideford an' pay up our debts,' said Stalky. 'I've got three quid out of my father—ad hoc. Don't owe more than thirty bob, either. Cut along, Beetle, and ask the Head for leave. Say you want to correct the "Swillingford Patriot."'

'Well, I do,' said Beetle. 'It'll be my last issue, and I'd like it to look decent. I'll catch him before he goes to his lunch.'

Ten minutes later they wheeled out in line, by grace released from five o'clock call-over, and all the afternoon lay before them. So also unluckily did King, who never passed without witticisms. But brigades of Kings could not have ruffled Beetle that day.

'Aha! Enjoying the study of light literature, my friends?' said he, rubbing his hands. 'Common mathematics are not for such soaring minds as yours, are they?'

('One hundred a year,' thought Beetle, smiling into vacancy.)

'Our open incompetence takes refuge in the flowery

202

paths of inaccurate fiction? But a day of reckoning approaches, Beetle mine. I myself have prepared a few trifling foolish questions in Latin prose which can hardly be evaded even by your practised arts of deception. Ye-es, Latin prose. I think, if I may say so—but we shall see when the papers are set—"Ulpian serves your need." "Aha! 'Elucescebat,' quoth our friend." We shall see! We shall see!'

Still no sign from Beetle. He was on a steamer, his passage paid into the wide and wonderful world—a thousand leagues beyond Lundy Island.

King dropped him with a snarl.

'He doesn't know. He'll go on correctin' exercises an' jawin' an' showin' off before the little boys next term—and next.' Beetle hurried after his companions up the steep path of the furze-clad hill behind the College.

They were throwing pebbles on the top of the gasometer, and the grimy gas-man in charge bade them desist. They watched him oil a turncock sunk in the ground between two furze-bushes.

'Cokey, what's that for?' said Stalky.

'To turn the gas on to the kitchens,' said Cokey. 'If so be I didn't turn her on, yeou young gen'lemen 'ud be larnin' your book by candlelight.'

'Um!' said Stalky, and was silent for at least a minute.

'Hullo! Where are you chaps going?'

A bend of the lane brought them face to face with Tulke, senior prefect of King's house—a smallish, white-haired boy, of the type that must be promoted on account of its intellect, and ever afterwards appeals to the Head to support its authority when zeal has outrun discretion.

The three took no sort of notice. They were on law-

203

ful pass.   Tulke repeated his question hotly, for he had
suffered many slights from Number Five study, and
fancied that he had at last caught them tripping.

'What the devil is that to you?' Stalky replied, with
his sweetest smile.

'Look here, I'm not goin'—I'm not goin' to be sworn
at by the Fifth!' sputtered Tulke.

'Then cut along and call a prefects' meeting,' said
M'Turk, knowing Tulke's weakness.

The prefect became inarticulate with rage.

'Mustn't yell at the Fifth that way,' said Stalky. 'It's
vile bad form.'

'Cough it up, ducky!' M'Turk said calmly.

'I—I want to know what you chaps are doing out of
bounds?' This with an important flourish of his ground-
ash.

'Ah!' said Stalky. 'Now we're gettin' at it.   Why
didn't you ask that before?'

'Well, I ask it now.   What are you doing?'

'We're admiring you, Tulke,' said Stalky.   'We think
you're no end of a fine chap, don't we?'

'We do! We do!' A dog-cart with some girls in it
swept round the corner, and Stalky promptly kneeled
before Tulke in the attitude of prayer; so Tulke turned
a colour.

'I've reason to believe—' he began.

'Oyez! Oyez! Oyez!' shouted Beetle, after the
manner of Bideford's town-crier, 'Tulke has reason to
believe!   Three cheers for Tulke!'

They were given. 'It's all our giddy admiration,'
said Stalky. 'You know how we love you, Tulke. We
love you so much we think you ought to go home and
die.   You're too good to live, Tulke.'

204

'Yes,' said M'Turk. 'Do oblige us by dyin'. Think how lovely you'd look stuffed!'

Tulke swept up the road with an unpleasant glare in his eye.

'That means a prefects' meeting—sure pop,' said Stalky. 'Honour of the Sixth involved, and all the rest of it. Tulke 'll write notes all this afternoon, and Carson will call us up after tea. They daren't overlook that.'

'Bet you a bob he follows us!' said M'Turk. 'He's King's pet, and it's scalps to both of 'em if we're caught out. We must be virtuous.'

'Then I move we go to Mother Yeo's for a last gorge. We owe her about ten bob, and Mary 'll weep sore when she knows we're leaving,' said Beetle.

'She gave me an awful wipe on the head last time—Mary,' said Stalky.

'She does if you don't duck,' said M'Turk. 'But she generally kisses one back. Let's try Mother Yeo.'

They sought a little bottle-windowed half-dairy, half-restaurant, a dark-browed, two-hundred-year-old house, at the head of a narrow side street. They had patronised it from the days of their fagdom, and were very much friends at home.

'We've come to pay our debts, mother,' said Stalky, sliding his arm round the fifty-six-inch waist of the mistress of the establishment. 'To pay our debts and say good-bye—and—and we're awf'ly hungry.'

'Aie!' said Mother Yeo, 'makkin' love to me! I'm shaamed of 'ee.'

''Rackon us wouldn't du no such thing if Mary was here,' said M'Turk, lapsing into the broad North Devon that the boys used on their campaigns.

'Who'm takin' my name in vain?' The inner door

opened, and Mary, fair-haired, blue-eyed, and apple-cheeked, entered with a bowl of cream in her hands. M'Turk kissed her. Beetle followed suit, with exemplary calm. Both boys were promptly cuffed.

'Niver kiss the maid when 'e can kiss the mistress,' said Stalky, shamelessly winking at Mother Yeo, as he investigated a shelf of jams.

''Glad to see one of 'ee don't want his head slapped no more!' said Mary invitingly, in that direction.

'Neu! 'Reckon I can get 'em give me,' said Stalky, his back turned.

'Not by me—yeou little masterpiece!'

'Niver asked 'ee. There's maids to Northam. Yiss —an' Appledore.' An unreproducible sniff, half contempt, half reminiscence, rounded the retort.

'Aie! Yeou won't niver come to no good end. Whutt be 'baout, smellin' the cream?'

''Tees bad,' said Stalky. 'Zmell 'un.'

Incautiously Mary did as she was bid.

'Bidevoor kiss.'

'Niver amiss,' said Stalky, taking it without injury.

'Yeou—yeou—yeou—' Mary began, bubbling with mirth.

'They'm better to Northam—more rich, laike—an' us gets them give back again,' he said, while M'Turk solemnly waltzed Mother Yeo out of breath, and Beetle told Mary the sad news, as they sat down to clotted cream, jam, and hot bread.

'Yiss. Yeou'll niver zee us no more, Mary. We'm goin' to be passons an' missioners.'

'Steady the Buffs!' said M'Turk, looking through the blind. 'Tulke has followed us. He's comin' up the street now.'

'They've niver put us out o' bounds,' said Mother Yeo. 'Bide yeou still, my little dearrs.' She rolled into the inner room to make the score.

'Mary,' said Stalky suddenly, with tragic intensity. 'Do 'ee lov' me, Mary?'

'Iss, fai! Talled 'ee zo since yeou was zo high!' the damsel replied.

'Zee 'un comin' up street, then?' Stalky pointed to the unconscious Tulke. 'He've niver been kissed by no sort or manner o' maid in hees borned laife, Mary. Oy, 'tees shaamful!'

'Whutt's to do with me? 'Twill come to 'un in the way o' nature, I rackon.' She nodded her head sagaciously. 'You niver want me to kiss un—sure-ly?'

' 'Give 'ee half-a-crown if 'ee will,' said Stalky, exhibiting the coin.

Half-a-crown was much to Mary Yeo, and a jest was more; but—

'Yeu'm afraid,' said M'Turk, at the psychological moment.

'Aie!' Beetle echoed, knowing her weak point. 'There's not a maid to Northam 'ud think twice. An' yeou such a fine maid, tu!'

M'Turk planted one foot firmly against the inner door lest Mother Yeo should return inopportunely, for Mary's face was set. It was then that Tulke found his way blocked by a tall daughter of Devon—that county of easy kisses, the pleasantest under the sun. He dodged aside politely. She reflected a moment, and laid a vast hand upon his shoulder.

'Where be 'ee gwaine tu, my dearr?' said she.

Over the handkerchief he had crammed into his mouth Stalky could see the boy turn scarlet.

'Gie I a kiss! Don't they larn 'ee manners to College?'

Tulke gasped and wheeled. Solemnly and conscientiously Mary kissed him twice, and the luckless prefect fled.

She stepped into the shop, her eyes full of simple wonder.

''Kissed 'un?' said Stalky, handing over the money.

'Iss, fai! But, oh, my little body, he'm no Colleger. 'Zeemed tu-minded to cry, laike.'

'Well, we won't. You couldn't make us cry that way,' said M'Turk. 'Try.'

Whereupon Mary cuffed them all round.

As they went out with tingling ears, said Stalky generally, 'Don't think there'll be much of a prefects' meeting.'

'Won't there, just!' said Beetle. 'Look here. If he kissed her—which is our tack—he is a cynically immoral hog, and his conduct is blatant indecency. "Confer orationes Regis furiosissimi" when he collared me readin' "Don Juan."'

''Course he kissed her,' said M'Turk. 'In the middle of the street. With his house-cap on!'

'Time, 3.57 p.m. Make a note o' that. What d'you mean, Beetle?' said Stalky.

'Well! He's a truthful little beast. He may say he was kissed.'

'And then?'

'Why, then!' Beetle capered at the mere thought of it. 'Don't you see? The corollary to the giddy proposition is that the Sixth can't protect 'emselves from outrages an' ravishin's. 'Want nursemaids to look after 'em! We've only got to whisper that to the Coll. Jam for the Sixth! Jam for us! Either way it's jammy!'

'By Gum!' said Stalky. 'Our last term's endin' well. Now you cut along an' finish up your old rag, and Turkey and me will help. We'll go in the back way. No need to bother Randall.'

'Don't play the giddy garden-goat, then?' Beetle knew what help meant, though he by no means objected to showing his importance before his allies. The little loft behind Randall's printing-office was his own territory, where he saw himself already controlling the 'Times.' Here, under the guidance of the inky apprentice, he had learned to find his way more or less circuitously about the case, and considered himself an expert compositor.

The school paper in its locked formes lay on a stone-topped table, a proof by the side; but not for worlds would Beetle have corrected from the mere proof. With a mallet and a pair of tweezers, he knocked out mysterious wedges of wood that released the forme, picked a letter here and inserted a letter there, reading as he went along and stopping much to chuckle over his own contributions.

'You won't show off like that,' said M'Turk, 'when you've got to do it for your living. Upside down and backwards, isn't it? Let's see if I can read it.'

'Get out!' said Beetle. 'Go and read those formes in the rack there, if you think you know so much.'

'Formes in a rack! What's that? Don't be so beastly professional.'

M'Turk drew off with Stalky to prowl about the office. They left little unturned.

'Come here a shake, Beetle. What's this thing?' said Stalky, in a few minutes. ''Looks familiar.'

Said Beetle, after a glance: 'It's King's Latin prose

209

exam. paper. "In—In Verrem: actio prima." What a lark!'

'Think o' the pure-souled, high-minded boys who'd give their eyes for a squint at it!' said M'Turk.

'No, Willie dear,' said Stalky; 'that would be wrong and painful to our kind teachers. You wouldn't crib, Willie, would you?'

'Can't read the beastly stuff, anyhow,' was the reply. 'Besides, we're leavin' at the end o' the term, so it makes no difference to us.'

''Member what the Considerate Bloomer did to Spraggon's account of the Puffin'ton Hounds? We must sugar Mr. King's milk for him,' said Stalky, all lighted from within by a devilish joy. 'Let's see what Beetle can do with those forceps he's so proud of.'

''Don't see how you can make Latin prose much more cock-eye than it is, but we'll try,' said Beetle, transposing an 'aliud' and 'Asiæ' from two sentences. 'Let's see! We'll put that full-stop a little further on, and begin the sentence with the next capital. Hurrah! Here's three lines that can move up all in a lump.'

' "One of those scientific rests for which this eminent huntsman is so justly celebrated."' Stalky knew the Puffington run by heart.

'Hold on! Here's a "vol—voluntate quidnam" all by itself,' said M'Turk.

'I'll attend to her in a shake. "Quidnam" goes after "Dolabella."'

'Good old Dolabella,' murmured Stalky. 'Don't break him. Vile prose Cicero wrote, didn't he? He ought to be grateful for—'

'Hullo!' said M'Turk, over another forme. 'What

price a giddy ode? "Qui—quis"—oh, it's "Quis multa gracilis," o' course.'

'Bring it along. We've sugared the milk here,' said Stalky, after a few minutes' zealous toil. 'Never thrash your hounds unnecessarily.'

' "Quis munditiis?" I swear that's not bad,' began Beetle, plying the tweezers. 'Don't that interrogation look pretty? "Heu quoties fidem!" That sounds as if the chap were anxious an' excited. "Cui flavam religas in rosa"—Whose flavour is relegated to a rose. "Mutatosque Deos flebit in antro." '

'Mute gods weepin' in a cave,' suggested Stalky. ' 'Pon my Sam, Horace needs as much lookin' after as— Tulke.'

They edited him faithfully till it was too dark to see.

.   .   .   .

' "Aha! 'Elucescebat,' quoth our friend." Ulpian serves my need, does it? If King can make anything out of that, I'm a blue-eyed squatteroo,' said Beetle, as they slid out of the loft window into a back alley of old acquaintance and started on a three-mile trot to the College. But the revision of the classics had detained them over long. They halted, blown and breathless, in the furze at the back of the gasometer, the College lights twinkling below, ten minutes at least late for tea and lock-up.

'It's no good,' puffed M'Turk. 'Bet a bob Foxy is waiting for defaulters under the lamp by the Fives Court. It's a nuisance, too, because the Head gave us long leave, and one doesn't like to break it.'

' "Let me now from the bonded ware'ouse of my knowledge," ' began Stalky.

'Oh, rot! Don't Jorrock. Can we make a run for it?' snapped M'Turk.

' "Bishops' boots Mr. Radcliffe also condemned, an' spoke 'ighly in favour of tops cleaned with champagne an' abricot jam." Where's that thing Cokey was twiddlin' this afternoon?'

They heard him groping in the wet, and presently beheld a great miracle. The lights of the Coastguard cottages near the sea went out; the brilliantly illuminated windows of the Golf Club disappeared, and were followed by the frontages of the two hotels. Scattered villas dulled, twinkled, and vanished. Last of all, the College lights died also. They were left in the pitchy darkness of a windy winter's night.

' "Blister my kidneys. It is a frost. The dahlias are dead!"' said Stalky. 'Bunk!'

They squattered through the dripping gorse as the College hummed like an angry hive and the dining-rooms chorussed, 'Gas! gas! gas!' till they came to the edge of the sunk path that divided them from their study. Dropping that ha-ha like bullets, and rebounding like boys, they dashed to their study, in less than two minutes had changed into dry trousers and coat, and, ostentatiously slippered, joined the mob in the dining-hall, which resembled the storm-centre of a South American revolution.

' "Hellish dark and smells of cheese."' Stalky elbowed his way into the press, howling lustily for gas. 'Cokey must have gone for a walk. Foxy 'll have to find him.'

Prout, as the nearest house-master, was trying to restore order, for rude boys were flicking butter-pats across chaos, and M'Turk had turned on the fags' tea-urn, so that many were parboiled and wept with an unfeigned dolor. The Fourth and Upper Third broke into the school song, the 'Vive la Compagnie,' to the accompaniment of drumming knife-handles; and the junior forms shrilled bat-like shrieks and raided one another's victuals. Two hundred and fifty boys in high condition, seeking for more light, are truly earnest inquirers.

When a most vile smell of gas told them that supplies had been renewed, Stalky, waistcoat unbuttoned, sat gorgedly over what might have been his fourth cup of tea. 'And that's all right,' he said. 'Hullo! 'Ere's Pomponius Ego!'

It was Carson, the head of the school, a simple, straight-minded soul, and a pillar of the First Fifteen, who crossed over from the prefects' table and in a husky, official voice invited the three to attend in his study in half an hour.

'Prefects' meetin'! Prefects' meetin'!' hissed the tables, and they imitated barbarically the actions and effects of the ground-ash.

'How are we goin' to jest with 'em?' said Stalky, turning half-face to Beetle. 'It's your play this time!'

'Look here,' was the answer, 'all I want you to do is not to laugh. I'm goin' to take charge o' young Tulke's immorality—a la King, and it's goin' to be serious. If you can't help laughin' don't look at me, or I'll go pop.'

'I see. All right,' said Stalky.

M'Turk's lank frame stiffened in every muscle and his eyelids dropped half over his eyes. That last was a war-signal.

The eight or nine seniors, their faces very set and sober, were ranged in chairs round Carson's severely Philistine study. Tulke was not popular among them, and a few who had had experience of Stalky & Company

213

doubted that he might, perhaps, have made an ass of himself. But the dignity of the Sixth was to be upheld. So Carson began hurriedly:

'Look here, you chaps, I've—we've sent for you to tell you you're a good deal too cheeky to the Sixth—have been for some time—and—and we've stood about as much as we're goin' to, and it seems you've been cursin' and swearin' at Tulke on the Bideford road this afternoon, and we're goin' to show you you can't do it. That's all.'

'Well, that's awfully good of you,' said Stalky, 'but we happen to have a few rights of our own, too. You can't, just because you happen to be made prefects, haul up seniors and jaw 'em on spec, like a house-master. We aren't fags, Carson. This kind of thing may do for Davies tertius, but it won't do for us.'

'It's only old Prout's lunacy that we weren't prefects long ago. You know that,' said M'Turk. 'You haven't any tact.'

'Hold on,' said Beetle. 'A prefects' meetin' has to be reported to the Head. I want to know if the Head backs Tulke in this business?'

'Well—well, it isn't exactly a prefects' meeting,' said Carson. 'We only called you in to warn you.'

'But all the prefects are here,' Beetle insisted. 'Where's the difference?'

'My Gum!' said Stalky. 'Do you mean to say you've just called us in for a jaw—after comin' to us before the whole school at tea an' givin' 'em the impression it was a prefects' meeting? 'Pon my Sam, Carson, you'll get into trouble, you will.'

'Hole-an'-corner business—hole-an'-corner business,' said M'Turk, wagging his head. 'Beastly suspicious.'

The Sixth looked at each other uneasily. Tulke had called three prefects' meetings in two terms, till the Head had informed the Sixth that they were expected to maintain discipline without the recurrent menace of his authority. Now, it seemed that they had made a blunder at the outset, but any right-minded boy would have sunk the legality and been properly impressed by the Court. Beetle's protest was distinct 'cheek.'

'Well, you chaps deserve a lickin',' cried one Naughten incautiously. Then was Beetle filled with a noble inspiration.

'For interferin' with Tulke's amours, eh?' Tulke turned a rich sloe colour. 'Oh no, you don't!' Beetle went on. 'You've had your innings. We've been sent up for cursing and swearing at you, and we're goin' to be let off with a warning! Are we? Now then, you're going to catch it.'

'I—I—I—' Tulke began. 'Don't let that young devil start jawing.'

'If you've anything to say, you must say it decently,' said Carson.

'Decently? I will. Now look here. When we went into Bideford we met this ornament of the Sixth— is that decent enough?—hanging about on the road with a nasty look in his eye. We didn't know then why he was so anxious to stop us, but at five minutes to four, when we were in Yeo's shop, we saw Tulke in broad daylight, with his house-cap on, kissin' an' huggin' a woman on the pavement. Is that decent enough for you?'

'I didn't—I wasn't.'

'We saw you!' said Beetle. 'And now—I'll be decent, Carson—you sneak back with her kisses' (not for nothing had Beetle perused the later poets) 'hot on your lips and call prefects' meetings, which aren't prefects' meetings, to uphold the honour of the Sixth.' A new and heaven-cleft path opened before him that instant. 'And how do we know,' he shouted—'how do we know how many of the Sixth are mixed up in this abominable affair?'

'Yes, that's what we want to know,' said M'Turk, with simple dignity.

'We meant to come to you about it quietly, Carson, but you would have the meeting,' said Stalky sympathetically.

The Sixth were too taken aback to reply. So, carefully modelling his rhetoric on King, Beetle followed up the attack, surpassing and surprising himself.

'It—it isn't so much the cynical immorality of the biznai, as the blatant indecency of it, that's so awful. As far as we can see, it's impossible for us to go into Bideford without runnin' up against some prefect's unwholesome amours. There's nothing to snigger over, Naughten. I don't pretend to know much about these things—but it seems to me a chap must be pretty far dead in sin' (that was a quotation from the school Chaplain) 'when he takes to embracing his paramours' (that was Hakluyt) 'before all the city' (a reminiscence of Milton). 'He might at least have the decency— you're authorities on decency, I believe—to wait till dark. But he didn't. You didn't! Oh, Tulke. You —you incontinent little animal!'

'Here, shut up a minute. What's all this about, Tulke?' said Carson.

'I—look here. I'm awfully sorry. I never thought Beetle would take this line.'

'Because-you've-no-decency-you-thought-I-hadn't,' cried Beetle all in one breath.

'Tried to cover it all up with a conspiracy, did you?' said Stalky.

'Direct insult to all three of us,' said M'Turk. 'A most filthy mind you have, Tulke.'

'I'll shove you fellows outside the door if you go on like this,' said Carson angrily.

'That proves it's a conspiracy,' said Stalky, with the air of a virgin martyr.

'I—I was goin' along the street—I swear I was,' cried Tulke, 'and—and I'm awfully sorry about it—a woman came up and kissed me. I swear I didn't kiss her.'

There was a pause, filled by Stalky's long, liquid whistle of contempt, amazement, and derision.

'On my honour,' gulped the persecuted one. 'Oh, do stop him jawing.'

'Very good,' M'Turk interjected. 'We are compelled, of course, to accept your statement.'

'Confound it!' roared Naughten. 'You aren't head-prefect here, M'Turk.'

'Oh, well,' returned the Irishman, 'you know Tulke better than we do. I am only speaking for ourselves. We accept Tulke's word. But all I can say is that if I'd been collared in a similarly disgustin' situation, and had offered the same explanation Tulke has, I—I wonder what you'd have said. However, it seems on Tulke's word of honour—'

'And Tulkus—beg pardon—kiss, of course—Tulkiss is an honourable man,' put in Stalky.

'—that the Sixth can't protect 'emselves from bein' kissed when they go for a walk!' cried Beetle, taking up the running with a rush. 'Sweet business, isn't it?

217

Cheerful thing to tell the fags, ain't it? We aren't prefects, of course, but we aren't kissed very much. 'Don't think that sort of thing ever enters our heads; does it, Stalky?'

'Oh no!' said Stalky, turning aside to hide his emotions. M'Turk's face merely expressed lofty contempt and a little weariness.

'Well, you seem to know a lot about it,' interposed a prefect.

''Can't help it—when you chaps shove it under our noses.' Beetle dropped into a drawling parody of King's most biting colloquial style—the gentle rain after the thunderstorm. 'Well, it's all very sufficiently vile and disgraceful, isn't it? I don't know who comes out of it worst: Tulke, who happens to have been caught; or the other fellows who haven't. And we'—here he wheeled fiercely on the other two— 'we've got to stand up and be jawed by them because we've disturbed their intrigues.'

'Hang it! I only wanted to give you a word of warning,' said Carson, thereby handing himself bound to the enemy.

'Warn? You?' This with the air of one who finds loathsome gifts in his locker. 'Carson, would you be good enough to tell us what conceivable thing there is that you are entitled to warn us about after this exposure? Warn? Oh, it's a little too much! Let's go somewhere where it's clean.'

The door banged behind their outraged innocence.

'Oh, Beetle! Beetle! Beetle! Golden Beetle!' sobbed Stalky, hurling himself on Beetle's panting bosom as soon as they reached the study. 'However did you do it?'

THE LAST TERM

'Dear-r man!' said M'Turk, embracing Beetle's head with both arms, while he swayed it to and fro on the neck, in time to this ancient burden—

'Pretty lips—sweeter than—cherry or plum,
Always look—jolly and—never look glum;
Seem to say—Come away. Kissy!—come, come!
Yummy-yum! Yummy-yum! Yummy-yum-yum!'

'Look out. You'll smash my gig-lamps,' puffed Beetle, emerging. 'Wasn't it glorious? Didn't I "Eric" 'em splendidly? Did you spot my cribs from King? Oh, blow!' His countenance clouded. 'There's one adjective I didn't use—obscene. 'Don't know how I forgot that. It's one of King's pet ones, too.'

'Never mind. They'll be sendin' ambassadors round in half a shake to beg us not to tell the school. It's a deuced serious business for them,' said M'Turk. 'Poor Sixth—poor old Sixth!'

'Immoral young rips,' Stalky snorted. 'What an example to pure-souled boys like you and me!'

And the Sixth in Carson's study stood aghast, glowering at Tulke, who was on the edge of tears.

'Well,' said the head-prefect acidly. 'You've made a pretty average ghastly mess of it, Tulke.'

'Why—why didn't you lick that young devil Beetle before he began jawing?' Tulke wailed.

'I knew there'd be a row,' said a prefect of Prout's house. 'But you would insist on the meeting, Tulke.'

'Yes, and a fat lot of good it's done us,' said Naughten. 'They come in here and jaw our heads off when we ought to be jawin' them. Beetle talks to us as if we were a lot of blackguards and—and all that. And

219

when they've hung us up to dry, they go out and slam the door like a house-master.   All your fault, Tulke.'

'But I didn't kiss her.'

'You ass!   If you'd said you had and stuck to it, it would have been ten times better than what you did,' Naughten retorted.   'Now they'll tell the whole school —and Beetle 'll make up a lot of beastly rhymes and nick-names.'

'But, hang it, she kissed me!'   Outside his work, Tulke's mind moved slowly.

'I'm not thinking of you.   I'm thinking of us.   I'll go up to their study and see if I can make 'em keep quiet!'

'Tulke's awf'ly cut up about this business,' Naughten began, ingratiatingly, when he found Beetle.

'Who's kissed him this time?'

'—and I've come to ask you chaps, and especially you, Beetle, not to let the thing be known all over the school.   Of course, fellows as senior as you are can easily see why.'

'Um!' said Beetle, with the cold reluctance of one who faces an unpleasant public duty.   'I suppose I must go and talk to the Sixth again.'

'Not the least need, my dear chap, I assure you,' said Naughten hastily.   'I'll take any message you care to send.'

But the chance of supplying the missing adjective was too tempting.   So Naughten returned to that still undissolved meeting, Beetle, white, icy, and aloof, at his heels.

'There seems,' he began, with laboriously crisp articulation, 'there seems to be a certain amount of uneasiness among you as to the steps we may think fit to take in

regard to this last revelation of the—ah—obscene. If
it is any consolation to you to know that we have decided—for the honour of the school, you understand—
to keep our mouths shut as to these—ah—obscenities,
you—ah—have it.'

He wheeled, his head among the stars, and strode
statelily back to his study, where Stalky and M'Turk
lay side by side upon the table wiping their tearful eyes
—too weak to move.

.   .   .   .

The Latin prose paper was a success beyond their
wildest dreams. Stalky and M'Turk were, of course,
out of all examinations (they did extra-tuition with the
Head), but Beetle attended with zeal.

'This, I presume, is a par-ergon on your part,' said
King, as he dealt out the papers. 'One final exhibition
ere you are translated to loftier spheres? A last attack
on the classics? It seems to confound you already.'

Beetle studied the print with knit brows. 'I can't
make head or tail of it,' he murmured. 'What does it
mean?'

'No, no!' said King, with scholastic coquetry. 'We
depend upon you to give us the meaning. This is an
examination, Beetle mine, not a guessing-competition.
You will find your associates have no difficulty in—'

Tulke left his place and laid the paper on the desk.
King looked, read, and turned a ghastly green.

'Stalky's missing a heap,' thought Beetle. 'Wonder
how King 'll get out of it?'

'There seems,' King began with a gulp, 'a certain
modicum of truth in our Beetle's remark. I am—er—
inclined to believe that the worthy Randall must have
dropped this in forme—if you know what that means.

221

Beetle, you purport to be an editor. Perhaps you can enlighten the form as to formes.'

'What, sir? Whose form? I don't see that there's any verb in this sentence at all, an'—an'—the Ode is all different, somehow.'

'I was about to say, before you volunteered your criticism, that an accident must have befallen the paper in type, and that the printer reset it by the light of nature. No—' he held the thing at arm's length—'our Randall is not an authority on Cicero or Horace.'

'Rather mean to shove it off on Randall,' whispered Beetle to his neighbour. 'King must ha' been as screwed as an owl when he wrote it out.'

'But we can amend the error by dictating it.'

'No, sir.' The answer came pat from a dozen throats at once. 'That cuts the time for the exam. Only two hours allowed, sir. 'Tisn't fair. It's a printed-paper exam. How're we goin' to be marked for it? It's all Randall's fault. It isn't our fault, anyhow. An exam.'s an exam.,' etc., etc.

Naturally Mr. King considered this was an attempt to undermine his authority, and, instead of beginning dictation at once, delivered a lecture on the spirit in which examinations should be approached. As the storm subsided, Beetle fanned it afresh.

'Eh? What? What was that you were saying to MacLagan?'

'I only said I thought the papers ought to have been looked at before they were given out, sir.'

'Hear, hear!' from a back bench.

Mr. King wished to know whether Beetle took it upon himself personally to conduct the traditions of the school. His zeal for knowledge ate up another fifteen minutes, during which the prefects showed unmistakable signs of boredom.

'Oh, it was a giddy time,' said Beetle, afterwards, in dismantled Number Five. 'He gibbered a bit, and I kept him on the gibber, and then he dictated about a half of Dolabella & Co.'

'Good old Dolabella! Friend of mine. Yes?' said Stalky tenderly.

'Then we had to ask him how every other word was spelt, of course, and he gibbered a lot more. He cursed me and MacLagan (Mac played up like a trump) and Randall, and the "materialised ignorance of the unscholarly middle classes," "lust for mere marks," and all the rest. It was what you might call a final exhibition—a last attack—a giddy parergon.'

'But of course he was blind squiffy when he wrote the paper. I hope you explained that?' said Stalky.

'Oh yes. I told Tulke so. I said an immoral prefect an' a drunken house-master were legitimate inferences. Tulke nearly blubbed. He's awfully shy of us since Mary's time.'

Tulke preserved that modesty till the last moment— till the journey-money had been paid, and the boys were filling the brakes that took them to the station. Then the three happily constrained him to wait awhile.

'You see, Tulke, you may be a prefect,' said Stalky, 'but I've left the Coll. Do you see, Tulke, dear?'

'Yes, I see. Don't bear malice, Stalky.'

'Stalky? Curse your impudence, you young cub,' shouted Stalky, magnificent in top-hat, stiff collar, spats, and high-waisted, snuff-coloured ulster. 'I want you to understand that I'm Mister Corkran, an' you're a dirty little schoolboy.'

'Besides bein' frabjously immoral,' said M'Turk. 'Wonder you aren't ashamed to foist your company on pure-minded boys like us!'

'Come on, Tulke,' cried Naughten, from the prefects' brake.

'Yes, we're comin'. Shove up and make room, you Collegers. You've all got to be back next term, with your "Yes, sir," and "Oh, sir," an' "No, sir," an' "Please, sir"; but before we say good-bye we're going to tell you a little story. Go on, Dickie' (this to the driver); 'we're quite ready. Kick that hat-box under the seat, an' don't crowd your Uncle Stalky.'

'As nice a lot of high-minded youngsters as you'd wish to see,' said M'Turk, gazing round with bland patronage. 'A trifle immoral, but then—boys will be boys. It's no good tryin' to look stuffy, Carson. Mister Corkran will now oblige with the story of Tulke an' Mary Yeo!'

SLAVES OF THE LAMP

(1897)

PART II

THAT very Infant who told the story of the cap-
ture of Boh Na-ghee[1] to Eustace Cleever,
novelist, inherited an estateful baronetcy, with
vast revenues, resigned the service, and became a land-
holder, while his mother stood guard over him to see
that he married the right girl. But, new to his position,
he presented the local volunteers with a full-sized
magazine-rifle range, two miles long, across the heart
of his estate, and the surrounding families, who lived
in savage seclusion among woods full of pheasants,
regarded him as an erring maniac. The noise of the
firing disturbed their poultry, and Infant was cast out
from the society of J. P.'s and decent men till such time
as a daughter of the county might lure him back to
right thinking. He took his revenge by filling the house
with choice selections of old schoolmates home on leave
—affable detrimentals, at whom the bicycle-riding
maidens of the surrounding families were allowed to
look from afar. I knew when a troopship was in port
by the Infant's invitations. Sometimes he would produce old friends of equal seniority; at others, young and
blushing giants whom I had left small fags far down in

[1] 'A Conference of the Powers' ('Many Inventions').

225

the Lower Second; and to these Infant and the elders expounded the whole duty of Man in the Army.

'I've had to cut the service,' said the Infant; 'but that's no reason why my vast stores of experience should be lost to posterity.' He was just thirty, and in that same summer an imperious wire drew me to his baronial castle: 'Got good haul; ex "Tamar." Come along.'

It was an unusually good haul, arranged with a single eye to my benefit. There was a baldish, broken-down captain of Native Infantry, shivering with ague behind an indomitable red nose—and they called him Captain Dickson. There was another captain, also of Native Infantry, with a fair moustache; his face was like white glass, and his hands were fragile, but he answered joyfully to the cry of Tertius. There was an enormously big and well-kept man, who had evidently not campaigned for years, clean-shaved, soft-voiced, and cat-like, but still Abanazar for all that he adorned the Indian Political Service; and there was a lean Irishman, his face tanned blue-black with the suns of the Telegraph Department. Luckily the baize doors of the bachelors' wing fitted tight, for we dressed promiscuously in the corridor or in each other's rooms, talking, calling, shouting, and anon waltzing by pairs to songs of Dick Four's own devising.

There were sixty years of mixed work to be sifted out between us, and since we had met one another from time to time in the quick scene-shifting of India—a dinner, camp, or a race-meeting here; a dak-bungalow or railway station up country somewhere else—we had never quite lost touch. Infant sat on the banisters, hungrily and enviously drinking it in. He enjoyed his baronetcy, but his heart yearned for the old days.

SLAVES OF THE LAMP

It was a cheerful babel of matters personal, provincial, and imperial, pieces of old call-over lists, and new policies, cut short by the roar of a Burmese gong, and we went down not less than a quarter of a mile of stairs to meet Infant's mother, who had known us all in our school-days and greeted us as if those had ended a week ago. But it was fifteen years since, with tears of laughter, she had lent me a gray princess-skirt for amateur theatricals.

That was a dinner from the Arabian Nights served in an eighty-foot hall full of ancestors and pots of flowering roses, and, this was more impressive, heated by steam. When it was ended and the little mother had gone away —('You boys want to talk, so I shall say good-night now')—we gathered about an apple-wood fire, in a gigantic polished steel grate, under a mantelpiece ten feet high, and the Infant compassed us about with curious liqueurs and that kind of cigarette which serves best to introduce your own pipe.

'Oh, bliss!' grunted Dick Four from a sofa, where he had been packed with a rug over him. 'First time I've been warm since I came home.'

We were all nearly on top of the fire, except Infant, who had been long enough at Home to take exercise when he felt chilled. This is a grisly diversion, but one much affected by the English of the Island.

'If you say a word about cold tubs and brisk walks,' drawled M'Turk, 'I'll kill you, Infant. I've got a liver, too. 'Member when we used to think it a treat to turn out of our beds on a Sunday morning—thermometer fifty-seven degrees if it was summer—and bathe off the Pebbleridge? Ugh!'

''Thing I don't understand,' said Tertius, 'was the

227

way we chaps used to go down into the lavatories, boil ourselves pink, and then come up with all our pores open into a young snowstorm or a black frost. Yet none of our chaps died, that I can remember.'

'Talkin' of baths,' said M'Turk, with a chuckle, ''member our bath in Number Five, Beetle, the night Rabbits-Eggs rocked King? What wouldn't I give to see old Stalky now! He is the only one of the two Studies not here.'

'Stalky is the great man of his Century,' said Dick Four.

'How d'you know?' I asked.

'How do I know?' said Dick Four scornfully. 'If you've ever been in a tight place with Stalky you wouldn't ask.'

'I haven't seen him since the camp at Pindi in '87,' I said. 'He was goin' strong then—about seven feet high and four feet thick.'

'Adequate chap. Infernally adequate,' said Tertius, pulling his moustache and staring into the fire.

'Got dam' near court-martialled and broke in Egypt in '84,' the Infant volunteered. 'I went out in the same trooper with him—as raw as he was. Only I showed it, and Stalky didn't.'

'What was the trouble?' said M'Turk, reaching forward absently to twitch my dress-tie into position.

'Oh, nothing. His colonel trusted him to take twenty Tommies out to wash, or groom camels, or something at the back of Suakin, and Stalky got embroiled with Fuzzies five miles in the interior. He conducted a masterly retreat and wiped up eight of 'em. He knew jolly well he'd no right to go out so far, so he took the initiative and pitched in a letter to his colonel, who was frothing at the mouth, complaining of the "paucity of

228

support accorded to him in his operations." Gad, it might have been one fat brigadier slangin' another! Then he went into the Staff Corps.'

'That—is—entirely—Stalky,' said Abanazar from his armchair.

'You've come across him too?' I said.

'Oh yes,' he replied in his softest tones. 'I was at the tail of that—that epic. Don't you chaps know?'

We did not—Infant, M'Turk, and I; and we called for information very politely.

' 'T wasn't anything,' said Tertius. 'We got into a mess up in the Khye-Kheen Hills a couple o' years ago, and Stalky pulled us through. That's all.'

M'Turk gazed at Tertius with all an Irishman's contempt for the tongue-tied Saxon.

'Heavens!' he said. 'And it's you and your likes govern Ireland. Tertius, aren't you ashamed?'

'Well, I can't tell a yarn. I can chip in when the other fellow starts. Ask him.' He pointed to Dick Four, whose nose gleamed scornfully over the rug.

'I knew you wouldn't,' said Dick Four. 'Give me a whisky and soda. I've been drinking lemon-squash and ammoniated quinine while you chaps were bathin' in champagne, and my head's singin' like a top.'

He wiped his ragged moustache above the drink; and, his teeth chattering in his head, began:

'You know the Khye-Kheen-Malot expedition when we scared the souls out of 'em with a field force they daren't fight against? Well, both tribes—there was a coalition against us—came in without firing a shot: and a lot of hairy villains, who had no more power over their men than I had, promised and vowed all sorts of things. On that very slender evidence, Pussy dear—'

229

'I was at Simla,' said Abanazar hastily.

'Never mind, you're tarred with the same brush. On the strength of those tuppenny-ha'penny treaties, your asses of Politicals reported the country as pacified, and the Government, being a fool, as usual, began road-makin'—dependin' on local supply for labour. 'Member that, Pussy? 'Rest of our chaps who'd had no look-in during the campaign didn't think there'd be any more of it, and were anxious to get back to India. But I'd been in two of these little rows before, and I had my suspicions. I engineered myself, summo ingenio, into command of a road-patrol—no shovellin', only marching up and down genteelly with a guard. They'd withdrawn all the troops they could, but I nucleused about forty Pathans, recruits chiefly, of my regiment, and sat tight at the base-camp while the road-parties went to work, as per Political survey.'

'Had some rippin' sing-songs in camp, too,' said Tertius.

'My pup'—thus did Dick Four refer to his subaltern —'was a pious little beast. He didn't like the sing-songs, and so he went down with pneumonia. I rootled round the camp, and found Tertius gassing about as a D. A. Q. M. G., which, God knows, he isn't cut out for. There were six or eight of the old Coll. at base-camp (we're always in force for a frontier row), but I'd heard of Tertius as a steady old hack, and I told him he had to shake off his D. A. Q. M. G. breeches and help me. Tertius volunteered like a shot, and we settled it with the authorities, and out we went—forty Pathans, Tertius, and me, looking up the road-parties. Macnamara's —'member old Mac, the Sapper, who played the fiddle so damnably at Umballa?—Mac's party was the last but one. The last was Stalky's. He was at the head of the road with some of his pet Sikhs. Mac said he believed he was all right.'

'Stalky is a Sikh,' said Tertius. 'He takes his men to pray at the Durbar Sahib at Amritzar, regularly as clockwork, when he can.'

'Don't interrupt, Tertius. It was about forty miles beyond Mac's before I found him; and my men pointed out gently, but firmly, that the country was risin'. What kind o' country, Beetle? Well, I'm no word-painter, thank goodness, but you might call it a hellish country! When we weren't up to our necks in snow, we were rolling down the khud. The well-disposed inhabitants, who were to supply labour for the road-making (don't forget that, Pussy dear), sat behind rocks and took pot-shots at us. 'Old, old story! We all legged it in search of Stalky. I had a feeling that he'd be in good cover, and about dusk we found him and his road-party, as snug as a bug in a rug, in an old Malot stone fort, with a watch-tower at one corner. It over-hung the road they had blasted out of the cliff fifty feet below; and under the road things went down pretty sheer, for five or six hundred feet, into a gorge about half a mile wide and two or three miles long. There were chaps on the other side of the gorge scientifically gettin' our range. So I hammered on the gate and nipped in, and tripped over Stalky in a greasy, bloody old poshteen, squatting on the ground, eating with his men. I'd only seen him for half a minute about three months before, but I might have met him yesterday. He waved his hand all sereno.

' "Hullo, Aladdin! Hullo, Emperor!" he said. "You're just in time for the performance."

231

'I saw his Sikhs looked a bit battered. "Where's your command? Where's your subaltern?" I said.

' "Here—all there is of it,' said Stalky. "If you want young Everett, he's dead, and his body's in the watch-tower. They rushed our road-party last week, and got him and seven men. We've been besieged for five days. I suppose they let you through to make sure of you. The whole country's up. 'Strikes me you walked into a first-class trap." He grinned, but neither Tertius nor I could see where the deuce the fun was. We hadn't any grub for our men, and Stalky had only four days' whack for his. That came of dependin' upon your asinine Politicals, Pussy dear, who told us that the inhabitants were friendly.

'To make us quite comfy, Stalky took us up to the watch-tower to see poor Everett's body, lyin' in a foot o' drifted snow. It looked like a girl of fifteen—not a hair on the little fellow's face. He'd been shot through the temple, but the Malots had left their mark on him. Stalky unbuttoned the tunic, and showed it to us—a rummy sickle-shaped cut on the chest. 'Member the snow all white on his eyebrows, Tertius? 'Member when Stalky moved the lamp and it looked as if he was alive?'

'Ye-es,' said Tertius, with a shudder. ' 'Member the beastly look on Stalky's face, though, with his nostrils all blown out, same as he used to look when he was bullyin' a fag? That was a lovely evening.'

'We held a council of war up there over Everett's body. Stalky said the Malots and Khye-Kheens were up together; havin' sunk their blood-feuds to settle us. The chaps we'd seen across the gorge were Khye-Keens. It was about half a mile from them to us as a bullet flies,

232

and they'd made a line of sungars under the brow of the hill to sleep in and starve us out. The Malots, he said, were in front of us promiscuous. There wasn't good cover behind the fort, or they'd have been there, too. Stalky didn't mind the Malots half as much as he did the Khye-Kheens. He said the Malots were treacherous curs. What I couldn't understand was, why in· the world the two gangs didn't join in and rush us. There must have been at least five hundred of 'em. Stalky said they didn't trust each other very well, because they were ancestral enemies when they were at home; and the only time they'd tried a rush he'd hove a couple of blasting-charges among 'em, and that had sickened 'em a bit.

'It was dark by the time we finished, and Stalky, always sereno, said: "You command now. I don't suppose you mind my taking any action I may consider necessary to reprovision the fort?" I said "Of course not," and then the lamp blew out. So Tertius and I had to climb down the tower steps (we didn't want to stay with Everett) and got back to our men. Stalky had gone off—to count the stores, I supposed. Anyhow, Tertius and I sat up in case of a rush (they were plugging at us pretty generally, you know), relieving each other till the mornin'.

'Mornin' came. No Stalky. Not a sign of him. I took counsel with his senior native officer—a grand, white-whiskered old chap—Rutton Singh, from Jullunder-way. He only grinned, and said it was all right. Stalky had been out of the fort twice before, somewhere or other, accordin' to him. He said Stalky 'ud come back unchipped, and gave me to understand that Stalky was an invulnerable Guru of sorts. All the same, I put the whole command on half rations, and set 'em to pickin' out loop-holes.

'About noon there was no end of a snowstorm, and the enemy stopped firing. We replied gingerly, because we were awfully short of ammunition. 'Don't suppose we fired five shots an hour, but we generally got our man. Well, while I was talking with Rutton Singh I saw Stalky coming down from the watch-tower, rather puffy about the eyes, his poshteen coated with claret-coloured ice.

'"No trustin' these snowstorms," he said. "Nip out quick and snaffle what you can get. There's a certain amount of friction between the Khye-Kheens and the Malots just now."

'I turned Tertius out with twenty Pathans, and they bucked about in the snow for a bit till they came on to a sort of camp about eight hundred yards away, with only a few men in charge and half-a-dozen sheep by the fire. They finished off the men, and snaffled the sheep and as much grain as they could carry, and came back. No one fired a shot at 'em. There didn't seem to be anybody about, but the snow was falling pretty thick.

'"That's good enough," said Stalky when we got dinner ready and he was chewin' mutton-kababs off a cleanin' rod. "There's no sense riskin' men. They're holding a pow-pow between the Khye-Kheens and the Malots at the head of the gorge. I don't think these so-called coalitions are much good."

'Do you know what that maniac had done? Tertius and I shook it out of him by instalments. There was an underground granary cellar-room below the watch-tower, and in blasting the road Stalky had blown a hole into one side of it. Being no one else but Stalky, he'd

234

kept the hole open for his own ends; and laid poor
Everett's body slap over the well of the stairs that led
down to it from the watch-tower. He'd had to remove
and replace the corpse every time he used the passage.
The Sikhs wouldn't go near the place, of course. Well,
he'd got out of this hole, and dropped on to the road.
Then, in the night and a howling snowstorm, he'd
dropped over the edge of the khud, made his way down
to the bottom of the gorge, forded the nullah which was
half frozen, climbed up on the other side along a track
he'd discovered, and come out on the right flank of the
Khye-Kheens. He had then—listen to this!—crossed
over a ridge that paralleled their rear, walked half a
mile behind that, and come out on the left of their line
where the gorge gets shallow and where there was a
regular track between the Malot and the Khye-Kheen
camps. That was about two in the morning, and, as it
turned out, a man spotted him—a Khye-Kheen. So
Stalky abolished him quietly, and left him—with the
Malot mark on his chest, same as Everett had.

' "I was just as economical as I could be," Stalky said
to us. "If he'd shouted I should have been slain. I'd
never had to do that kind of thing but once before, and
that was the first time I tried that path. It's perfectly
practicable for infantry, you know."

' "What about your first man?" I said.

' "Oh, that was the night after they killed Everett,
and I went out lookin' for a line of retreat for my
men. A man found me. I abolished him—privatim—
scragged him. But on thinkin' it over it occurred to me
that if I could find the body (I'd hove it down some
rocks) I might decorate it with the Malot mark and
leave it to the Khye-Kheens to draw inferences. So I

235

went out again the next night and did. The Khye-Kheens are shocked at the Malots perpetratin' these two dastardly outrages after they'd sworn to sink all blood-feuds. I lay up behind their sungars early this morning and watched 'em. They all went to confer about it at the head of the gorge. Awf'ly annoyed they are. Don't wonder." You know the way Stalky drops out his words, one by one.'

'My God!' said the Infant explosively, as the full depth of the strategy dawned on him.

'Dear-r man!' said M'Turk, purring rapturously.

'Stalky stalked,' said Tertius. 'That's all there is to it.'

'No, he didn't,' said Dick Four. 'Don't you remember how he insisted that he had only applied his luck? Don't you remember how Rutton Singh grabbed his boots and grovelled in the snow, and how our men shouted?'

'None of our Pathans believed that was luck,' said Tertius. 'They swore Stalky ought to have been born a Pathan, and—'member we nearly had a row in the fort when Rutton Singh said Stalky was a Sikh? Gad, how furious the old chap was with my Pathan Jemadar! But Stalky just waggled his finger and they shut up.

'Old Rutton Singh's sword was half out, though, and he swore he'd cremate every Khye-Kheen and Malot he killed. That made the Jemadar pretty wild, because he didn't mind fighting against his own creed, but he wasn't going to crab a fellow-Mussulman's chances of Paradise. Then Stalky jabbered Pushtu and Punjabi in alternate streaks. Where the deuce did he pick up his Pushtu from, Beetle?'

'Never mind his language, Dick,' said I. 'Give us the gist of it.'

'I flatter myself I can address the wily Pathan on occasion, but, hang it all, I can't make puns in Pushtu, or top off my arguments with a smutty story, as he did. He played on those two old dogs o' war like a—like a concertina. Stalky said—and the other two backed up his knowledge of Oriental nature—that the Khye-Kheens and the Malots between 'em would organise a combined attack on us that night, as a proof of good faith. They wouldn't drive it home, though, because neither side would trust the other on account, as Rutton Singh put it, of the little accidents. Stalky's notion was to crawl out at dusk with his Sikhs, manœuvre 'em along this ungodly goat-track that he'd found, to the back of the Khye-Kheen position, and then lob in a few long shots at the Malots when the attack was well on. "'That'll divert their minds and help to agitate 'em," he said. "Then you chaps can come out and sweep up the pieces, and we'll rendezvous at the head of the gorge. After that, I move we get back to Mac's camp and have something to eat."'

'You were commandin'?' the Infant suggested.

'I was about three months senior to Stalky, and two months Tertius's senior,' Dick Four replied. 'But we were all from the same old Coll. I should say ours was the only little affair on record where some one wasn't jealous of some one else.'

'We weren't,' Tertius broke in, 'but there was another row between Gul Sher Khan and Rutton Singh. Our Jemadar said—he was quite right—that no Sikh living could stalk worth a damn; and that Koran Sahib had better take out the Pathans, who understood that kind of mountain work. Rutton Singh said that Koran Sahib jolly well knew every Pathan was a born deserter, and every Sikh was a gentleman, even if he couldn't crawl on his belly. Stalky struck in with some woman's proverb or other, that had the effect of doublin' both men up with a grin. He said the Sikhs and the Pathans could settle their claims on the Khye-Kheens and Malots later on, but he was going to take his Sikhs along for this mountain-climbing job, because Sikhs could shoot. They can too. Give 'em a mule-load of ammunition apiece, and they're perfectly happy.'

'And out he gat,' said Dick Four. 'As soon as it was dark, and he'd had a bit of a snooze, him and thirty Sikhs went down through the staircase in the tower, every mother's son of 'em salutin' little Everett where It stood propped up against the wall. The last I heard him say was, "Kubbadar! tumbleinga!"[1] and they tumbleingaed over the black edge of nothing. Close upon 9 p. m. the combined attack developed; Khye-Kheens across the valley, and Malots in front of us, pluggin' at long range and yellin' to each other to come along and cut our infidel throats. Then they skirmished up to the gate, and began the old game of calling our Pathans renegades, and invitin' 'em to join the holy war. One of our men, a young fellow from Dera Ismail, jumped on the wall to slang 'em back, and jumped down, blubbing like a child. He'd been hit smack in the middle of the hand. 'Never saw a man yet who could stand a hit in the hand without weepin' bitterly. It tickles up all the nerves. So Tertius took his rifle and smote the others on the head to keep them quiet at the loopholes. The dear children wanted to open the gate and go in at 'em generally, but that didn't suit our book.

[1]"Look out; you'll fall!'

'At last, near midnight, I heard the "wop, wop, wop," of Stalky's Martinis across the valley, and some general cursing among the Malots, whose main body was hid from us by a fold in the hillside. Stalky was brownin' 'em at a great rate, and very naturally they turned half right and began to blaze at their faithless allies, the Khye-Kheens—regular volley firin'. In less than ten minutes after Stalky opened the diversion they were going it hammer and tongs, both sides the valley. When we could see, the valley was rather a mixed-up affair. The Khye-Kheens had streamed out of their sungars above the gorge to chastise the Malots, and Stalky—I was watching him through my glasses—had slipped in behind 'em. Very good. The Khye-Kheens had to leg it along the hillside up to where the gorge got shallow and they could cross over to the Malots, who were awfully cheered to see the Khye-Kheens taken in the rear.

'Then it occurred to me to comfort the Khye-Kheens. So I turned out the whole command, and we advanced "a la pas de charge," doublin' up what, for the sake of argument, we'll call the Malots' left flank. Even then, if they'd sunk their differences, they could have eaten us alive; but they'd been firin' at each other half the night, and they went on firin'. Queerest thing you ever saw in your born days! As soon as our men doubled up to the Malots, they'd blaze at the Khye-Kheens more zealously than ever, to show they were on our side, run up the valley a few hundred yards, and halt to fire again. The moment Stalky saw our game he duplicated it his side the gorge; and, by Jove! the Khye-Kheens did just the same thing.'

'Yes, but,' said Tertius, 'you've forgot him playin'

"Arrah, Patsy, mind the baby" on the bugle to hurry us up.'

'Did he?' roared M'Turk. Somehow we all began to sing it, and there was an interruption.

'Rather,' said Tertius, when we were quiet. No one of the Aladdin company could forget that tune. 'Yes, he played "Patsy." Go on, Dick.'

'Finally,' said Dick Four, 'we drove both mobs into each other's arms on a bit of level ground at the head of the valley, and saw the whole crew whirl off, fightin' and stabbin' and swearin' in a blinding snowstorm. They were a heavy, hairy lot, and we didn't follow 'em.

'Stalky had captured one prisoner—an old pensioned Sepoy of twenty-five years' service, who produced his discharge—an awf'ly sportin' old card. He had been tryin' to make his men rush us early in the day. He was sulky—angry with his own side for their cowardice, and Rutton Singh wanted to bayonet him—Sikhs don't understand fightin' against the Government after you've served it honestly—but Stalky rescued him, and froze on to him tight—with ulterior motives, I believe. When we got back to the fort, we buried young Everett —Stalky wouldn't hear of blowin' up the place—and bunked. We'd only lost ten men, all told.'

'Only ten, out of seventy. How did you lose 'em?' I asked.

'Oh, there was a rush on the fort early in the night, and a few Malots got over the gate. It was rather a tight thing for a minute or two, but the recruits took it beautifully. Lucky job we hadn't any badly wounded men to carry, because we had forty miles to Macnamara's camp. By Jove, how we legged it! Half way

240

in, old Rutton Singh collapsed, so we slung him across four rifles and Stalky's overcoat; and Stalky, his prisoner, and a couple of Sikhs were his bearers. After that I went to sleep. You can, you know, on the march, when your legs get properly numbed. Mac swears we all marched into his camp snoring, and dropped where we halted. His men lugged us into the tents like gram-bags. I remember wakin' up and seeing Stalky asleep with his head on old Rutton Singh's chest. He slept twenty-four hours. I only slept seventeen, but then I was coming down with dysentery.'

'Coming down! What rot! He had it on him before we joined Stalky in the fort,' said Tertius.

'Well, you needn't talk! You hove your sword at Macnamara and demanded a drumhead court-martial every time you saw him. The only thing that soothed you was putting you under arrest every half-hour. You were off your head for three days.'

' 'Don't remember a word of it,' said Tertius placidly. 'I remember my orderly giving me milk, though.'

'How did Stalky come out?' M'Turk demanded, puffing hard over his pipe.

'Stalky? Like a serene Brahmini bull. Poor old Mac was at his Royal Engineer's wits' end to know what to do. You see I was putrid with dysentery, Tertius was ravin', half the men had frost-bite, and Macnamara's orders were to break camp and come in before winter. So Stalky, who hadn't turned a hair, took half his supplies to save him the bother o' luggin' 'em back to the plains, and all the ammunition he could get at, and, "consilio et auxilio" Rutton Singh, tramped back to his fort with all his Sikhs and his precious prisoner, and a lot of dissolute hangers-on that he and the prisoner

had seduced into service. He had sixty men of sorts—
and his brazen cheek. Mac nearly wept with joy when
he went. You see there weren't any explicit orders to
Stalky to come in before the passes were blocked: Mac
is a great man for orders, and Stalky's a great man for
orders—when they suit his book.'

'He told me he was goin' to the Engadine,' said Tertius. 'Sat on my cot smokin' a cigarette, and makin'
me laugh till I cried. Macnamara bundled the whole
lot of us down to the plains next day. We were a
walkin' hospital.'

'Stalky told me that Macnamara was a simple god-
send to him,' said Dick Four. 'I used to see him in
Mac's tent listenin' to Mac playin' the fiddle, and, between the pieces, wheedlin' Mac out of picks and shovels
and dynamite cartridges hand-over-fist. Well, that was
the last we saw of Stalky. A week or so later the passes
were shut with snow, and I don't think Stalky wanted
to be found particularly just then.'

'He didn't,' said the fair and fat Abanazar. 'He
didn't. Ho, ho!'

Dick Four threw up his thin, dry hand with the blue
veins at the back of it. 'Hold on a minute, Pussy; I'll
let you in at the proper time. I went down to my regiment, and that spring, five months later, I got off with
a couple of companies on detachment: nominally to
look after some friends of ours across the Border; actually, of course, to recruit. It was a bit unfortunate,
because an ass of a young Naick carried a frivolous
blood-feud he'd inherited from his aunt into those hills,
and the local gentry wouldn't volunteer into my corps.
Of course, the Naick had taken short leave to manage
the business; that was all regular enough; but he'd

stalked my pet orderly's uncle. It was an infernal shame, because I knew Harris of the Ghuznees would be covering that ground three months later, and he'd snaffle all the chaps I had my eyes on. Everybody was down on the Naick, because they felt he ought to have had the decency to postpone his—his disgustful amours till our companies were full strength.

'Still the beast had a certain amount of professional feeling left. He sent one of his aunt's clan by night to tell me that, if I'd take safeguard, he'd put on to a batch of beauties. I nipped over the Border like a shot, and about ten miles the other side, in a nullah, my rapparee-in-charge showed me about seventy men variously armed, but standing up like a Queen's company. Then one of 'em stepped out and lugged round an old bugle, just like—who's the man?—Bancroft, ain't it?—feeling for his eyeglass in a farce, and played "Arrah, Patsy, mind the baby. Arrah, Patsy, mind"—that was as far as he could get.'

That also was as far as Dick Four could get, because we had to sing the old song through twice, again and once more, and subsequently, in order to repeat it.

'He explained that if I knew the rest of the song he had a note for me from the man the song belonged to. Whereupon, my children, I finished that old tune on that bugle, and this is what I got. I knew you'd like to look at it. Don't grab.' (We were all struggling for a sight of the well-known unformed handwriting.) 'I'll read it aloud:

"Fort Everett, February 19.
"Dear Dick, or Tertius: The bearer of this is in charge of seventy-five recruits, all pukka devils, but desirous of

243

leading new lives. They have been slightly polished, and after being boiled may shape well. I want you to give thirty of them to my adjutant, who, though God's Own ass, will need men this spring. The rest you can keep. You will be interested to learn that I have extended my road to the end of the Malot country. All headmen and priests concerned in last September's affair worked one month each, supplying road-metal from their own houses. Everett's grave is covered by a forty-foot mound, which should serve well as a base for future triangulations. Rutton Singh sends his best salaams. I am making some treaties, and have given my prisoner—who also sends his salaams—local rank of Khan Bahadur.

"A. L. Corkran."'

'Well, that was all,' said Dick Four, when the roaring, the shouting, the laughter, and, I think, the tears, had subsided. 'I chaperoned the gang across the Border as quick as I could. They were rather homesick, but they cheered up when they recognised some of my chaps, who had been in the Khye-Kheen row, and they made a rippin' good lot. It's rather more than three hundred miles from Fort Everett to where I picked 'em up. Now, Pussy, tell 'em the latter end o' Stalky as you saw it.'

Abanazar laughed a little nervous, misleading, official laugh.

'Oh, it wasn't much. I was at Simla in the spring, when our Stalky, out of his snows, began corresponding direct with the Government.'

'After the manner of a king?' suggested Dick Four.

'My turn now, Dick. He'd done a whole lot of things

he shouldn't have done, and constructively pledged the Government to all sorts of action.'

'Pledged the State's ticker, eh?' said M'Turk, with a nod to me.

'About that; but the embarrassin' part was that it was all so thunderin' convenient, so well reasoned, don't you know. Came in as pat as if he'd had access to all sorts of information—which he couldn't, of course.'

'Pooh!' said Tertius, 'I back Stalky against the Foreign Office any day.'

'He'd done pretty nearly everything he could think of, except strikin' coins in his own image and superscription, all under cover of buildin' this infernal road and bein' blocked by the snow. His report was simply amazin'. Von Lennaert tore his hair over it at first, and then he gasped, "Who the dooce is this unknown Warren Hastings? He must be slain. He must be slain officially! The Viceroy 'll never stand it. It's unheard of. He must be slain by His Excellency in person. Order him up here and pitch in a stinger." Well, I sent him no end of an official stinger, and I pitched in an unofficial telegram at the same time.'

'You!' This with amazement from the Infant, for Abanazar resembled nothing so much as a fluffy Persian cat.

'Yes—me,' said Abanazar. ''T wasn't much, but after what you've said, Dicky, it was rather a coincidence, because I wired:

> "Aladdin now has got his wife,
> Your Emperor is appeased.
> I think you'd better come to life:
> We hope you've all been pleased."

Funny how that old song came up in my head. That was fairly non-committal and encouragin'. The only flaw was that his Emperor wasn't appeased by very long chalks. Stalky extricated himself from his mountain fastnesses and loafed up to Simla at his leisure, to be offered up on the horns of the altar.'

'But,' I began, 'surely the Commander-in-Chief is the proper—'

'His Excellency had an idea that if he blew up one single junior captain—same as King used to blow us up —he was holdin' the reins of empire, and, of course, as long as he had that idea, Von Lennaert encouraged him. I'm not sure Von Lennaert didn't put that notion into his head.'

'They've changed the breed, then, since my time,' I said.

'P'r'aps. Stalky was sent up for his wiggin' like a bad little boy. I've reason to believe that His Excellency's hair stood on end. He walked into Stalky for one hour— Stalky at attention in the middle of the floor, and (so he vowed) Von Lennaert pretending to soothe down His Excellency's top-knot in dumb show in the background. Stalky didn't dare to look up, or he'd have laughed.'

'Now, wherefore was Stalky not broken publicly?' said the Infant, with a large and luminous leer.

'Ah, wherefore?' said Abanazar. 'To give him a chance to retrieve his blasted career, and not to break his father's heart. Stalky hadn't a father, but that didn't matter. He behaved like a—like the Sanawar Orphan Asylum, and His Excellency graciously spared him. Then he came round to my office and sat opposite me for ten minutes, puffing out his nostrils. Then he said, "Pussy, if I thought that basket-hanger—"'

'Hah! He remembered that,' said M'Turk.

' "That two-anna basket-hanger governed India, I swear I'd become a naturalised Muscovite to-morrow. I'm a 'femme incomprise.' This thing's broken my heart. It'll take six months' shootin'-leave in India to mend it. Do you think I can get it, Pussy?" '

'He got it in about three minutes and a half, and seventeen days later he was back in the arms of Rutton Singh—horrid disgraced—with orders to hand over his command, etc., to Cathcart MacMonnie.'

'Observe!' said Dick Four. 'One colonel of the Political Department in charge of thirty Sikhs on a hilltop. Observe, my children!'

'Naturally, Cathcart not being a fool, even if he is a Political, let Stalky do his shooting within fifteen miles of Fort Everett for the next six months; and I always understood they and Rutton Singh and the prisoner were as thick as thieves. Then Stalky loafed back to his regiment, I believe. I've never seen him since.'

'I have, though,' said M'Turk, swelling with pride.

We all turned as one man.

'It was at the beginning of this hot weather. I was in camp in the Jullunder doab and stumbled slap on Stalky in a Sikh village, sitting on the one chair of state, with half the population grovellin' before him, a dozen Sikh babies on his knees, an old harridan clappin' him on the shoulder, and a garland o' flowers round his neck. 'Told me he was recruitin'. We dined together that night, but he never said a word of the business of the Fort. 'Told me, though, that if I wanted any supplies I'd better say I was Koran Sahib's bhai; and I did, and the Sikhs wouldn't take my money.'

'Ah! That must have been one of Rutton Singh's

247

villages,' said Dick Four; and we smoked for some time in silence.

'I say,' said M'Turk, casting back through the years. 'Did Stalky ever tell you how Rabbits-Eggs came to rock King that night?'

'No,' said Dick Four.

Then M'Turk told.

'I see,' said Dick Four, nodding. 'Practically he duplicated that trick over again. There's nobody like Stalky.'

'That's just where you make the mistake,' I said. 'India's full of Stalkies—Cheltenham and Haileybury and Marlborough chaps—that we don't know anything about, and the surprises will begin when there is really a big row on.'

'Who will be surprised?' said Dick Four.

'The other side. The gentlemen who go to the front in first-class carriages. Just imagine Stalky let loose on the south side of Europe with a sufficiency of Sikhs and a reasonable prospect of loot. Consider it quietly.'

'There's something in that, but you're too much of an optimist, Beetle,' said the Infant.

'Well, I've a right to be. Ain't I responsible for the whole thing? You needn't laugh. Who wrote "Aladdin now has got his wife"—eh?'

'What's that got to do with it?' said Tertius.

'Everything,' said I.

'Prove it,' said the Infant.

And I have.

THE END